The Political Economy of Development Policy Change

Gustav Ranis
and
Syed Akhtar Mahmood

BLACKWELL
Cambridge MA & Oxford UK

First published 1992

Blackwell Publisher
3 Cambridge Center
Cambridge, Massachusetts 02142, USA

108 Cowley Road
Oxford OX4 1JF, UK

Library of Congress Cataloging in Publication Data
Ranis, Gustav.
    The political economy of development policy change / Gustav Ranis,
Syed Mahmood.
        p.   cm.
    Includes bibliographical references and index.
    ISBN 1-55786-250-8
    1. Developing countries – Economic policy – Case studies.
    2. Economic development. I. Mahmood, Syed (Syed Akhtar)
    II. Title.
    HC59.7.R268   1991
    338.9′009172′4 – dc20   91-14513
                                                                         CIP

British Library Cataloguing in Publication Data

A CIP catalogue record for this book is available from the British
Library.

Typeset in Times Roman on L-202 10 on 11.5 pt
by Huron Valley Graphics, Inc.
Printed in the USA

This book is printed on acid-free paper.

Contents

TO OUR FAMILIES

Preface

The dramatic divergence of postwar performance within what used to be considered a more or less monolithic "Third World" has been well documented. Thanks largely to a generally buoyant international economy in the 1960s and the flow of commercial bank capital in the 1970s, some of that divergence remained hidden until exposed during the debt-ridden 1980s. As to the "whys" and "wherefores" of that underlying divergence, however, we are much less certain. Clearly, different macroeconomic policy choices made over the years by different developing countries have played a dominant role. In fact, most academic research, as well as most of the advice of the international donor agencies over the past two decades, has focused heavily on an examination of the precise content and phasing of policy change in the Third World as the critical explanatory variable.

What remains shrouded in mystery, however, is the "why" at a more fundamental level. It is impossible, writing in and for the 1990s, to carry on with the (at least implicit) assumption that in less-developed countries (LDC) policymakers "know not what they do" and that, given enough training and advice from the more enlightened academic and donor community abroad, all policy errors would eventually be exposed to the sun of rationality and eliminated.

This easy set of assumptions flies in the face of the often-forgotten fact that, both by virtue of education and accumulated experience, the technical competence of LDC decision makers has increased by leaps and bounds over the past two decades. Thus, while no one would claim that development economics is a perfect science or that any group of analysts would necessarily agree on the precise contours of any country-specific reform program, it has become increasingly evident that "they know well what they do." In other words, decisions on macroeconomic policy change – or its absence – are made on the basis of rational decisions by those in control of the apparatus, not because of any lack of technical ability. We must, therefore, address the question of the causes of the observed divergence of policy choice and performance at a more fundamental level, e.g., whether there are other features of the landscape that prompt decision makers to react very differently to their less-developed status as well as their changing international environment.

This volume is intended not to provide answers to this complicated problem but to begin to address it. It is our basic premise that a country's initial conditions play a major role in determining not only its "ideal" development path, but also – and more to the point here – its freedom of action to adopt the "ideal" policy package at different stages of its development.

The point of departure for our analytical effort in this volume is the notion that such freedom of action may be circumscribed by political obstacles arising out of varying degrees of vested-interest resistance to change. Thus, our idea of the "political economy of policy change" represents but one, rather special, component of the growing mosaic of activity in this general field. We will not attempt to model explicitly the action of various interest groups that have a stake in the policy package adhered to. Nor do we accept the view that the state is either predatory on its own account or platonic in terms of seeking the "best outcome" for the majority of its citizens. Instead, we accept the concept that the typical LDC state is an instrument of the most powerful – if often myopic – interest groups, the new industrialist class, public or private, and that the resistance of these vested interests can be overcome only when the system has no other way of avoiding the required adjustment. In other words, it has to be "up against it," without any easy alternative by which the day of reckoning can be delayed – either because a country's own resources or the resources made available from the outside are considered insufficient to keep the system operating along the old rails.

To test out this general hypothesis, we selected three pairs of countries differing in terms of various dimensions of their initial conditions and examined their policy responses to external shocks as well as their consequent performance over periods spanning the end of their early import-substitution phase and the early 1980s. This includes one long period of relative improvement in the external conditions (pre-1973) and one long period of relative deterioration (post-1973), something approaching as close to a laboratory condition as social science usually permits. At the end, we hope to have been persuasive that societies indeed, like individuals, respond more readily to the realities of a changing environment when there is no buffer, or "easy way out," provided either by the inherent bounties of nature or all-too-accommodating foreign friends or investors.

We chose not to pursue our analysis into the more recent period, the decade of the so-called debt crisis of the late 1980s. Had we done so, we undoubtedly would have observed a direct relationship between the severity of that crisis and countries' willingness to effect large structural reforms – as perhaps more dramatically demonstrated by the major post-1986 policy changes in Mexico. In order to determine the empirical validity of our approach, we restricted our analysis to the contrast in behavior across our three pairs of countries over a single cycle, a long upswing followed by a long downswing.

More work clearly needs to be done in testing varying political economy responses to exogenous shocks, including not only changes in the international environment but possibly also those of domestic origin, e.g., major crop fluctuations, national disasters, wars, and so on. Nor do we deny that the specifics of the political process of how vested interests are overcome in some types of LDCs and prove unremittingly stubborn in others still need to be spelled out. But we at least hope to have indicated a fruitful direction for future research – in the belief that greater transparency represents a potentially critical contribution to improved policies.

The authors would like to thank the World Bank for supporting our work on Colombia, the Agency for International Development for supporting our work on the Philippines and Thailand, and Taiwan's Academia Sinica for supporting our work on Korea and Taiwan. We are grateful to John Fei of Yale for his contribution at an early stage of this project and to Yale graduate students Juan Carlos Buitrago, David Carbon, John Clark, Ruthanne Deutsch, Kolleen Rask, Wooheon Rhee, Jai-Won Ryou, James Shapiro, and Clifford Tan for their research assistance. Permission to utilize materials from Gustav Ranis's "The Political Economy of Development Policy Change," in Meier, Gerald, ed., *Politics and Policy-Making in Developing Countries: Perspectives on the New Political Economy* (San Francisco: International Center for Economic Growth, 1991) is gratefully acknowledged.

Gustav Ranis
Syed Akhtar Mahmood
New Haven, 1991

1

Introduction

For most of the so-called Third World, the post-1950 era represents a unique period of attempted transition from colonial agrarianism to the epoch of modern economic growth. This transition effort has constituted an extremely growth-conscious period during which – given a wide variety of initial conditions – a wide range of macroeconomic policy instruments were brought to bear in these countries in order to promote growth.

The record of the postwar period, however, also reveals that the extent of success or failure of this effort, in terms of the achievement of a combination of growth and distributional objectives, has varied enormously across countries. All the statistical evidence that can be brought to bear clearly indicates that of all the postwar LDCs, the newly industrializing countries of East Asia (i.e., the so-called "Gang of Four" – Taiwan,[1] South Korea, Singapore, and Hong Kong), have registered by far the best development performance – in terms of such bottom-line indicators as GDP growth rates and Gini coefficients – over the past 35 years, whereas performance has been relatively more modest in other parts of the developing world, e.g., Latin America and other parts of Asia, and worst in sub-Saharan Africa.

This is clearly demonstrated in the data presented in table 1.1(a). While East Asian economies such as Taiwan and South Korea have achieved very remarkable rates of growth of real per capita GDP virtually throughout the postwar period performance has been relatively modest in other countries. Within Latin America, for example, Colombia achieved per capita income growth rates exceeding 2 percent per annum during the seventies only; Costa Rica performed relatively better during the sixties and seventies but suffered negative growth during the eighties. Mexico had an impressive record until the end of the sixties, but its performance has declined since then. Even Brazil, whose track record

---

[1] Taiwan is referred to as a country only for convenience without implying any political judgements.

Table 1.1   Postwar performance indicators of a sample of LDCs

(a) Average real per capita GDP growth rates (percent per year)

	1960–69	1970–79	1980–86
Taiwan	5.9	8.1	5.6
South Korea	4.9	7.5	4.3
Thailand	5.0	5.0	3.1
Philippines	2.1	3.3	−1.5
Pakistan	3.9	2.0	3.6
Sri Lanka	2.2	2.1	3.4
Colombia	1.9	3.9	0.7
Mexico	4.1	1.9	−0.7
Costa Rica	3.1	3.5	−1.1
Brazil	2.4	5.7	0.5
Kenya	3.2	0.9	−1.5
Tanzania	4.7	1.8	−2.6

(b) Income distribution (Gini coefficient)

	1950	1960	1970	1980
Taiwan	.56	.44 ('59)	.29	.29 ('78)
South Korea	–	–	.37	.38 ('76)
Thailand	–	.41 ('62)	.44 ('68)	–
Philippines	.49 ('56)	.50 ('61)	.49 ('71)	.50 ('77)
Pakistan	–	.36 ('64)	.33 ('70)	.36 ('79)
Sri Lanka	.46 ('53)	.45 ('63)	.35 ('73)	.45 ('82)
Colombia	–	.53	.56	.52 ('82)
Mexico	–	.54	.58	.50 ('77)
Costa Rica	–	.50 ('61)	.43 ('71)	.42 ('82)
Kenya	–	–	–	.59 ('77)

Sources:
G. S. Fields, *A Compendium of Data on Inequality and Poverty for the Developing World,* mimeo, (Ithaca, N.Y.: Cornell University, March 1989).
J. Fei, G. Ranis and S. Kuo, *Growth with Equity: The Taiwan Case,* (Oxford: Oxford University Press, 1979).
S. Jain, *Size Distribution of Income* (Washington, D.C.: The World Bank, 1975).
United Nations, *National Income Statistics,* various issues.
World Bank, *World Tables,* and *World Development Report,* various issues.
National Income of the Republic of China, various issues.
Statistical Yearbook of the Republic of China, various issues.

with respect to growth is one of the best in Latin America, performed only modestly compared to the East Asian representatives in table 1.1(a). Within Asia, performance is very modest in the South Asian economies, as exemplified by the record of two representatives from this region, Pakistan and Sri Lanka. Southeast Asian economies represented intermediate cases, as shown by the performance of the Philippines and Thailand. Finally, growth performance has been the worst in sub-Saharan Africa, as illustrated by Kenya, one of the relatively better performing African cases, and Tanzania.

The exceptionally high growth rates of East Asia have, moreover, been accompanied by an unusual, increasingly equitable, distribution of the fruits of that growth (see table 1.1(b)). The Gini coefficient of family income in Taiwan, for example, fell from 0.56 in 1950 to 0.29 by 1970 and has remained at more or less that level, the lowest in the nonsocialist developing world. In contrast, the Latin American countries have been characterized not only by slower growth but also by a greater concentration of income; in Colombia and Mexico, for example, Gini coefficients have exceeded 0.50 in all periods, and there is no consistent trend of improvement in evidence. Costa Rica has done better both in terms of levels and trends – there is a consistent improvement over time – but nowhere near the East Asians. Thailand is intermediate in terms of income distribution while the Philippines is typically Latin American. The South Asian representatives, especially Pakistan, have a better record, but performance is quite bad in the only African example in that table.

Different LDCs have not only achieved very different degrees of "bottom-line" success but have also made substantially different organizational and policy choices in the course of their efforts to achieve modern growth. It is a well-recognized fact that most LDCs started out as mixed economies marked by a substantial volume of government intrusion and control, partly as a reaction to prior, colonial patterns of resource allocation, and partly to help create a unified national entity capable of starting on an independent national development-oriented path in the first place. Most LDCs, in other words, initiated their transition growth efforts with strong political forces penetrating their mixed economies.

Subsequently, however, there has been a more or less universal trend toward depoliticization, or a changing role of government, combined with the increased utilization of various markets, but with a different gradient in evidence in different parts of the developing world. Indeed, that gradient itself is determined by the extent to which policies oscillate in a "stop-go" pattern or maintain a measure of monotonicity. In the successful East Asian countries, which, like virtually every other LDC, initiated their development efforts under a policy regime characterized by direct controls and interventions, there has been in evidence over time a linear trend toward greater external orientation and liberalization in various markets. In other parts of the developing world, on the other hand, once this primary import-substitution subphase came to an end, the statistical record of economic performance has been accompanied by a somewhat different, less clear-cut, and more oscillatory pattern of organizational choice, with more market-oriented episodes temporarily followed by a return to import-substitution-type policies in a more or less continuous fashion. This pattern is particularly evident in the case of the Latin American countries but is also observable in other parts of the developing world.

The more pronounced external orientation of the East Asian systems and their greater overall willingness to subject themselves to the competitive discipline of the market have been identified by many, including academicians as well as practitioners such as the World Bank and the IMF, as the major contributory factors to their relative success. The associated trends toward greater external orientation and greater market liberalization have helped to transform fundamentally the systems of the small group of East Asian countries. These trends made them more successful by instilling in them a flexibility, a sensitivity to technological change, and an ability to adjust to (inevitable) exogenous shocks, which are the hallmarks of the industrially advanced market economies. Successful LDCs, in other words, seem to converge toward a liberalizing pattern of organizational and institutional choice as well as toward the well-known Kuznetsian stylized structural characteristics of the "mixed" mature developed economy.

Given the strong link that seems to exist between policy choice and performance, a study of differential LDC performance over time must, therefore, include an analysis not only of *what* happened but also of *why* it happened, including an effort to understand the difference in the organizational and policy choices made along the way. This effort to begin to endogenize policy choice made over time in different LDC settings represents the main purpose of this volume. It should also help us understand why the often very similar policy advice proffered by the international financial and academic community is so differently received in different contexts.

To explain the continued divergence in organizational and policy choices largely on the basis of intrinsic cultural and human capital differences or other "special case" dimensions is, in our opinion, inappropriate; such an approach not only challenges the intelligence of a large body of LDC decision makers, but it is also probably factually incorrect. Instead, we believe it is more likely that the bulk of the explanation for the observed divergence of performance is to be found in a combination of the initial typological differences among developing countries when the curtain rises, plus various political and economic forces that shape governments' adoption or rejection of different institutional and policy changes over time.

A government can usually exercise political intrusion via three basic powers: the power to block trade, the power to transfer income to itself and other favored parties, and the power to decide on the specific allocation of its own expenditures. The major macropolicy instruments of development – the interest rate, the foreign exchange rate, the rate of protection, the rate of monetary expansion, and the tax rate – can, therefore, be interpreted as political instruments to promote growth through the exercise of these powers, in particular via the indirect transfer of income among social groups, that is, by "manufacturing" profits for one class at the expense of others. In a political process, such indirect transfers are usually sanctioned by the powerful need of governments (especially the newly independent) to try to solve current problems, while putting aside the possibility of a social conflict arising later, i.e., with a time lag.[2] Once political force has penetrated the postindependence developing country, it is thus necessary not only to trace this pattern over time but also to attempt to differentiate between the conventional "on-the-table" or overt, revenue-and expenditure-related policies of government and the much more pervasive deployment of the "under-the-table," i.e., indirect or implicit, income transfers among groups.

When the familiar macroeconomic variables are interpreted as growth-promoting policy instruments to effect income transfers, the concrete meaning of liberalization becomes the gradual withdrawal of such political forces from the economic arena over time. Differentiating between the covert and overt types of policy, moreover, permits us to render the analysis more politically sensitive, as well as realistic. Shifting from the former to the latter clearly does not necessarily mean a diminished role for government but merely a different role; its indirect functions may actually increase with the continued process of liberalization, even as its direct functions diminish. This way of looking at the application of macropolicy and the overt and covert transfer of resources will help us explain the divergent paths of organizational and policy evolutions referred to earlier. In fact, it is our basic hypothesis that relative policy linearity occurs when the role of government does not atrophy but is consistently transformed from implicit to explicit actions. Policy oscillation is more likely to occur when covert policies that are adopted for short-term political convenience sooner or later self-destruct because of the insufficiently anticipated and delayed adverse impact on some groups whose income is being transferred in the absence of a clear political consensus.

The political process underlying policy change or its absence, in turn, is likely to be influenced by the initial conditions of the system, in particular its initial resource endowment. The contrast between relative

---

[2] One leading example of this is, of course, a policy of monetary expansion that seems to solve a growth or unemployment problem today but leads to inflation after a time lag, culminating in conflict among various constituent groups within the body politic.

monotonicity and oscillation, en route ultimately to "modern-growth" organizational characteristics, can thus be explained by a combination of initial typological differences and the alternative ways in which the responding political economy of policy change plays itself out over time. In trying to understand the fundamental causes of divergent performance and differential patterns of policy evolution and organizational change, we therefore intend to proceed beyond a mere description of divergent growth performances and toward the generation of a comparative, typologically sensitive development perspective that includes the evolution of organizational and policy changes as part of the explanatory framework – a framework that endogenizes policy change. Because policy change is clearly achieved through a political process, our analysis proceeds beyond the normal confines of descriptive comparative economics and includes an investigation of the political economy of policy change. It should be recalled that such considerations represented an essential component of classical economies and were artificially excised from the profession's consideration by the neoclassical school only after the last quarter of the nineteenth century.

It should also be pointed out that, given the record of the almost four decades of postwar development efforts behind us, we are now in a position to examine LDC policy evolution in a fashion that is complementary rather than antithetical to the empirically focused policy-neutral analysis that we are accustomed to. Traditionally, policy analysis stresses the economic impact, for example, on employment, labor reallocation, the pattern of trade, growth, and the distribution of income of various policy options, without much reference to political arguments – including the processes of adoption and/or abandonment of policies within a particular political milieu. It stresses comparative statics, i.e., the situation before and after some individual reform or package of reforms, but it has little to offer on the dynamics of getting from here to there and in what preferable sequence. A fruitful alternative approach would be one that recognizes that a search for any sort of economic determinism relating policy sequences and economic events in some rigid monolithic fashion would be highly inappropriate. It also acknowledges the need for reasoning about both economic and political phenomena in order to understand the logical necessity of differential orderings of policy events, that is, the timely adoption and/or abandonment of particular policy measures within the total matrix of the essential components of a liberalizing trend. We are by no means ready to present a deterministic model of such a complex set of relations and interrelations but hope to demonstrate an approach to be followed, with the help of specific country cases.

The methodology of studying transitional economies by grouping them into different types based on some set of initial conditions is, of course, not novel. Starting with the seminal work by Kuznets, much past work has been done by Chenery (and his associates), by Bhagwati and Krueger, and Fei and Ranis, among others, in analyzing the way an LDC typically changes its economic structure as it moves toward modern growth. But the role played by organizational and policy choices in this analytical context has received much less attention.

Kuznets preferred to think of policies as either obstructing or accommodating the natural evolution of a system over time but essentially excluded policy formation from his descriptive canvas. Chenery (1960), on the other hand, incorporated policy considerations in an informal way. Starting with the notion that there is a "typical" developing country whose expected performance over time can be captured by cross-sectional analysis across all economies at varying levels of income and population, he left deviations from this pattern to be explained by further analysis, including policy differences.

From these beginnings Chenery's work became increasingly sensitive to the need to disaggregate, certainly between developed and developing, but also among developing countries, and, taking advantage of the accumulating record of more than three decades of postwar LDC growth, he increasingly turned to the use of the LDC historical laboratory as a complement to his initial cross-sectional analysis. Thus, in the later 1960s, in collaboration with Taylor, he for the first time fitted a regression line to time series data plotted alongside those fitted to cross-sectional data and also paid much more attention than before to the role of international trade (Chenery and Taylor, 1968).

The accumulation of postwar data for LDCs of course also meant that individual contemporary LDCs could now be studied longitudinally. It thus became increasingly possible to observe family resemblances, so to speak, among groups of countries and to move toward a typology of countries according to some set of economic and/or institutional criteria. Chenery accordingly proposed the identification of three country types – large, small, and, within the small, primary oriented and industry oriented. Since primary or industrial orientation is, to a considerable extent, a function of economic policy, this typology is itself at least partly based on the nature of the policies pursued. Such use of policy differences as part of the "initial" typological environment became more pronounced in his later work. In collaboration with Syrquin, Chenery, for example, developed a classification of development patterns that separated countries by identifiable development strategies, including primary specialization, balanced development, import substitution, and industrial specialization (Chenery and Syrquin, 1975).

A common denominator of these approaches, shared also by Bhagwati/ Krueger, Fei/Ranis, and others, has thus been an attempt to stratify the LDC sample, depending on some mix of initial conditions and political-economic decisions in the course of the subsequent transition growth effort. Whatever their intellectual point of departure, the approaches all clearly assume that there exists a meaningful family affinity among subsets of developing countries giving them a certain uniqueness not necessarily shared by other LDCs, while recognizing that, even within any one subfamily, there may, and usually do, exist important, instructive differences between countries. What clearly seems to be evolving therefore is the recognition that we are all looking for some sort of halfway house between an ever-elusive general theory of development and the unacceptable notion that every country differs so fundamentally from every other at every point in time that nothing can be said of generalizable value. A readily helpful typological approach, no matter what school it emanates from, should thus help bring into clear focus the important elements of family affinity without suppressing meaningful intrafamily differences.

There is also a common recognition, implicit if not explicit in these approaches, as well as the research and advice emanating from the World Bank and the International Monetary Fund over recent decades, that the organizational and policy choices made are basic to the explanation of developmental success and failure. For example, it is now quite widely, though by no means universally, accepted that increased openness and reduced government intervention are generally associated with improved development performance. Indeed the diminishing role of the existence and pursuit of rents in various markets has opened up an important and closely related area of inquiry. But what has still eluded observers and constitutes an important field for investigation is just how to begin to endogenize policy change over time.

Our alternative typological approach represents an attempt at tackling this challenge. Instead of classifying countries on the basis of policies adopted – an approach that leaves open the awkward possibility that countries may have to be switched from one category to another following changes in the ministry of finance (and thus making it difficult to carry out a meaningful study of differential policy evolution over time) – our approach groups countries on the basis of their initial resource endowments, natural and human, while policy is treated at least as partly endogenous. It bases itself on three elements in order to trace the evolution of a society over time: (1) development theory sensitive to different initial conditions; (2) the evolutionary tracing of events, both in the economic performance sense and in terms of a focus on policy events over time; and (3) the quantification of both of the above in the context of an effort to trace causal relations among them.

The theoretical framework linking differential patterns of development policy evolution to differences in initial resource endowments and in the subsequent evolution of political economy forces is developed in chapter 2. The rest of the volume is devoted to the empirical application of this framework to the experience of six LDCs: Colombia, Mexico, South Korea, Taiwan, the Philippines, and Thailand. These countries have been selected as representatives of three different "families" of LDCs, the definition of families based on our chosen criterion of typological differentiation, i.e., initial endowments of natural and human resources.[3] The empirical studies carry out inter- as well intrafamily comparisons of policy evolution.

Colombia and Mexico represent the moderately labor-surplus, relatively natural-resources- and human-resources-rich, "Latin American" type. As the data in table 1.2(a) indicate, the initial natural resource endowment was relatively favorable in Mexico as reflected in its position as a significant producer of a large range of mineral products. Colombia is somewhat less rich than Mexico in mineral resources, but this is partly compensated for by its endowments of cash crops, notably coffee – endowments that, as will be clear from our discussion in the next chapter, can often have implications for development policy formulation similar to that of a rich natural resource base. The data in tables 1.2(b) and 1.2(c) confirm the moderate nature of the labor surplus and human capital endowments in both these countries.

South Korea and Taiwan, on the other hand, belong to the heavily labor-surplus, relatively natural-resources-poor and human-resources-rich "East Asian" family. The natural resources poverty of the East Asian pair is clearly brought out in Table 1.2(a); except for some coal and gold in South Korea and Taiwan, natural gas in Taiwan and tungsten in South Korea, these countries are virtually bereft of any natural resource base. Not only were there no large deposits of exportable minerals or reproducible raw materials in existence in the East Asian countries, but the amount of good arable land was limited to only 22 percent of the total land area in Taiwan and to about 25 percent in South Korea, Ranis (1991). Given the large population, this implied exceptionally low land/man ratios in both cases. In contrast, as indicated in table 1.2(c), they were both relatively favorably endowed in terms of human resources, sharing a common Chinese cultural heritage characterized, among other things, by such features as pragmatism, a capacity for hard work, and a reverence for learning. Such cultural traits defined initial human capacities that undoubtedly proved conducive to modern growth. But it was policy changes over the past 30-plus years that built upon and modified that initially favorable environment. The secret of the success of these countries thus must clearly be found in their ability to carry out a pattern of policy evolution that effectively mobilized and enhanced these human resources.

The Philippines and Thailand constitute the "intermediate" Southeast

---

[3] Since our focus of attention is the postwar period, the year 1950 is taken as representing the "initial" position.

Table 1.2   Initial conditions (approximately 1950)

(a) Natural resource endowment

per capita production in 1950

(all units of measurement are in metric tons per thousand population unless otherwise indicated)

Natural resource	Colombia	Mexico	South Korea	Taiwan	Philippines	Thailand
Coal	47.10	34.70	31.10	187.80	7.84	–
Lignite	–	–	1.30	–	–	–
Natural gas[a]	–	66.74	–	54.14	–	–
Crude petroleum	423.80	394.30	–	–	–	–
Manganese ore	–	0.60	–	–	0.59	–
Iron ore	–	10.90	–	–	15.90	–
Copper ore	–	2.30	–	–	0.51	–
Lead ore	–	9.10	–	–	0.04	–
Zinc ore	–	8.50	–	–	–	–
Tin concentrates	–	0.02	–	–	–	0.54
Chrome ore	–	–	–	–	4.67	–
Tungsten ore	–	0.001	0.026	–	–	0.38
Antimony ore	–	0.20	–	–	–	0.005
Mercury	–	0.005	–	–	–	–
Gold[b]	1.04	0.48	0.008	0.13	0.51	–
Silver	–	0.06	–	–	0.004	–
Round Wood[c]	–	–	–	–	0.15	0.16
Natural rubber	–	0.03	–	–	–	5.80
Cash Crops						
Coffee	29.83	2.51	–	–	–	–
Tea	–	–	–	1.58	–	–

[a] in cubic meters per thousand population
[b] in kgs. per thousand population
[c] in thousand cubic meters per thousand population
. . nil or not significant
Source: United Nations, *Statistical Yearbook*, 1953.

(b) Size and extent of labor surplus

	Size[a]	Labor surplus[b]
Colombia	11,334	3.0 ('51)
Mexico	25,826	1.0 ('50)
South Korea	20,513	8.3 ('49)

Table 1.2 (cont.)

(b) Size and extent of labor surplus

	Size[a]	Labor surplus[b]
Taiwan	7,981	4.0 ('50)
Philippines	19,910	2.2 ('48)
Thailand	18,488	3.3[c]('47)

(c) Human capital resources

	Adult literacy rate (in %)		School enrollment ratios (adjusted)[d] first and second level		
	'50	'60	'50	'55	'60
Colombia	60.0	63.0	30	41	50
Mexico	56.8	64.5	37	43	53
South Korea	76.8[e]	82.2	54	60	64
Taiwan	51.1	73.0	47	57	74
Philippines	60.0[f]	74.9	89	70	70
Thailand	52.0[h]	67.7	48	50	58

[a] population (in thousands)
[b] Rural population–arable land ratios (in person per hectare)
[c] Arable land refers to land devoted to main crops only
[d] These are the ratios of total enrollment at the two levels to the estimated population in the age group corresponding to the actual duration of schooling in each country
[e] 1955
[f] 1948
[g] 1958
[h] 1947.
Sources: United Nations, *Demographic Yearbook;* FAO, *Production Yearbook;* UNESCO, *Statistical Yearbook;* United Nations, *Statistical Yearbook.*

Asian pair; their initial conditions place them between the Latin American and East Asian families in the typological spectrum. Compared to the East Asian cases they are relatively better endowed with natural resources, but there are also differences within the pair; the Philippines, while not as rich as Mexico, is particularly well endowed in a wide range of minerals (e.g., coal, iron, copper, lead, chromite, timber) while Thailand's natural resources are more narrowly concentrated (in tin, rubber, tungsten, and timber). Although this is not the focus of table 1.2(a), the Philippines is also relatively richer in a variety of cash crops such as copra and sugar, while Thailand is basically a major rice exporter, recently supplemented by tapioca.

These three "families" differ with respect to the demonstrated sequencing of their subphases of transition to modern growth. All six countries in our sample, as virtually every LDC, initially (during the

1950s) pursued a strategy of primary import substitution (PIS), the active promotion of domestic production with the help of a well-known array of protectionist, interventionist policies. But the intensity and length of time over which PIS was pursued differed substantially. In the case of the East Asian and Southeast Asian countries, significant industrialization readily started in the early 1950s, while Colombia and Mexico, like many other Latin American countries, started this industrialization process much earlier, partly due to their earlier independence from colonial rule and partly due to certain developments in the international economy – notably the instability caused by the Great Depression and, in particular, the cutting off of the normal channels of trade during the two world wars, which induced them to industrialize. This early import-substituting industrialization may be called "natural," i.e., resulting from a response to market forces, to be followed by a PIS phase largely resulting from government interventions. These earlier beginnings of import-substituting industrialization in Latin America are also reflected in the primary import-substitution indices, defined as the proportion of consumer nondurable imports in total imports, presented in table 1.3. These ratios, on average, were already considerably lower by the early 1950s for our Latin American pair when compared to the East Asian and Southeast Asian pairs. In fact, for Mexico the ratio had already reached a low plateau by 1950, indicating that the inevitable termination of this subphase with the exhaustion of domestic markets had nearly been reached.

Partly because the scope for further primary import substitution had already become restricted in the Latin American countries, especially Mexico, by the beginning of the 1950s, the follow-on secondary import-substitution regime here was of a relatively severe character. By contrast, while the PIS phase in Taiwan and South Korea was characterized by the presence of all the features of a typical import-substitution policy mix – protectionism, repressed money markets, overvalued exchange rates, large government budget deficits, and neglect of the agricultural sector – it is especially noteworthy that, by international standards, both these cases chose a relatively mild version of that syndrome. Thus, for example, the fiscal system was, from the beginning, called upon to begin to replace the inflation tax. Interest rates were raised early on and government deficits brought under control, with the timely help of foreign aid, during the 1950s. Consolidated income tax reforms were promulgated in Taiwan as early as 1955, for example, and budgetary surpluses started appearing in the early 1960s. While there have been consistently greater fluctuations in policy in the case of South Korea, the effort to reduce budget deficits here has also evoked a consistent search for new taxes during the PIS period. Thus, from the beginning, the East Asians tried to move away from "under-the-table," covert taxation and were able increasingly to

Table 1.3 Primary import-substitution index[a]

	1950	1960	1970	1980	1986
Colombia	13.1 ('51)	6.1	5.0	4.6	4.8
Mexico	5.7	3.6	5.5	2.7	2.3 ('85)
South Korea	10.9 ('54)	7.5	7.3	3.2	4.8
Taiwan	17.2	8.1	5.8	2.9 ('77)	3.6 ('86)
Philippines	23.3 ('52)	8.1	5.5	3.2	5.5
Thailand	22.6 ('54)	18.6	9.1	2.9	4.8

[a] Primary import-substitution index-imports of manufactured consumer nondurables as a percentage of total imports. Manufactured consumer nondurables are those that correspond to the following SITC categories: i) 61-leather, etc.; ii) 64-paper, paper board etc.; iii) 65-textiles; iv) 84-clothing; v) 851-footwear; and vi) 892-printed matter.
Source: United Nations, *Yearbook of International Trade Statistics, various issues*

implement rounds of tax reform to generate adequate direct or "on-the-table" government revenues. Once again, the Southeast Asian pair represent an intermediate case with regard to the flexibility of their PIS phase, with Thailand closer to the East Asian pattern and the Philippines approximating the Latin American syndrome. Fei and Pauuw (1973) report that traditional agriculture-based exports still dominated the scene in Thailand in the 1950s, with a relatively mild form of primary import substitution in evidence at least until the midsixties, according to Akrasanee (1977), Corden (1967), and Ingram (1971). There is a substantial consensus that Thailand's primary import-substitution subphase was considerably milder than the typical LDC case, both in terms of the relatively low levels of tariff – which principally retained their revenue function – and the severity of the other customary instruments of import-substitution intervention.

As table 1.3 indicates, "easy" import substitution had reached its inevitable end by the 1960s. Countries now faced a rather critical decision about what future path to follow. There were primarily two alternatives. The first, followed only by a minority of LDCs, notably Taiwan and South Korea, was to move to a strategy of primary export substitution (PES), i.e., the production for export of the same commodities – consumer nondurables – earlier directed exclusively toward the domestic market.[4] This transition was a politically difficult task since it required radical changes in the "rules of the game," as economic agents now had to be persuaded to start operating in an environment that was much more competitive than the hitherto protected domestic market and to shift from

[4] The strategy is termed "primary export substitution" because the basis for comparative advantage in foreign trade now gradually shifts from land to unskilled labor, with exports of manufactured goods gradually "substituting" for agricultural exports.

a regime of earning certain and large unit profits on a small volume to one of uncertain small unit profits on a large volume.

The political difficulty associated with a shift to a PES strategy explains why, once PIS had run out of steam, most LDCs, including Colombia, Mexico, the Philippines and, to a lesser extent, Thailand, opted for the alternative route, that of secondary import substitution (SIS), i.e., the production at home of consumer durables and capital goods previously imported. This route is politically easier since it does not require liberalization in various markets and the withdrawal of rents from various favored interest groups. Import substitution continued to be the basic strategy of industrialization in these countries, although, over time, this became tinged increasingly with an element of export promotion (EP), reflecting a desire to export manufactured goods, which, of course, could be accomplished only through the direct or indirect subsidization of such exports. The strategy typically followed by the Latin American prototype may, therefore, be properly termed one of secondary import substitution cum export promotion (SIS/EP). In that sense these countries can also be said to have entered an era of external orientation at the end of their PIS phases but one based on changing comparative advantage. For virtually all countries in our sample, with the exception of Colombia, the beginnings of some form of external orientation can be dated in the early 1960s.

While all six countries in our sample moved toward substantially greater external orientation during the 1960s, the subsequent trends in the degree of external orientation and in the composition of exports diverged significantly, as indicated in table 1.4(a). In 1960, the initial degree of external orientation, defined as the export/GDP ratio, was no higher for our East Asian pair than for the Latin American and South-

Table 1.4(a)   External orientation ratios (exports/GDP: in percent)

	1950	1960	1970	1980	1986
Taiwan	10.1	11.1	29.6	52.2	60.6
South Korea	2.1	3.3	14.3	37.7	40.7
Colombia	10.9	15.7	14.6	16.3	18.9
Mexico	17.0	10.6	8.2	22.4	17.0
Thailand	15.0	17.0	18.7	25.8	28.2
Philippines	10.5	11.0	18.1	17.1	24.5

Sources:
IMF, *International Financial Statistics: Yearbook*, various issues.
World Bank, *World Tables*, and *World Development Report*, various issues.
Statistical Yearbook of the Republic of China, various issues.
Philippine Statistical Yearbook, various issues.
National Income of the Republic of China, various issues.

east Asian countries. By 1970, that picture had changed substantially. External orientation fell in the Latin American countries, remained virtually stagnant in Thailand, increased moderately in the Philippines, and more than doubled in East Asia.

A more remarkable change took place in the composition of exports. In the East Asian countries, the proportion of manufactured exports in total exports increased dramatically over the sixties: from 14 percent in 1960 to 77 percent in 1970 in South Korea and from 16 percent to 74 percent in Taiwan over the same period (see table 1.4(b)). By contrast, manufactured exports continued to figure relatively insignificantly in the export composition of the Latin American and Southeast Asian countries, with Mexico something of an exception. In other words, the Latin American and Southeast Asian countries continued to rely on traditional primary and mineral-based exports to finance the importation of producers' goods necessary to fuel their increasingly capital- and technology-intensive industrialization effort while, in the East Asian countries, the burden of financing continued industrialization was dramatically shifted to the exportation of nondurable consumer goods.

The success of the PES strategy in East Asia was based on the continuous absorption of abundant labor reallocated from the agricultural to the fast-growing export-oriented nonagricultural sectors. However, as the PES phase ran its course and labor reallocation at rates of more than 6 percent annually gradually exhausted the system's labor surplus, relatively stable unskilled real wages gave way to rising real wages. Taiwan and South Korea reached this point of labor scarcity or "commercialization" of the agricultural labor force during the late sixties and early seventies, respectively. The growth rate of unskilled real wages, modest during the first half of the sixties, accelerated in the second half of the decade before virtually exploding in the seventies.

The emergence of labor shortage and the associated increase in real wages implied that these countries were losing their comparative advantage in labor-intensive exports and facing increased competition in international markets from LDCs, which, lagging behind in the growth process, still enjoyed the benefits of cheap labor. Given their substantial liberalization effort in various markets, the East Asians followed the signals of a changing comparative advantage and moved into a "secondary-import-cum-export-substitution" (SIS/SES) subphase of transition. This essentially involved a "natural" shift in the composition of output, for domestic as well as export markets, toward the production of capital goods, consumer durables, and the domestic processing of raw materials. Since this represents an output mix substantially more skill-, technology-, and capital-intensive than PES, it also required institutional/organizational changes in the educational and financial spheres, as we shall see.

Table 1.4(b)   The composition of exports (as percentage of total exports)

	1960	1970	1980	1986
Colombia				
i) agricultural (non–fuel primary)	78.8	80.6	76.7	71.2
ii) mineral	18.9	11.3	2.8	13.2
iii) manufactured	2.3	8.1	20.6	15.5
Mexico				
i) agricultural (non–fuel primary)	64.2	48.6	14.2	23.0
ii) mineral	15.0	18.7	71.1	51.0
iii) manufactured	20.7	32.5	14.6	25.9
South Korea				
i) agricultural (non–fuel primary)	58.0	16.6	8.9	5.8
ii) mineral	27.8	6.7	1.1	2.3
iii) manufactured	14.2	76.7	89.9	91.8
Taiwan				
i) agricultural (non–fuel primary)	82.1	24.5	10.9	8.5
ii) mineral	2.1	1.9	1.5	1.4
iii) manufactured	15.8	73.6	87.6	90.0
Philippines				
i) agricultural (non–fuel primary)	80.4	69.9	41.7	32.5
ii) mineral	13.0	22.5	21.3	10.0
iii) manufactured	6.6	7.4	37.0	57.5
Thailand				
i) agricultural (non–fuel primary)	90.8	74.3	56.9	52.4
ii) mineral	7.1	14.9	13.9	2.9
iii) manufactured	2.1	10.7	29.0	44.6

The categorization of exports follows the Standard International Trade Classification (SITC), Series M, No. 34, Revision 1. Agricultural (non–fuel primary) exports include commodities in SITC categories 0 (food and live animals); 1 (beverages and tobacco); 2 (crude materials excluding fuel) but excluding SITC division 27 (minerals and crude fertilizers) and 28 (metaliferrous ores); and 4 (animal and vegetable oils and fats). Mineral exports include commodities in SITC categories 3 (mineral fuels etc.); divisions 27, 28, and 68 (nonferrous metals). Manufactured exports include all commodities in SITC categories 5 (chemicals and related products); 6 (basic manufactures) but excluding division 68; 7 (machinery and transport equipment); 8 (miscellaneous manufactured goods) and 9 (goods not classified by kind). Figures may not add up to 100 due to rounding off decimals. Source: Computed from data in United Nations, *Yearbook of International Trade Statistics,* various issues; Inspector General of Customs, Taiwan, Statistical Department, *The Trade of China,* various issues.

The small size of the East Asian economies combined with the appearance of industries with substantial economies of scale for the first time made it necessary to combine secondary export substitution with secondary import substitution in the product-cycle context. The experience of operating in international markets, acquired during the PES phase, was undoubtedly helpful in permitting the East Asians to adjust continuously to a changing endowment and demand situation over time. By contrast, in the Latin American and, to a lesser extent, Southeast Asian countries, the continued efforts during the 1970s to promote exports within a basically unchanged structure of import-substitution interventions rendered increased external orientation and a more diversified composition of exports difficult and costly. In the East Asian countries, as we have seen, both the degree of external orientation as well as the proportion of manufactured exports in total exports increased dramatically during the 1970s and 1980s.

The differences in the nature of the transitional subphases followed by the "majority" Latin American and Southeast Asian countries vis-a-vis those in the "minority" East Asian typology are, of course, reflected in the differential pattern of development policy evolution over time, particularly in the differential responses to similar external shocks, shocks to which countries become more susceptible once they shift to an external orientation. A theoretical framework is developed in chapter 2 that attempts to capture the main characteristics of this pattern of policy evolution in a typical LDC context. It posits the likely links between initial conditions, the subsequent interplay of political economy forces, and the resulting long-run trends for various crucial policy parameters. The empirical application of our hypothetical pattern is the subject of chapter 3, which examines the policy experience of Colombia and Mexico, two typical LDCs. Chapter 4 analyzes the contrasting pattern of the "deviant" East Asian cases of Taiwan and South Korea, while chapter 5 traces the policy evolution and performance in the "intermediate" Southeast Asian cases of the Philippines and Thailand. Finally, chapter 6 summarizes our findings and their implications for development policy generally.

The manner in which the empirical studies have been structured reflects our belief that while no country is *sui generis,* i.e., differing so fundamentally from the others at every point in time that nothing of transferable value can be learned from its experience, there is also no "average" behavioral pattern followed by all LDCs and no "average" transition growth path common to all. Each of the empirical studies attempts to bring out the features of policy evolution unique to a particular family, but it also tries to show that important and instructive differences in behavior may exist within a family. Such intrafamily differences are, of course, partly due to differences in initial conditions even within families but they also arise because policy evolution over time is affected not only by external shocks, which may be more or less common to members of one family, but also by domestic shocks specific to individual countries. In other words, while our formal analysis is heavily focused on the relationship between a system's initial natural resource endowment, differences in policy behavior, and in "bottom-line" outcomes across country types, intrafamily differences, e.g., as to the precise nature of colonial footprints and even of the commodity composition of traditional exports, can also play a role. This is illustrated especially by such intermediate cases as the Philippines and Thailand, geographic neighbors and similar in some dimensions of our initial conditions, but belonging to different types in other dimensions.

2

Theoretical Framework

2.1 Introduction

During their transition growth effort, so-called "open dualistic" developing economies generally seem to pass through two by now well-recognized subphases, namely, an early (or primary) import-substitution subphase (IS), followed by some form of an external-orientation subphase (EO), both definable in terms of certain observable statistical time series.[1] Superimposed on this long-run trend of growth and structural change en route to modern growth are disturbances that can be traced to various kinds of exogenous shocks, including those originating from swings in the prices of primary products in world markets as well as the international business cycle. This mainly "externally originated" cause of instability in LDCs is basically different from the mainly "internally originated" instability in DCs. Thus, while aggregate demand management in the DCs is largely directed at "internally originated instability," demand management in LDCs is primarily directed at maintaining growth in the context of externally originated instability. This does not, of course, exclude the possibility of other shocks of the business cycle or crop failure variety in the typical LDC, which we will not, however, be dealing with here.

In their early IS subphase, LDCs almost without exception adopt an internally oriented policy as an essential component of a growth-promotion strategy in which macropolicies are deployed to provide protection for their fledgling industrialists from the threat of exogenous disturbances. During this period, a cardinal element of the customary strategy is growth promotion through protection via QRs and/or tariffs and government spending, i.e., the deployment of various macropolicies, both intended to assist private entrepreneurs by "manufacturing" profits on their behalf. A corrupted version of the "Keynesian" mone-

---

[1] See Kuznets (1966), who defined modern economic growth but did not concern himself with the phases of the transition process.

tary approach transferred from the DCs lurks beneath the surface here as policy practice seems to be based on the conviction that (1) interest rates can be repressed to an artificially low level to generate profits; and (2) government can acquire all the goods and services it needs from the market by "covert taxation without consent," i.e., inflation. All such growth-promotion tasks can be undertaken without great difficulty as the government of a sovereign state has the power to monopolize the printing of money. All it really takes is the political will to use this power persistently, giving the typical LDC a virtually perpetual inflationary bias.[2] The government's political will penetrates the market system to determine not only the overall volume of aggregate demand but the precise direction in which resources are to be transferred and even individual investment decisions and allocations.[3]

With the arrival of the EO phase, a "liberalization" process then usually sets in as the market mechanism that regulates the exchange behavior among economic actors is gradually depoliticized. There is inevitably a gradual atrophying of the growth-focused political will in the sense that Keynesian monetarism is gradually abandoned and replaced by a monetary policy that is based on the recognition that money (M) should serve primarily as an internal medium of exchange, while the foreign exchange reserve stock (R) should serve primarily as an external medium of exchange. The manipulation of these quantities as vehicles for exercising the monopoly power of the government is gradually eroded.

The pace at which such Keynesian monetarism is abandoned over time, does, however, seem to differ markedly across the developing world. For example, it seems to occur more slowly and hesitatingly in Latin America than in East Asia. This is, of course, relevant to the differential choice made by societies at the end of their early IS, that is, between continued or secondary import substitution (SIS) complemented by export promotion (EP), as in Latin America, and the shift to export substitution (ES), as in East Asia, as described earlier.

---

[2] To refer to this approach as Keynesian is somewhat misleading as an expansion of the money supply meant to create a "liquid asset" in the Cambridge tradition to meet the demand for liquidity; no such roundabout way of thinking is needed in the LDC where monetary expansion is a convenient way to create purchasing power to allow the beneficiary (i.e., the government and/or favored private entrepreneurs) to "costlessly" acquire goods and services from the market. As long as money must be accepted, involuntarily, as a medium of exchange, this convenient method of finance can be practiced extensively.

[3] The multiple exchange rates, the import licensing system, the differential interest rate structure, and/or the availability of bank credit to "favored" public or private sector industries are typical examples. This contrasts sharply with the normal directional neutrality of macropolicies in the DCs where, under the U.S. Federal Reserve System, for example, the monetary authorities control only the overall levels of new bank lending, generally leaving the market system, i.e., banks and the money market, to determine the precise direction of individual allocations.

The more or less gradual movement toward liberalization of most LDCs also represents a movement toward greater rationalism, a more organic nationalism, and away from the notion that an "all-powerful" newly independent government, trying to synthetically "create" nationalism, can and should "take care of everything." The movement also suggests, however, that the government ultimately can no longer shy away from the onerous task of seeking social compromises in order to narrow budgetary gaps through "taxation with consent," replacing "under-the-table" taxes, and that private entrepreneurs must learn, sooner or later, to earn profits through their competitive productive performance in internal and world markets rather than via rent-seeking activities. These trends, while starting earlier and more pronounced in strength in East Asia, now seem to be gaining ascendancy elsewhere, from Latin America to Eastern Europe. Seen in long-run historical perspective they seem to constitute a natural organizational companion to the Kuznetsian economic characteristics of modern economic growth – especially in the so-called mixed economies.[4]

This liberalization process is, however, clearly not smooth and linear. In particular, in the archetypal Latin American case, the pursuit of organizational and policy reforms tends to be a slow, painful process, as the very existence and abundance of economic rents (arising in the production of the exported primary products) invites competitive "rent-seeking" activities by various interest groups to remain on the political stage; moreover, anything smacking of a tendency toward laissez-faire continues to be suspect of neocolonial designs and to run counter to the lingering political ideology that holds that growth is a public concern that must be managed directly, via the exercise of political power.

This inevitable, if sometimes slow, sometimes faster depoliticization process is disturbed, moreover, by exogenous shocks, such as fluctuations in the prices of primary products in the world markets, the business cycle, and so on, clearly yielding what appear to be periodic revivals of an earlier IS phase with all its well-known observable "symptoms." The superimposition of cyclical fluctuations on this long-run gradual liberalization trend (showing the IS subphase and the various EO subphases) will be developed first (see section 2.2 and figure 2.1). The analysis of the political economy at work within a typical cycle, in terms of policy behavior culminating in the periodic, if only temporary, revival of IS "regimes" constitutes the main analytical focus of this chapter. Section 2.3 then proceeds to identify the internal (or domestic) and the external

---

[4] Even in contemporary still-avowedly-socialist LDCs, e.g., mainland China, the authorities have rationalized their own brand of liberal reform (post-1979) by tracing it, with considerable justification, to what they now call the "fundamental teachings of Marx," according to which "forces of production" will always be liberated from institutional constraints, and the party only expedites the process.

(or foreign-trade- and foreign-capital-related) dimensions of the macro-policies that will then be treated separately in sections 2.4 and 2.5.

In the LDCs, the monopoly of the management of the foreign exchange reserves by political power, i.e., the prohibition of private international financial transactions in order to isolate domestic interest rates from international rates, is usually a cornerstone of the government's pursuit of an independent low interest rate policy combined with the printing of money.[5] Under the condition of a centralized reserve system (that is, with government control of capital movements) and given the prospect that inflation will continue for some time to come, the art of management of the foreign exchange rate and foreign exchange reserves becomes a critical reform issue. Clean and/or dirty floats in LDCs represent another aspect of the short-run political economy choice and will also be analyzed in section 2.5.

Unionism, and minimum-wage legislation, conspicuous by its presence in the Latin American archetype and its relative absence in the East Asian archetype, represent another political economy phenomenon; its macropolicy implications are discussed in section 2.6. Unlike the developed country case, in LDCs, given their typical underlying labor surplus condition, union and bargaining power generally derive from government rather than from the marketplace. Nevertheless, union unrest, strikes, and the agitation for minimum-wage legislation and indexation may be likened to a thermometer of social unrest traceable to unevenness, for different social groups, of the impact of price inflation over each cycle. In most instances social upheavals with union responses are induced by monetary malpractices. However, a differentiated wage structure (i.e., a much higher union wage for an elite minority of the labor force) can be damaging to the cause of export diversification in the natural-resource-abundant LDCs as the export of labor-intensive manufactured goods is effectively blocked, contributing to the persistence of unemployment. A tight monetary policy (or at least a more modest pace of inflation) represents a more effective and equitable way of keeping union power in check as long as labor surplus persists.

These various arguments will be combined into an overall theory of policy oscillation in section 2.7, where we also hope to begin to answer the question of the comparative evolution of policy in typologically dif-

---

[5] This is not to suggest that full integration with world financial markets is foreseeable anywhere in the near future. Given completely free international capital movements, the sovereign economic power of the LDC government would collapse. Given rapid inflation, the inverse of Gresham's Law implies that a stable foreign currency (e.g., the U.S. dollar) would drive out the domestic currency as a standard of value and even as a medium of exchange when not protected by the political force of "legal tender." Even in contemporary liberated Taiwan, full integration of its domestic financial market with the rest of the world is still stubbornly resisted.

ferent parts of the LDC world. If we can show why the periodic revival of an IS-like regime is more likely to occur in the natural-resource-abundant Latin American type and less likely in the natural-resource-poor East Asian type of LDC we will have come a long way toward beginning to understand the political economy of development policy change.

2.2 Basic framework

As pointed out earlier, the postwar LDC transition growth process has been almost universally characterized by the appearance of a primary IS (import-substitution) phase, succeeded by an EO (external-orientation) phase. This phasing process can be measured, first of all, by the *degree of external orientation E/Q* (i.e., total exports as a fraction of GDP) as well as by the *degree of export diversification E_q/E* (i.e., nonprimary product exports as a percentage of total exports). As figures 2.1(a) and 2.1(b) show, both of these indices increase markedly during the EO phase.

Superimposed on these long-term trends of E/Q and E_q/E are fluctuations that are causally traceable to externally originated instability, e.g., the price fluctuations of primary products in world markets C_i and/or business cycles in the industrially advanced countries.[6] In case the two exogenous cycles coincide, we can identify a "recovery" or boom (+) and a "recession" or bust (−) subphase within each C_i (see figure 2.1(c)). The recovery phase (+) provides the exogenous background favorable for external orientation and export diversification and hence E/Q and E_q/E temporarily accelerate above their respective trend values (shown in figure 2.1(a)). The reverse holds for the recession subphase.

In long-run perspective, the evolution of the LDCs in the direction of modern economic growth tends to repeat the historical experience of the DCs in terms of statistically measurable structural change. As empha-sized earlier, this is equally true in the organizational sense, i.e., there is a general evolutionary trend from heavy direct-market interference and a greater reliance on the market mechanism, complemented by the type of government interference characteristic of the DC. This long-run trend of "liberalization" is, however, not a smooth process and is usually marked by short-run policy oscillations as liberalization packages are adopted and experimented with for a time, only to be abandoned once again under the impact of external shocks pictured in figure 2.1(c). Policy oscillation be-

---

[6] Such externally originated fluctuations causing instability in the less-developed countries of course are likely to be more pronounced the smaller the country and the less diversified its primary exports.

Figure 2.1   Trends and exogenous shocks

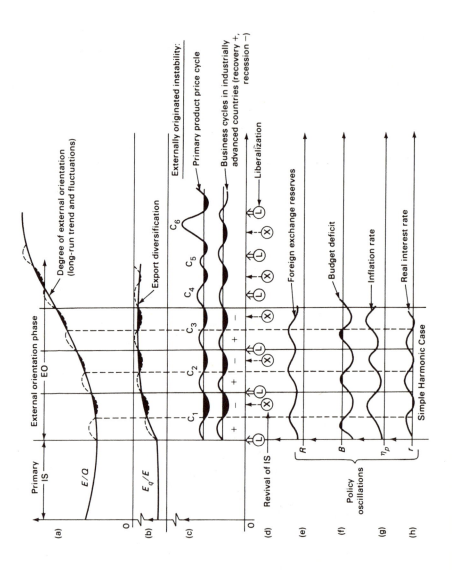

tween "more liberalization" and a "return to import substitution" (indicated by the Ls and Xs, respectively, in figure 2.1(d)) is thus a combined product of growth and externally originated fluctuations.

In the DCs the initial long period of postwar prosperity (1950–73) was characterized by transferring substantial producers' incomes to nonproducers after the fact, through social welfare and other redistributive programs, and maintaining countercyclical monetary and fiscal policies in order to smooth out any, mainly internally originated, signs of instability. Thus, while the economic role of DC governments expanded rapidly after World War II, macropolicies were aimed mainly at creating an environment for the private sector to make the "right" growth-relevant decisions, that is, policy instruments were used mainly to minimize instability and inequity as well as to accommodate growth rather than to promote growth directly. This may be labeled as a growth-neutral (at best an only indirectly growth-oriented) set of policies.

The typical LDC, in contrast, anxious to "catch up" right from the outset, has been concerned with direct growth promotion via the use of macropolicies, as was typical in the IS subphase. As a consequence, during the inevitably ensuing EO subphase, liberalization experiments began hesitantly because its relatively laissez-faire connotations ran counter to the lingering political ideology, which identifies the market with colonialism and holds that growth is a public concern that must be managed, directly, via the exercise of political power. Accordingly, all the major policy instruments (the interest rate, the money supply, the budget, the foreign exchange rate, the rate of protection) are viewed as tools for such direct growth-oriented activism by government. Liberalization thus proceeds in an oscillating manner as the idea of "growth through controls" can be expected to atrophy only slowly.

When the EO phase is reached, the growth process, in other words, has to contend with the legacy of a prior primary IS phase, which typically contains a substantial control-oriented institutional and organizational package. Import-licensing procedures and such deeply ingrained practices as monetary expansion and the protection of infant industries continue to have a heavy influence. The periodic revival of IS then usually occurs during difficult periods of "recession," i.e., it may be viewed as a temporary retreat to a comfortable heritage. It was, after all, the fear of the unfavorable impact of externally originating fluctuations, such as the decline of primary product prices, that provided the underlying rationale for the inward-oriented strategy of primary IS in the first place. The occasional dipping of E/Q below the trend line during the recession phase (see figure 2.1(b)) suggests a temporary revival of that policy syndrome.

In order to generalize this inductive approach let us start with the "simple harmonic case" by assuming that the phases of the primary product price cycle C_i and of the business cycle coincide as they occur in succession over time (e.g., C_1, C_2, C_3 in figure 2.1).[7] Liberalization efforts are assumed to start at the end of primary IS or the beginning of C_1. The actual analysis of time series, such as R (the foreign exchange reserves), B (the government's budget deficit), η_p (the inflation rate), r (the real rate of interest), dM/dt (the rate of monetary expansion), t (the effective rate of protection), to empirically corroborate our thesis will be based on the historical experience of the six countries in our sample.

2.3 Exogenous instability and the activation of government policies

Real variable indicators

The exogenous fluctuations of "foreign purchasing power" (as proxied by C_i, shown in figures 2.2(a) and 2.2(b)), transmitted by the international market mechanism, produce domestic impacts on the GNP growth rate (η_Q), the external orientation rate ($\eta_{E/Q}$), as well as the trade balance (D), with an over-the-cycle pattern that is naturally harmonic with C_i (as shown in the dotted curves of figures 2.2(c), 2.2(d), and 2.2(e).[8] During the recovery (recession) phase η_Q and $\eta_{E/Q}$ are higher (lower) than their long-run trend values, as it is a time of relatively rapid (slow) growth and a relatively higher (lower) rate of external orientation. As induced by exogenous fluctuations, the sense of success (failure) of the growth performance, measurable by the speed of GDP growth during the recovery (recession) years, creates the sociopolitical underpinnings for domestic policy reactions.

The underlying "natural" domestic response may not, however, be really observable because it is affected by political forces that induce policy reactions. What can be statistically observed, *ex post*, are the magnified fluctuations of η_Q and $\eta_{E/Q}$, i.e., exacerbated in the recovery (recession) period by the expansion (contraction) of domestic monetary purchasing power (see figures 2.2(c) and (d)). As compared with the broken curves that indicate the "natural" response, the solid curves in figures 2.2(c) and (d) indicate the *ex post* (observable) pattern and show a sharp contrast between the relatively greater external orientation and more rapid growth of the recovery period and the more pronounced internal orientation and slower growth of the recession period. Similarly, as the result of such political economy effects, the solid (*ex post*) D or trade balance curve (figure 2.2(e)) shows an export-surplus-raising bias at the beginning of the recovery phase (before t') and an import-surplus-

---

[7] Treatment of the more complicated and, luckily, also less likely to occur nonharmonic case, e.g., C_4, C_5, C_6, is not attempted here.

[8] Throughout $\eta_x = (dx/dt)/x$ stands for the growth rate of the time variable $x(t)$.

reducing bias at the end of the recession phase (after t'''), with a hastening of the arrival of the relative import surplus in between (e.g., at time t''.)

The vertical arrows in figures 2.2(c), (d), (e), and (f) indicate the direction of the distortion exercised by the political force underlying macroeconomic policies (fiscal and monetary) in relation to what would have happened "naturally" through time in the absence of such market interferences. A time marking the beginnings of an externally originating downturn (e.g., at t') is "naturally" a time of relatively slow growth and more internal orientation; the exercise of macropolicies to overcome this, in fact, will hasten both the return to an internal orientation (i.e., when η_Q becomes negative) and of a relative import surplus (i.e., a negative D), as indicated in figures 2.2(d) and (e).

Sources of government's power to spend

The typical interventionist LDC government springs into action (or alternately, relative inaction) during the recovery (recession) period of the cycle, not only because of its sense of a growth-promotion mission but also, and just as important, due to the waxing and waning of the feeling that it has the power to spend. Exogenous fluctuations induce the government to be active (passive) during the recovery (recession) period by way of two channels: via its foreign exchange reserves, R, i.e., its accumulated external purchasing power (as shown in figure 2.2(f)), and via its tax revenue, T, plus the possible running of a deficit, i.e., its internal spending power (as shown in figure 2.2(k)). The relative dependence of an LDC government on the externally generated rather than the domestically generated power to spend of course varies from case to case, indicating differences in the over-the-cycle characteristics that can be statistically verified.

Foreign exchange (FE) reserves (R) as a source of government power

The stockpiling (dissipation) of FE reserves, R (or external purchasing power), during the recovery (recession) years ($D = dR/dt$ for D and R in figures 2.2(e) and (f)) represents an accumulation (decumulation) of the windfall political power to spend bestowed on the government by exogenous events. In a politicized economic system, R represents something considerably more than international reserve assets to help defend against short-run fluctuations in the balance of payments. The memory of the experience of previous cycles often leaves the LDC government with little doubt that mercantilist affluence ($dR/dt > 0$) is necessarily good, while the opposite ($dR/dt < 0$) is surely a sign of government weakness that causes national anxiety of crisis proportions. Thus, an externally sensitive LDC government seldom fails to try to stockpile R

Figure 2.2 Intracycle policy performance

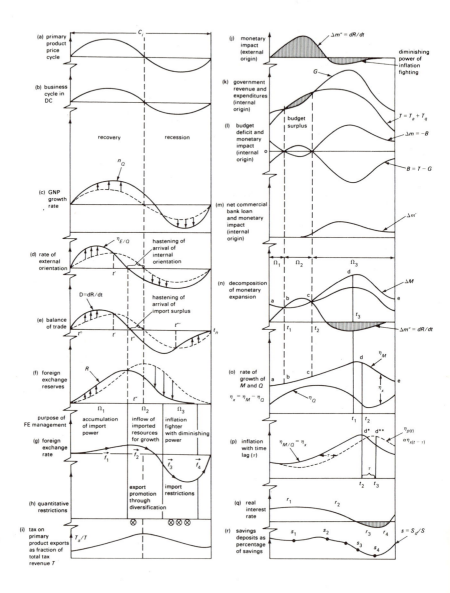

as much as it can at the beginning of each cycle C_i for later use. The drive to accumulate FE reserves is made possible by the fact that the mainly natural-resources-based (relative) export surplus provides the necessary precondition, which the government can try to exploit fully. This is what lies behind the temporary EO bias (before t' in figure 2.2(e)). Moreover, a sovereign government can always "promote exports" by buying foreign exchange, thus permitting its own exchange rate to decline in value. In figure 2.2(f), the "natural" (dotted) R-path is distorted to become the *ex post* (solid) R-path. Toward the end of each C_i, on the other hand, as the government's political power is threatened by the depletion of the FE reserves, it becomes increasingly reluctant to release the rapidly diminishing foreign exchange reserves, implying that the import surplus is politically curtailed. Thus the cyclical pattern of foreign exchange management, as depicted in figure 2.2(f), amounts to a distortion of the trade deficit within each C_i by encouraging it to "borrow from both tails," i.e., to promote exports (during t_0 to t') or cut imports (during t''' to t_n) to allow more imported resources to flow in to "finance the middle," (i.e., between t' and t'') to accommodate its interventionist objectives. Warning signals of trouble ahead (i.e., $dR/dt < 0$ at t'' when an import surplus threatens) usually appear in this middle period.

Tax revenue and the power of government spending   Positive exogenous events also give the government an enhanced sense of the domestic power to spend as total government revenues T increase during the recovery period (see figure 2.2(k)). The opposite, of course, holds for a negative shock from abroad. While the patterns of R holdings are "discretionary" and those of T are "built in," the harmonic motion of T and R can be explained only on the grounds that the "boom" and "bust" nature of the political power to spend is mainly traceable to the appropriation of windfall economic rents from primary producers, which become more (less) abundant in the recovery (recession) period. This is indicated by the relative tax burden T_d/T, i.e., the proportion of total taxes based on natural resource rents, which rises during the recovery period (see figure 2.2(i)). Such an involuntary expansion of the political power to spend then emboldens the government to promote growth through the voluntary act of spending even more, i.e., via expansionary fiscal policies. Total expenditures of government, G, are accordingly likely to zoom and, with a time lag, to yield, first a brief (relative) budget surplus B ($= T - G$), quickly followed by a deficit, as shown in figure 2.2(l). As compared with the typical DC, we note here the trendal characteristic of B toward a budget deficit, such that deficit years (more frequent and longer than surplus years) can occur right in the middle of prosperity, giving fiscal policy a noncompensatory cast. In other words, in good times, government spending is justified by the need for growth;

in bad times, the rationale becomes "Keynesian" spending. This internal asymmetry tends to further magnify rather than ameliorate the impact of unavoidable exogenous fluctuations (see figures 2.2(a), (b), and (c)).

2.4 Internal purchasing power creation

Money variable indicators

Soon after the recovery the activist government is emboldened to assist domestic entrepreneurs by manufacturing profits through the "printing of additional money" (dM/dt) by the banks to accommodate the demand for money for private investment finance. The inverse U-shaped $\Delta m'$ curve of figure 2.2(m) represents the time path for such "net lending" (i.e., new loans minus the repayment of old loans) by commercial banks to accommodate the demand for money for private investment finance. By way of a footnote to the history of monetary thought, the notion of a "demand for finance," that is, a demand for monetary purchasing power to command goods and services in the market, was rendered all but obsolete by the "liquidity preference" theory of Keynes, according to which an increase in the quantity of money has mainly psychological effects. In LDCs, money creation is more appropriately interpreted as the creation of "market power" granted to private entrepreneurs and state enterprises by the political act of the sovereign government's monopoly power to manufacture money.

The decomposition of the growth of money

Accordingly, money is printed to solve three types of growth-related problems. First, as a complement to the "centralized foreign exchange" system, it allows the government to acquire foreign exchange reserves at zero cost, as the foreign exchange earnings of exporters can be forcibly acquired via money creation, $\Delta m'' = dR/dt = D$, reproduced in figure 2.2(j) to show what is referred to in the literature as the "external origin" of dM/dt. Second, it allows control over domestic resources without the inconvenience of taxation, i.e., $\Delta m = -B$ as shown by the symmetrical curve in figure 2.2(l), one of the components of dM/dt that is of "internal origin." Third, it allows the government to manufacture profits for private entrepreneurs by accommodating their demand for finance, $\Delta m'$, (shown in figure 2.2(m)), with impunity. Money creation (dM/dt) can thus become an all-problem-solving device for the typical LDC government.

The three additive components of dM/dt ($=\Delta m + \Delta m' + \Delta m''$) are shown by the time path abcde in figure 2.2(n), with three regions (Ω_1, Ω_2, Ω_3) marked off. In Ω_1, dM/dt is small because the increase of the money of external origin, $\Delta m''$, is offset by the decrease of Δm. In Ω_2, dM/dt is moderate because the increase of money of "external origin" ($\Delta m''$) is partly offset by the government budget surplus (Δm). In Ω_3, dM/dt is inverse U-shaped, zooming rapidly to a peak (at d) before it declines. Thus, it is in the "middle period," between t_2 and t_3, that the government finds it difficult to resist the temptation to use its powers of money creation to solve conveniently its growth-related problems. During Ω_3, $\Delta m''$ gradually declines to zero, signifying that the government's capacity to fight inflation by drawing down its reserves rapidly diminishes.

The existence of these three phases can be statistically verified by the so-called "money-base" approach to the decomposition of dM/dt (or inflation). Thus dM/dt is attributable increasingly to the "external" source ($\Delta m''$) in Ω_2 and to the internal sources ($\Delta m + \Delta m'$) in Ω_3 as *the* dominant cause. However, the usual mechanics of the money-base approach, by treating Δm, $\Delta m''$, and ΔF (the increase of central bank credit) as the "high-powered money base" that is multiplied by u to become dM/dt (i.e., $dM/dt = u(\Delta m + \Delta m'' + \Delta F)$) is spuriously misleading in two ways. First, dM/dt is not linked up with the political motivation for its creation. Second, when it is so linked, in the absence of central bank autonomy the expansion of central bank credit is merely a meaningless formal *ex post* accommodation to an expansionary political will that is not to be denied. Moreover, it often has direct investment allocation functions, as we shall see.

Monetary expansion thus constitutes the most important policy instrument in a "typical" LDC. Its citizens have no choice but to accept money, involuntarily, as the medium of exchange – even when the monetary system functions very badly (e.g., at times of hyperinflation). In the absence of the tradition of some central bank autonomy, the convenient power of money printing is thus monopolized by the government – with the central bank performing merely as an arm of the executive branch. It is primarily for these reasons that a change in monetary philosophy is essential if the liberalization trend is to become more dependably "linear."

Analysis of inflation

When the government persistently indulges in the convenience of money printing this will, sooner or later, produce inflation – if with a time lag. Let $x = M/Q$ be the supply of money, as the medium of exchange, per unit of real GNP. Then the growth rate $\eta_x = \eta_M - \eta_Q$ is indicated as the difference between η_M (derived from ΔM in figure 2.2(n)) and η_Q (in figure 2.2(c)), as shown in figure 2.2(o). The fact that η_Q is higher (lower) in the good (bad) years implies that a peak value of η_x occurs (i.e., at t_2). The inflationary pressure is thus much stronger toward the latter part of C_i because, with a decline of η_Q, less money is then needed for transactions purposes. A second peak postponement occurs because the inflation rate (η_P) occurs with a time lag (i.e., of τ years, say 1–2) after the change in η_x as indicated by the relation $\eta_P(t) = a\eta_x(t - \tau)$ (shown in figure 2.2(p)). This equation shows that a stabilized inflation rate (η_P) can be achieved if and only if η_x has been constant for some time in the past. A solution of this differential equation implies a dynamic version of the equation of exchange $p(t) = a(M(t - \tau))/Q(t - \tau) -$ which shows that a constant price level ($\eta_P = 0$) can be achieved when and only when the condition $\eta_M = \eta_Q$ is fulfilled. This implies that monetary conservatism has been practiced in the past so that the addition to the supply of money is approximately the same as the additional transactions demand for money.

Thus we see that the "monetarism" of price inflation, especially pronounced in the late phase of C_i, is primarily traceable to the political activism exhibited during the recovery phase. At that time the government indulges in the convenience of money printing (by taking advantage of the necessity of acceptance of money as a medium of exchange by the nonbank public) while reaping the harvest of inflation only later, via a number of time lags (d, d*, d** in figures 2.2(o) and (p)). It is the durability of the circulation of the artificially created purchasing power (η_M) that produces these time lags, which "blind" almost everyone into believing in a cost-push theory of inflation. Secondary inflation pressures are, of course, also bound to build, depending on the strength of expectations that raise the value of "a" (the velocity of circulation in the dynamic-exchange equation), as we shall see below.

Covert transfers and forced savings

When the government and/or private entrepreneurs borrow (i.e., B and $\Delta m'$ in figures 2.2(l) and (m)), the repayment burden that falls due at a later date can be lightened or even rendered negative by inflation.[9] The printing of money by government acts as a covert tax on savers through inflation. When banks create money to finance investment, investors similarly receive newly created purchasing power that they can use in the marketplace to bid resources away from would-be consumers. The total of such "forced savings" that can be generated as a percentage of total out-

---

[9] It is an historical misfortune that the elementary fact that bank loans must be repaid becomes almost an irrelevant minor detail in the liquidity preference theory of interest. To put the emphasis on the total money *stock* (M) rather than the *flow* of its creation (dM/dt) renders the Keynesian theory almost entirely irrelevant to the political economy of LDCs. Far more relevant are the Swedish and the forced-saving schools of thought based on the loanable funds theory in which the obligation of the repayment of a bank loan is formally recognized.

put (s') depends on the increase in the money supply that is generated in this fashion (dM/dt) and the velocity of money (V).[10] An upward change in the velocity is one way in which the consuming public can "fight back" to resist the excessive resort to forced savings. What results is inflation. Moderate amounts of forced savings (sometimes called the "seigniorage" tax) are standard in both DCs and LDCs – though generally larger in LDCs where more currency is held in private hands. But if it is used excessively it may generate a response, via increases in velocity and inflation, until yields *ex post* fall with a lowered forced savings rate. Avoiding such an inflation-sensitive range for money supply increases thus effectively constitutes a ceiling to the covert efforts at financing growth.

This can be illustrated with the help of figure 2.3, in which the rate of growth of the money supply η_M is shown on the vertical axis and the forced savings rate s' on the horizontal axis. The V_i curves ($V_3 < V_2 < V_1$) indicate different possible velocity responses governing the relationship between given rates of growth of the money supply and achievable forced savings rates in different societies. It should be noted that diminishing returns to increasing levels of η_M are likely to be observed along each of the V curves; indeed lower forced savings rates will result at some (high) level of money supply increase as the system enters its inflation-sensitive region. Different societies are likely, for institutional, historical, and psychological reasons, to be on different V curves. It is also possible due to some exogenous shock, e.g., the experience with hyperinflation in interwar Germany, for economies to switch from one to another V response curve, e.g., from V_3 to V_2 or vice versa. Thus, as the money supply increase shifts from η_{M2} to η_{M3} the system, initially at point 2, may end up at point 4 instead of point 3. The temptation to resort to forced savings and possibly to "overdo" is thus clearly present and likely to be more severe during the downturn.

The cyclical pattern of real interest rates r (i.e., $r = i - \eta_p$, the difference between the commercial bank lending rate and the inflation rate) is also likely to become negative toward the end of the recession phase, providing an inflationary benefit (see figure 2.2(q)). It is in this dynamic sense that the manufacture of profits via the creation of purchasing power to meet the investment demands of an earlier date is used as a covert transfer device to promote growth. LDC businessmen are well aware that this process helps them substantially as they benefit from negative real interest rates, i.e., the delayed price inflation lightens the repayment burden. This manufacture of purchasing power plus inflation represents a key growth-promotion mechanism in the LDCs. It has been likened to an "act of burglary" by classical monetary theorists.

---

[10] If forced savings, in real terms, is defined as $S' = (dM/dt)/P$, $s' = S'/Q = \eta_{M/V}$ (using $MV = PQ$, the equation of exchange).

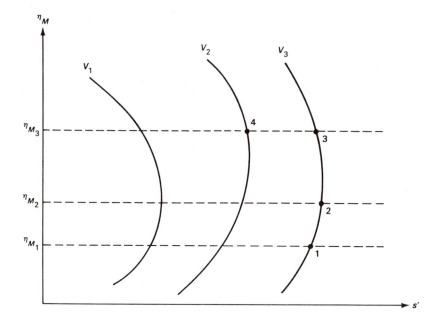

Figure 2.3   Monetary expansion and forced savings

Given a dualistic financial system, that is, the coexistence of commercial banks cum money markets and informal or curb markets, savings deposits in commercial banks, S_d, as a percentage of total savings, S, decline when r declines, especially when r becomes negative (figure 2.2(r)). Though this is more controversial, the prevailing view is that total savings are themselves also interest elastic at least to some extent, i.e., in response to large changes. When savings decline the government is forced to rely even more on money printing – a fact that lies behind the increase of η_M in figure 2.2(o). Under these circumstances, to permit commercial banks to continue raising their "formal" savings deposits, real interest rates must be raised under the competitive pressures of the "money market." The same holds for the so-called "black" or "parallel" markets.[11] While competitive pressures will ultimately force the elimination of the customary "legal ceiling" on interest rates as an LDC approaches modern growth, this often brings about efforts at "indexing" in the LDC setting during the latter half of C_i. In the mixed economy the right to borrow and lend among private parties always imposes some

[11] There is always a tendency to refer to the "informal" free market as "black" because it threatens not only the official savings institutions but also the entire manufacture-of-profits mechanism based on the exploitation of savers.

upper bound to the possible exploitation powers inherent in government monetary policies.

Indexing as a monetary institution

When a sequence of cycles C_1, C_2, C_3, . . . is viewed in a longer-term perspective, the periodicity of the pattern of the real rate of interest (see figure 2.2(q)) is thus a concrete illustration of the occasional "official theft" emphasized by the "rational expectations" school of thought, i.e., when savers are not yet fully "rational" they take defensive measures since the real interest-depressing effects of inflation are only "perceived" *ex post* rather than fully anticipated *ex ante*. It is only in such a long-run context, as savers gradually learn from experience, that indexing can become a permanent monetary institution and weaken the government's capacity to "get away with it."

According to the monetarists, the expansion of the money supply will lead to inflation with a time lag; inflation will stop only when the money stock is held for transactions purposes with a more or less constant velocity, as money demand is interest inelastic.[12] With the expectation of price stability the entrepreneurial class must rely on its own capacity to make a real profit, not augmented by political patronage, once the market rate of interest is closer to its equilibrium level. But this scenario becomes irrelevant at times of unpredictable inflation, as monetary chaos renders all rational calculations extremely difficult.

It should be noted that, under a complete indexing arrangement for bank deposits, money creation can no longer be as effective a policy instrument to manufacture profits for the entrepreneurial class, since the market rate of interest is now closer to its equilibrium level. In order to manufacture profits by political force, the exploitation of a victim class – the savers in the present case – is required, and this is clearly diminished by indexing.

The experience of wartime finance has shown that the government can resort to money printing (or taxation without consent) indefinitely as long as there is a public consensus to support the purposes of the war. In the case of Latin American indexing, governments have resorted to money printing to promote growth, also an avowed national purpose, which, however, does not for long receive the same sort of public support. Since the required sacrifices (in terms of tax dollars) are not openly debated,

---

[12] Newly inflation-sensitive post-Keynesians tend to interpret the difference between them and the monetarists as one concerning the positiveness of this elasticity. Such a compromise on the equilibrium level of the inflation rate is not likely to be helpful, however, for understanding the real issue of the causation of inflation, which we believe is related to the difference between the spending desires of the monetarists and the hoarding philosophy of Keynes.

compromised, and ultimately assessed to different social groups, the victims of price inflation (mainly the workers and savers) ultimately become dissatisfied and restless and reveal their sentiments by strikes and work stoppages.

The apportionment of such *ex post* growth burdens among various social groups by means of a time-lagged inflation can never make everyone feel that they are being treated fairly, with or without indexing. It is not difficult to see why "total indexing" is so crude that, as a policy, it constitutes a very imperfect substitute for a formal process of political compromise where tax burdens are overtly agreed upon *ex ante*. But "crudeness" is a secondary argument. For while its nominal purpose is to be equitable, it is more likely that countries resort to total indexing only because they hope to avoid the inconvenience of a political process in which a meaningful compromise, i.e., one that resists social unrest, is an impossibility. "Equity through total indexing" is really a contradiction in terms because an "agreement" on "total indexing" (at best a pseudounstable agreement) is achieved only when citizens cannot reach an agreement on equity under the customary methods of political bargaining in a constitutional democracy.[13] The very fact that governments continue to print money (for deficit finance) in spite of "total indexing" is concrete proof of this contradiction. For if the body politic has the capacity to agree on something equitable (e.g., "total indexing") the same capacity would have made it possible for citizens to agree on some level of "taxation with consent" in the first place.

In an evolutionary perspective, however, the practice of indexing the interest rate is contributory to the cause of liberalization over the longer term. It leads to the emergence and firming up of the idea, as loanable funds theory contended,[14] that a government, in spite of all its (possibly) good intentions, cannot persistently use an expansionary monetary policy to suppress the interest rate to artificially low levels, i.e., much below the "natural rate." Monetary maturity paves the way to political maturity when citizens demand an explicit accounting of the "costs of growth" expressed in terms of the tax burdens on various groups, instead of the "under-the-table" covert transfers of resources to the government by

---

[13] Taxation with consent can be more readily realized through fiscal reforms in East Asian countries because their higher capacity to agree is ensured by deep-rooted cultural traits that emphasize "obligation" (to oneself and to the society) rather than "human rights," a Western cultural trait. This Chinese cultural trait has often been crudely seen through "Western" eyes as "Oriental despotism" or the acceptance of an "authoritarian" government.

[14] We really cannot blame LDCs for their slow acceptance of such a non-Keynesian idea popularized in the United States only in the seventies through a combination of monetarists, the rational expectations school, and the practitioners of the Federal Reserve System.

money printing while relying on price inflation as the mollifier, with or without indexing.

2.5 Growth-oriented foreign exchange management

Foreign exchange reserve management

The just-described "politicized" monetary expansion in the middle of the recovery period creates a tight real resources situation domestically. This, in turn, induces an inflow of imported resources. The relative export surplus consequently turns into a relative import surplus at some point t'' during the "prosperity" phase when the accumulated FE reserves begin to be dissipated in order to buy the needed imports (figures 2.2(e) and (f)). Within each cycle C_i, R thus has a three-stage political life (see figures 2.2(f) and (g)). The first stage ($dR/dt > 0$) pictures a drive to accumulate import power, as we have just explained. In the second stage ($dR/dt < 0$) the reserves decline as the expanded domestic purchasing power puts pressure on the provision of resources through imports. This represents a calculated, intentional dissipation of reserves to achieve growth. Finally, in the "recession" phase, the unintentional further dissipation of reserves serves a negative purpose, i.e., as an "inflation fighter" (see $\Delta m''$ in figures 2.2(j) and (n)). We may thus observe that the FE reserves management in this type of country is a growth-related art that bears little resemblance to its use as a first line of defense related to the floating of the FE rate as in the DC case. There is, moreover, an almost imperceptible change in the art of FE reserve management that takes place over each cycle as objective circumstances change.

In the assumed absence of a clear-cut "precautionary motive" (e.g., the stockpiling of reserves for national defense by the Taiwan government) and in the absence of short-term capital movements of the speculative or "hot money" type, reserves move up and down to accommodate trade balances. There is no assurance that FE reserve stocks will not be substantially drawn down in the same prosperous phase instead of in the rainy days of the next downturn. This is, in fact, almost certain to happen when there is a political election cycle to contend with, since it is foolish to leave the external purchasing power to be spent by the *next* administration when it can be used to enhance the popularity of *this* administration. Under conditions of synthetic nationalism or weak forms of democracy, in other words, the government does not have the capacity to hold on to a growing FE reserve stock if it engages in non-compensatory, growth-oriented fiscal policy during the recovery phase. We see furthermore that the inseparability of monetary management, both internal and external, from politics (the absence of central bank autonomy) lies at the heart of the difficulties in the context of a politicized market system.

Another important lesson to be learned here is that while the EO phase represents a "natural" phenomenon (see figure 2.2(d)), the noncompensatory monetary and fiscal policies of government are likely to shorten that phase and hasten an "unnatural" early return to an internal orientation. Other things being equal, an expansionary policy brings about an import surplus. The application of this principle in an evolutionary perspective implies that the seeds of a temporary revival of an "internal-orientation" phase are planted right in the middle of the boom and then blossom fully into a return to the import-substitution policy syndrome during the recession.

But even if reserves move up and down to accommodate changes in the trade balance, i.e., there are no short-term capital movements under a centralized system of foreign exchange holdings, there is still the issue of long-term capital movements to be considered. Some level of long-term capital movements, predominantly concessional in the fifties, predominantly commercial in the sixties and seventies, and a mixture in the eighties, can be considered endemic, and that is why we have described our trade surpluses and deficits over the cycle as "relative." But there are also fluctuations around such trends which need to be taken into account. One would expect that changes in the size of the net long-term capital inflows would be countercyclical, i.e., positive during the downturn and negative during the upturn. If that were the case this could ameliorate some of the political economy effects over the cycle we have analyzed here. But it is indeed more likely that foreign investors become more bullish at a time of a relative terms-of-trade upturn and more bearish at the time of a relative downturn. Not only does the natural resource bonanza attract additional long-term investor interest when prices (e.g., of oil) are high, but the whole system is viewed as a better investment opportunity; vice versa for the downturn. Long-term capital movements may then indeed be seen as likely to be procyclical in character, reinforcing the perverse political responses we are analyzing.

Foreign exchange rate management

Given the basic rules of a more or less automatic market adjustment mechanism, a cardinal principle of interference is that the government can control prices or quantities, but not both, i.e., a political suppression of both price and quantity must be accompanied by some sort of rationing. The political economy that explains the foreign exchange reserve (or R) path implies, by this principle, that the foreign exchange rate, f, and/or quantitative restrictions, are determined, endogenously, at the closed end of the "cyclic model." Thus we can predict the movement of the foreign exchange rate and/or of import controls. All we have to remember is that, other things being equal, the domestic currency appreciates (depreciates) against the foreign currency when the central bank takes the initiative of drawing down (adding to) its FE reserves, which amounts to an increase (decrease) in the supply of the foreign currency in the controlled FE market. Accordingly, we also observe three stages in the behavior of the foreign exchange rate over the cycle.

As shown in figure 2.2(g), the FE rate depreciates in the first stage (indicated by an arrow f_1 pointing upward) because here the FE reserves are being stockpiled. In the second stage, the FE rate appreciates (the arrow f_2 pointing downward) to accommodate the inflow of resources. In this phase the overvaluation of the domestic currency represents a direct response to the political request of industrialists that producers of primary product exports be discriminated against in order to supply them with the necessary resources. It is at this juncture that the government also begins to think about "export promotion" (e.g., by means of an export bonus scheme) to compensate partially for the overvaluation of the currency. Such selective export-promotion schemes are likely to fail because of the basic contradiction between the government's desire to discriminate against traditional exports and to promote (i.e., to diversify into) new, potentially profitable, exports, which is normally beyond the ability of bureaucrats to accomplish.

In the final stage, i.e., during the downturn or recession phase, the domestic currency appreciation becomes more pronounced (represented by a sudden drop of the arrow f_3). Some now claim that the FE rate is overvalued due to inflation. Believers in the "import cost-pushed theory of inflation" assert that devaluation at such a time would "cause" more inflation. In the midst of such confusion only one thing is clear, namely that the artificially overvalued domestic currency becomes an "inflation fighter" as devaluation is postponed.[15]

The analysis is facilitated, however, if we again take a longer-term view and remember that the seeds of this process were planted earlier, during the upturn, with a time lag. The rapid dissipation of the FE reserves (i.e., the rapid decline of the R curve) can only mean that their inflation-fighting power is rapidly diminishing (i.e., $dR/dt < 0$ and $d^2R/dt^2 > 0$). Given the customary national anxiety about devaluation, such action is postponed as long as possible, usually until the FE rate has to be devalued abruptly (represented by a sharp upturn in f, e.g., to f_4) as the reserves near complete exhaustion.

---

[15] The fact that an overvalued domestic currency (conducive to an import surplus) can act as an "inflation fighter" was a popular idea in the United States around 1984 and is currently popular in the United Kingdom. The same notion is routinely in vogue in the recession phase of most LDCs.

At this point, the conclusion is frequently drawn that inflation is virtually uncontrollable. But the economy is really only belatedly paying the price for its earlier growth-oriented activism. The rapid dissipation of the FE reserves implies the loss of the power to import (figure 2.2(e)) as a way to fight inflation. The behavior of the FE rate in this situation has only psychological significance, as rumors of impending devaluation can become self-fulfilling, leading to the immediate overdiscounting of a future rise in import costs and into instantaneous price inflation, with the actual (later) arrival of the devaluation, having already been anticipated, making little difference to the inflation rate. The government probably tends to postpone the devaluation in order to forestall its further psychological effects – but usually to no avail since the depletion of the country's reserves is an open secret – and is often accelerated by speculation and capital flight. Finally, when it comes, the devaluation has a "big bang" effect (f_4). In the wake of this crisis atmosphere, the economy then makes a resolute effort to try liberalization once again, thus starting a new cycle (C_{t+1}).

Trade restrictions

Like the FE rate, the cyclical behavior of tariffs or, more relevantly, quantitative trade restrictions, can be explained perfectly well at the closed end of the model. First of all, as we have indicated, we can expect the government to initiate export-promotion schemes during the latter half of the recovery or upturn. Since such export diversification efforts are likely to be futile, as no rational amount of export subsidy can cope with severe currency overvaluation when devaluations have been continually postponed, they will ultimately have to be abandoned. When the government tries to control both its "price" (i.e., postpone a devaluation) and its "quantity" (i.e., restrict the sale of FE reserves in order to support the overvalued currency) foreign exchange must be rationed. It is at such a time that restrictions once again appear on the scene – either in the form of "temporary" tariff increases or import licensing. This return to controls is intended to protect the nearly exhausted foreign exchange reserves or, in fact, to protect the "life" of the centrally controlled reserve system.[16] Only when a large devaluation is finally forced can these important restrictions once again be abandoned as we enter the next cycle (C_{t+1}).

---

[16] Since there is no reason for us to believe that the economy would collapse if the centrally controlled FE reserve system were abandoned (i.e., if the "Hong Kong system" were adopted, with a capital market fully integrated with that of the rest of the world) the reserve crisis at such a juncture represents an "organizational" or "political" crisis threatening the heart of the political philosophy of government control. Liberalization in C_{t+1} represents a partial response to such a crisis.

The possibly nonharmonic movement of exogenous disturbances

To modify the "simple harmonic" model focused on thus far we may wish to note that the international business cycle cited earlier may also be relevant and that it may in addition have a different periodicity and amplitude, i.e., the two cycles may not be harmonic. For example, the primary product price cycle may exhibit a ten-year cycle that is somewhat counterharmonic with the business cycle abroad (figure 2.1(c)), which affects the demand for nonprimary product exports. However, as long as coffee exports, for example, represent a dominant component of economic activity (e.g., as in Colombia), we can still assume that the period of a coffee price boom (decline) is also a period of recovery (recession). Thus the external orientation ratio, as we have analyzed, is still higher (lower) in the recovery (recession) phase. The above framework would thus need to be modified somewhat to take into account policy sensitivity relative to the expansion or decline of new or nontraditional exports sensitive to the business cycle rather than to C_i, as, for example, in the case of the East Asian NICs.

Under a single (unified) exchange rate the emergence of nontraditional exportable products (e.g., manufactured goods and noncoffee primary products in the Colombian case) is obviously discouraged at a time of prosperity and encouraged at a time of recession as the domestic currency appreciates and depreciates because of the favorable (unfavorable) trend of primary product prices.[17] Thus the rate of export diversification will slow down (accelerate) during recovery (recession) and hence η_Q and $\eta_{E/Q}$ may become counterharmonic. We can then predict that the government will move toward an intensification of export-promotion schemes (e.g., an export-bonus scheme) for reasons quite independent of those discussed in relation to figure 2.2(h).

A growth-conscious government with vested ideas (in this case, export diversification) is likely to try either to compensate for an appreciated exchange rate distorted by the political will of the government itself or even to battle the world market forces at the time of a primary product price boom. What often happens is that the exchange rate adjustment is "overdone" – either overcompensated or undercompensated for – as a manifestation of government "activism." As compared with the simple harmonic case, the nonharmonic case thus only reveals the complexity of external shocks in the real world and hence the possibly less predictable nature of the political economy response.

---

[17] When C_i and the business cycle move counterharmonically, the expansion of new exports thus suffers a "double jeopardy" at a time of prosperity as, on top of unfavorable external demand, it is "squeezed out" by the expansion of primary product exports, which causes exchange rate appreciation.

Figure 2.4 Intracycle and long-run stabilization of exchange rate

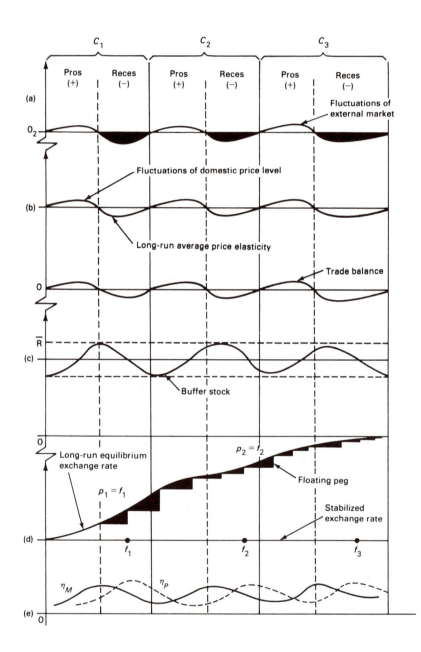

A possible floating exchange rate system

The "typology" of foreign exchange management is a topic for specialists in international finance who have developed schemes of classification of various FE systems. One key criterion is the extent to which the domestic financial market is integrated with the international market (or the degree to which the free movement of capital is allowed). Almost all LDCs (with exceptions such as Hong Kong) have historically opted initially for a centralized FE management system under which the central bank has the power to purchase all FE earnings from exporters, while the volitional choice of private citizens to convert their domestic currency into foreign currency for any motives unrelated to trade is absent or tightly regulated. For lack of a better name, what we have discussed earlier may thus be labeled as an interventionist, centralized FE management system, which, together with the internal government monopoly to print money, constitutes the foundation of the typical monetary philosophy in many LDCs.

When an LDC adopts a floating exchange rate system[18] this means that, given the price cycle C_i (figure 2.4(a)), the FE reserves R may be used as a buffer stock (figure 2.4(c)) to cushion the impact of the trade imbalance D (solid curve, figure 2.4(c), a reproduction of figure 2.2(e)) and thus to stabilize absolutely the FE rate (horizontal line, figure 2.4(d)). Although domestic prices will increase (decrease) in the recovery (recession) phase (dotted curve, figure 2.4(e)), since positive (negative) dR/dt induces an expansionary (contractionary) money supply, the price level is constant in the long run in the "average" sense (see dotted horizontal line in figure 2.4(b)). Let us begin our reasoning about the floating exchange rate system (LDC style) from this imaginary and "ideal" situation in order to emphasize the difference between a long-run (i.e., inter-C_i) and short-run (i.e., intra-C_i) perspective.

While the intentions (aiming at long-run price stability) may be good, the fact is that the fluctuations of C_i can be so violent that the intracycle price fluctuation may be intolerably severe in an LDC where one or two primary product exports represent a dominant component of economic life. It would thus require a huge FE reserve stock to defend against such severe price fluctuations. This the LDC cannot afford, not only in the economic sense, (i.e., a large R is seen as a "luxury") but also in the political sense because, once accumulated, it is difficult to keep it from being spent, given all the existing growth-related demands.

---

[18] We should add the remark here that the "floating" of an exchange rate in the case of LDCs has a somewhat different meaning from the corresponding expression in the case of industrially advanced countries due to the customary absence of short-run capital movements based on the volitional choice of private citizens.

Figure 2.5 Intracycle fluctuations of floating exchange rate

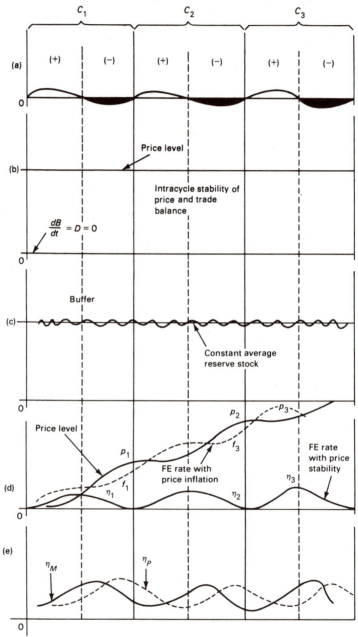

It would thus have been far better for the managers of R in the LDC to interpret these intracycle trade imbalances as an indication of "fundamental disequilibrium." The alternative paradigm is shown in figure 2.5, where the FE rate is permitted to float (see the horizontal waves in figure 2.5(d), and the FE reserve stock is used as a buffer against truly erratic and random fluctuations, with a constant average value ($\bar{R}$) and a small standard deviation (shown by the small "wiggles" in figure 2.5(c)). This in turn implies price stability within each cycle (figure 2.5(d)) since, as compared with figure 2.4, the external cause of the variation in the money supply is less violent, and thus a root cause of price fluctuations is eliminated. Moreover, given that the floating exchange rate encourages imports (exports) during the recovery (recession) years there tends to be a balance-of-payments equilibrium at all times ($D = dR/dt = 0$ in figure 2.5(b)).

There are several advantages for the short-run (i.e., intracycle) floating exchange system of figure 2.5. First of all, in a capital-short LDC, the foreign exchange earnings should be used to import producers' goods for development rather than for hoarding reserves mercantilistically. In good years the LDC should consequently grow faster. By contrast, in recession years, as the "coffee" price falls, a depreciation of the exchange rate encourages export diversification. This is a period of natural austerity. Furthermore, the absence of a trade imbalance eliminates one major "externally originated" monetary cause of inflation. Finally, the government's mind is taken off the accumulation of FE reserves viewed as "spending power." Thus, at the risk of oversimplification, if the "art" of clean floating is, in fact, exercised, this tends to: (1) promote intracycle stability; (2) avoid violent fluctuations in the reserve stock; and (3) restore foreign exchange rate flexibility, as summarized in figure 2.5.

On dirty and clean floats

A floating exchange rate system is, of course, not just a piece of pure economic logic, since it may be either a *clean* or a *dirty* float. The first implies that the foreign exchange rate defies political management and challenges the growth-oriented political will, while the latter is submissive to it and accommodates it. We should remember that there are few, if any, cases of really clean floats in existence anywhere, least of all in the LDCs. The art of management of a floating exchange rate system depends entirely on the position of the FE manager (i.e., the central banker), who may be either independent of or submissive to political pressures. In this regard, the extent of the central banker's external independence is just as important as his internal independence, the absence of which is likely to convert him into an "obliging" money printer.

A floating exchange rate system is, of course, much more "liberal" than a movable peg as it puts relatively greater reliance on the market and individual institutions and relatively less on government intervention.[19] The management of an FE reserve stock becomes infinitely easier because it requires only steadfast adherence to a longer-term vision rather than judgments about the short-run complexities of the real world. What the central banker mainly needs to do is watch the quantity of reserves and be "color blind" with respect to the foreign exchange rate.[20] While one may argue that exports or imports may not be FE rate elastic, the fact is that a clean floating system has probably never been tried over a significant period of time during the EO phase of any LDC. The trouble usually starts in the recovery phase, i.e., there is a tendency to accumulate reserves with a view to spending them later (as we saw earlier), while the foreign exchange rate is meticulously watched as an instrument of policy to promote growth.

The rules governing a clean float, i.e., following the principle of PPP (purchasing power parity), imply a political discipline that is crucial when domestic purchasing power is manipulated for growth-promotion purposes. A symmetrical economic interpretation of PPP is, however, misleading because it is far more important for the FE managers to weather the pressure of monetary expansion when the "heat is on," so to speak. The basic task of an FE manager is to protect the opportunity offered by international trade, especially once the economy opens up in the EO phase. The central banker often fails in this mission because he acts simultaneously as both an internal and external money manager.

Suppose the central banker as a money printer allows money creation (η_M) and price inflation (η_p) to occur (see figure 2.5(e)), producing a long-run increasing price trend (with an accelerated increase of the price level at p_1, p_2, p_3, as shown in figure 2.5(d)). If the central banker is a conscientious clean floater, the time path of the FE rate, following the principle of PPP, would lead to the time path of f_1, f_2, f_3, in figure 2.4(d) ($f_i = n_i \times p_i$, the product of the inflated price level p_i and the natural real FE rate n_i in the absence of price inflation). In this way he would have at

---

[19] The difference, however, between a frequently adjusted movable peg and a managed floating rate system becomes mainly one of the extent of transparency, which may itself, of course, have substantive content.

[20] In this regard, the advice to FE managers in an LDC is quite similar to the advice to the central banker domestically, namely to keep an eye on the long-run growth rate of money M and forget the short-run interest rate (i.e., to be color blind to i). This represents an extension of our view of money to the stock of foreign exchange. While both represent mediums of exchange, only the former can, of course, be created by the monopoly power of government.

least protected the country's international trade opportunities, as the natural exchange rate (i.e., the one that obeys PPP and reflects a country's competitiveness) leaves the upper part of figure 2.4 unchanged. In particular, the constancy of R implies that central bankers refuse to release external resources to accommodate the political pressures for growth. A clean float prevents domestic interference with emerging international trade opportunities. However, we should not necessarily expect a (domestic) money printer to also emerge as a clean floater externally, as that would imply a politically split personality, i.e., submitting to the domestic pressure for monetary expansion while simultaneously protecting the opportunities for trade by resisting these pressures internationally.

Notice that the central banker is less likely to have a split personality the other way around, i.e., as a nonprinter of money domestically but a dirty floater internationally. The stability of domestic prices is largely the result of a determination to fight off domestic political pressures. When he is relatively faithful to his internal monetary independence, the resulting price stability only makes his job as a clean floater easier. In other words, a domestic money printer is likely also to be a dirty floater as the same political pressures are encountered. An assessment of the relevant political, institutional, and monetary pressures will be seen to be relevant to our general policy discussion later.

Our typical FE manager might have started with a far-sighted long-run foreign exchange rate–stabilizing paradigm in mind (see figure 2.4). When price inflation occurs, producing the long-run trend of prices (p_i in figure 2.4(d)), an initially relatively clean float leads to the time path of the FE rate $p_1 = f_1$, $p_2 = f_2$, $p_3 = f_3$.[21] However, all these *ex ante* good intentions can be distorted out of shape once the FE manager becomes a dirty floater. This happens when the FE management makes excessive concessions to the political demands for imports needed as a resource for growth. These concessions can be seen in terms of the subsequent "pegging" of the floating exchange rate as represented by the step function that lags behind the planned or *ex ante* long-run clean float path in figure 2.4(d).[22] Let the time path of the FE rate be reproduced in figure 2.6. A shaded triangle (e.g., abc) of this step function has a horizontal component ($\bar{h}$), representing the temporary postponement of devaluation (or tolerance of temporary overvaluation), and a vertical component ($\bar{v}$), representing the devaluation necessary to catch up with PPP. It is the cumulative effect of such "concessions" (i.e., temporary overvalua-

---

[21] Notice that $f_1 = f_2 = f_3$ are stabilized as planned.
[22] The long-run equilibrium exchange rate of figure 2.4(d) reflects fully the PPP when the "effective exchange rate" equals 1. For the step function the effective exchange rate is shown to be persistently less than 1. Notice that the η_M and η_p curves of figures 2.2(o) and (p) are reproduced in figures 2.4(e) and 2.5(e) for purposes of comparative reference.

Figure 2.6 Cyclical perspective of floating exchange rate

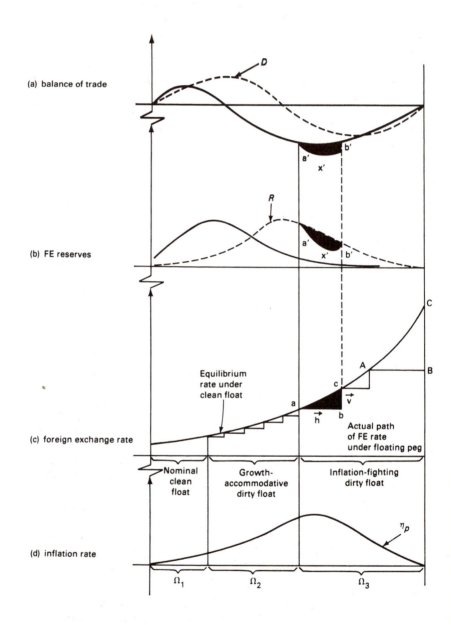

Figure 2.6 Cyclical perspective of floating exchange rate

tions represented by the step functions) that make an inflow of imported resources possible.

The three stages (Ω_i, i = 1, 2, 3) in figures 2.2(f) and (g) are reproduced in figures 2.6(b) and (c), which provide more of a microscopic view of the day-to-day operations of the FE market. In Ω_1, when the government accumulates R, the FE rate resembles something of a clean float system. However, the monetary discipline required of a "clean float" is met only nominally since the inflation rate at this time is relatively low (see figure 2.6(d), a reproduction of figure 2.2(p)), and a clean float system would become operationally significant only at times of substantial inflation. In Ω_2, when inflationary pressures build up, the "floating" system has a chance to meet its challenge for the first time as the FE rate is "pegged," i.e., small concessions are made to the political pressures by "using up" R via increased imports. In Ω_3, the camel is already well inside the tent, with the FE manager now reduced to the role of futile inflation fighter as he deliberately keeps on postponing devaluations. The horizontal steps ($\bar{h}$) becomes more elongated as devaluation is postponed and hence the vertical steps ($\bar{v}$) are getting steeper, and the whole process more discontinuous. This can only lead, finally, to a "big bang" devaluation (triangle abc in figure 2.6(c)) because the very postponement of devaluations discourages exports, cumulatively contributing to a rapid loss of foreign exchange reserves and ultimately, a large-sized devaluation.[23]

The return to the IS growth syndrome thus comes about *ex post*, while nobody planned it that way. The basic reason is that there was insufficient realization of the seriousness of the political commitment that had been made (i.e., one that separates FE management from politics) when the "floating rate" was first announced. The FE managers might have promptly devalued the currency to nip the expansionary policies in the bud, but the political economy got in the way. Growth promotion through artificial purchasing power expansion is clearly not without its social costs and should be reflected promptly in terms of the endearment of imported resources. An increasingly dirty float basically results from an incomplete commitment to the "rationalism" of a persistent, if gradual, liberalization trend.

---

[23] From the point of view of a day-to-day operational perspective, the cardinal principle of market interference (namely, in the absence of rationing, the government can control price or quantity, but not both), is illustrated in figures 2.6(a) and (b) where the time paths of D and R (of figures 2.2(e) and (f)) are reproduced. The postponement of the devaluation (i.e., a price interference abc) led, with time lags, to the enlarging of the import surplus and rapid dissipation of FE reserves (represented by dips in the D-path and R-path to a'x'b' in figures 2.6(a) and (b) and predictably brought on increased import restrictions (see figure 2.2(h)).

2.6 The organized labor market

The political significance of unions

The postwar experience of unionism and minimum-wage legislation in the labor-abundant LDCs has shown rather conclusively that the phenomenon is primarily a political one, stemming from the government's efforts to establish a political base and to demonstrate its concern for the working classes. While the wages, working conditions, and prestige of organized workers can be raised, the impact of unionization and minimum wages on the rewards of the laboring class as a whole has been negligible or even negative. Political power resting on a confrontational foundation cannot achieve full employment for all workers at higher real wages, i.e., as long as a labor surplus persists unions exist mainly for a political purpose since it is impossible to legislate against the system's factor endowment. If unions and minimum wages have any influence at all, e.g., on raising the real wages of the elite labor force – which may constitute 5 to 10 percent of the country's total – that "benefit" is likely to be secured at a cost to the 90 percent nonunionized or "uncovered" workers and to the growth of the total pie rather than at a cost to the "capitalists."[24]

Unionism and minimum-wage legislation thus represent political forces that can provide coverage only for a very small, elite portion of the total labor force (i.e., that which is politically active and employed in the large-scale urban establishments), although it pretends to represent the interests of the entire working class. Differentials between union and non-union wages represent a form of discrimination against the latter because capitalists, operating in imperfectly competitive markets, can usually protect their profits by increasing the price of the product. The burden of the bilateral oligopoly thus usually falls on the unemployed and underemployed and on consumers.

The economic impact of unionism and minimum-wage legislation

In case an LDC is "naturally" (i.e., from the point of view of comparative advantage) capable of exporting labor-intensive, manufactured goods to the rest of the world during the EO phase, artificially created wage differentials can be a serious handicap. Producers of such products stand to lose the intrinsic comparative advantage of the low wage cost generated by the system's relative labor surplus condition. In making profit calculations to guide their investment decisions, foreign or domestic entrepreneurs con-

---

[24] While job security is gradually displacing wage increases as the main objective in the DC context, many LDC's continue to emulate DC union practices and objectives of an earlier vintage.

templating the building up of large-scale factories must use the official or minimum wage as the "base." The nonunion or informal sector wage (which may be as low as one-third of the union wage) is irrelevant as everyone knows that unions will move in to organize the factory and/or government enforcement officials will insist on minimum wages being paid. Consequently, the capitalist is likely to opt for a more capital-intensive factory, seek labor-saving technology changes, or decide not to invest at all and leave the surplus labor untapped. In this way a small minority (10 percent) of the labor force can effectively deprive their nonunionized brethren, i.e., the majority, of employment opportunities as it denies the country the comparative advantage of low labor costs in international trade. The coexistence of high wages with substantial open or disguised urban unemployment for the majority makes a mockery of elementary ILO justice. Avoiding it represents a basic development tenet that has been crucial for the early success of the labor surplus economies of East Asia.

Sooner or later, LDCs must become aware of the fact that a labor surplus system faces a choice between the high wages for the minority with unemployment for the majority and fuller employment at moderate and more equal wages for all. Once labor shortage has been achieved in the course of successful transition growth real wages can, of course, be expected to rise across the board as a result of market pressures. The evolution of a pluralistic society can give the nonunionized majority substantially more "political protection" en route as the labor surplus condition gradually terminates. However, even before that point is reached the best "political protection" that can be given to the majority of workers is to liberalize the labor market, so that real wage rates in nonagriculture can be more competitively determined and the existing labor surplus more rapidly mopped up. As a consequence, a working family's total wage income will rise even as the wage rates of each of the now more numerous employed members of the family moderate.

Cyclical labor unrest

In typical developing countries organized labor or union unrest (e.g., work stoppages or strikes) are also a cyclical phenomenon, an endemic component of the politicized cycle, C_i, of economic development, especially at a time of inflation, (see figure 2.2(p)) when workers feel they have been unfairly hurt. At such junctures (i.e., between t_2 and t_3 in figure 2.2(p)) unions may lead or support protest movements on behalf of all workers against the unfair burdens of covert taxation by inflation. Strikes and unrest can almost be predicted, using η_M and η_p as leading indicators. In that sense labor unrest is an endogenous cyclical phenomenon, an endemic result of the money-printing process through time.

Within the politicized growth cycle, C_i, unions thus play an odd role as they represent both a "curse" and a "blessing" for the working man. In the recovery phase, a strong union stand by insisting on a higher wage differential (in favor of the minority) hurts the cause of the majority by preventing labor-intensive investment projects and output mixes, including exports, from being realized. Since union power, along with minimum-wage legislation and civil service emoluments, usually derives from the government, this is in part a political response to the previously discussed "rent-seeking" surge associated with the prosperity phase. In the recession phase, on the other hand, union leaders are likely to act as spokesmen for all workers and protest against the "unfairness" of the inequality of the adjustment process that they are themselves partly responsible for having created. Unions typically care about all working men at one point in the cycle and only about their own members at another. Two monopolistic political powers – the money-printing state and the wage-gap-creating union – thus combine to create an odd politicoeconomic cycle of growth with its own dynamic logic.

2.7 Toward a theory of policy oscillation in the EO phase

When we look at these "evolutionary events" over a typical cycle C_i in their entirety, we see that, especially in the downturn, with inflation (figure 2.2(p)), currency overvaluation (figure 2.2(g)), higher tariffs and quantitative controls (figure 2.2(h)), negative real interest rates (figure 2.2(q)), and so on, that there is a tendency for the earlier IS policy syndrome to be temporarily restored. The sequence of such cycles C_1, C_2, C_3, . . . (see figure 2.1) then portrays a picture of the periodic revival of IS-type growth. A liberalization package initiates each cycle only to be abandoned as the field is yielded once again to the IS pattern that nobody wanted in the first place. The revival of IS thus occurs almost as a natural result of policy oscillations, traceable via the political economy of a growth-activist LDC – rather than as a consequence of any design or conspiracy. Several factors that lie behind this "natural" oscillation that have been hinted at in the discussion above may now be more explicitly summarized.

Economic-geographic background: natural resource abundance

The relative natural resources abundance of the typical primary export-producing LDC is clearly a crucial factor because of the size of the "under-the-table" rents to be reallocated and the greater sensitivity to externally originated instability which that condition implies. The fact that every cycle tends to start with the accumulation of foreign exchange reserves and ends with a more or less abrupt devaluation can only be explained by the fact that relative resource abundance, in combination with the inevitability of exogenous shocks, represents a "precondition" for policy oscillation. The accumulation of FE reserves and the expansion of government revenue (figures 2.2(f) and (k)) are based on the government's capacity to appropriate part of the windfall rents of primary product producers that is possible only in a natural-resources-abundant economy.

Every C_i thus induces a political economy cycle that is relevant for "typical" natural-resources-rich LDCs but much less relevant for the natural-resources-poor East Asian countries, by contrast. It is, of course, also true that these latter systems expect their governments to perform growth-related functions with a missionary passion during their primary IS phase. However, their IS phase is likely to be shorter and less severe. Moreover, as they move into their EO phase, they are influenced mostly by the business cycle, whose fluctuations are milder than those of the primary product cycle C_i. Moreover, as they liberalize more and more increasingly monotonically, i.e., as they follow the export-substitution (ES), rather than the secondary import-substitution (SIS) cum export-promotion (EP) path (see chapter 1), their production and export structures become more diversified and, as relatively small open economies, they become less affected even by the business cycle.

As a consequence, a basic difference that emerges is that at the time of recovery, while total government revenue and FE reserves increase, this is not at the expense of the producers of the export product which, in the East Asian case, are increasingly represented by manufactured rather than primary products. In other words, while in the more typical LDC case, the government and the urban elite seek to exploit the usually spatially dispersed primary product producers, this income transfer cum profit manufacture mechanism cannot operate as well in the natural-resources-poor LDC context since, in the relative absence of a "victim class," there is also no pronounced "beneficiary class." Soon after entering the EO phase, these countries discovered that the diversification into nontraditional exports, indeed the lifeline of their economic future, can only be carried out by the entrepreneurs themselves. Consequently there never existed here the same political temptation to return to an internal orientation once it had been left behind because the government never had the same economic power to generate a big "push" for growth in the middle of C_i in the first place.

Economic theory background

The policies or actual practices of typical LDCs during the postwar years could probably have been somewhat rationalized by some theory, e.g., that of the structuralists or the "big push" adherents. However, the short-run Keynesian message – i.e., that large government deficits are necessary; that inflation is cost pushed; that an increase in the supply of money lowers the rate of interest; that commercial bank lending does not represent the creation of additional purchasing power for investment finance; and, above all, that governments *can* and *should* manage economic affairs across the board was really the dominant intellectual support, especially when accepted out of context.

When all is said and done, what gives some unity to the usual malfunctioning of the economic systems we have been witnessing – described by the 15–20 policy-related variables summarized in figure 2.2 – is a misconception of the monetary phenomenon – a complex subject "not one in a million comprehends" (Keynes). Government spending without adequate taxation and the possibility of the artificial suppression of the interest cost to manufacture profits – the cornerstone of macropolicies in the typical LDC – are predicated on a single feature of the monetized economy: namely that government monopolizes the vast power to acquire goods and services from the market through "money printing." Maintaining a linear trend toward depoliticization of the LDC system depends, to a large extent, on increased maturity in monetary thinking, i.e., to increasingly regard money and the stock of foreign exchange as domestic and international mediums of exchange to be increasingly separated from the objectives of growth promotion.

Political background: growth and equity under synthetic nationalism

During each recovery phase, as we have seen, the LDC government can be typically expected to take on more growth-oriented tasks – e.g., the accumulation of FE reserves and the use of expansionary purchasing power in ways that few DC governments would attempt. The practice of covert income transfers, i.e., the absence of on-the-table calculations of the "benefits and burdens" of taxes and expenditures, thus becomes a root cause of the policy oscillation observed. Given the political convenience of money creation, growth and income distribution objectives then attain a different dimension.

A growth-activist LDC government is typically antiliberalization in its reactions since, in an evolutionary perspective, "liberalization" essentially means moving in the direction of the advanced countries' organizational choice, i.e., featuring an increasing role for markets. The covert forms of income transfers typically linger on or recur because the LDC is not yet a "pluralistic society" in which each of the multiplicity of interest groups can exercise only a relatively small influence on the political stage, so that future costs and benefits of government policy are more likely to be calculated and negotiated in order to reach an *ex ante* political compromise. Ideological change in the direction of economic liberalization and the emergence of a differentiated, equity-sensitive political pluralism clearly represents a more long-run evolutionary "organizational" accomplishment. That is why policy oscillations ($C_1, C_2, C_3, \ldots$) occur in succession during the EO phase. What we can realistically hope for is a rising trend and diminishing amplitude of fluctuations around that trend in the future.

Let us assume for a moment, not unreasonably, in projecting the long-run economic impact of policy, that the quality of the key policymakers in all these countries (Latin American, East Asian and Southeast Asian) is equally high. A question that then arises is whether it is easier for authoritarian systems whose policymakers can afford to take a longer view and not have to placate public opinion in the short term to act responsibly in terms of that long-run view of the institutional as well as economic requirements of success; or, alternatively whether relatively stable democracies have a better chance to shift to increased transparency and a political consensus negotiated among interest groups. Is a tax reform, for example, more readily implemented when, in the final analysis, interest groups do not dare to protest or when they are part and parcel of a sometimes painful public debate and legislative process? Much depends, of course, on the realism of the expectations about government actions in the first place and on the art of governing to unify the country without inducing its citizens to form unrealistic expectations. In our sample, the apparently more authoritarian one-party regimes of East Asia (see chapter 4), seem to have done best – but, when one looks more closely, they also seem to have had more decentralization and participation at the local level than some other regimes, e.g., those of Latin America or the Philippines, which have more of the trappings of democracy. A comparison of Colombia and Mexico (see chapter 3), moreover, might lead one to the conclusion that, *ceteris paribus,* a genuine two-party system, even if highly centralized and elitist, generally does better than a one-party system. However, the world is clearly more complicated, and *ceteris paribus* never holds true.

We intend to return to some of these issues in our summary chapter, chapter 6. What we shall emphasize in this volume is differences in the initial conditions as they affect the political economy of policy change – working their mysterious way through both economy and polity. This includes paying attention to the importance of the strength of a preexisting organic nationalism, itself undoubtedly related to the extent of the population's ethnic and/or cultural homogeneity. But most of all it means tracing the differential impact of the strength of the natural resource endowment. What we are able to probe in the three empirical chapters that follow clearly will not solve all the mysteries of an undoubtedly very complicated many-dimensional story. But we do believe that it is in this general arena that the more fundamental question as to the "why" of development success and failure must be addressed; and we hope to have taken a substantial step in that direction.

3

The "Typical" Latin American Case: Mexico and Colombia

The first of the three sets of country case studies carried out in this volume is concerned with the pattern of development policy evolution in two Latin American countries, Mexico and Colombia, whose situation is viewed as historically "typical" of the majority of LDCs. While this chapter attempts to bring out the common features of policy evolution in this archetypal case, it also highlights instructive intrafamily differences.

3.1 External shocks

The first step in the empirical application of the theoretical framework outlined in chapter 2 is the identification of the external shocks. Here, external shocks are specifically identified as changes in the external terms of trade, defined as the unit value of exports divided by the unit value of imports. Indices of external terms of trade were derived for the years 1960 to 1985 for both countries. The beginning of external orientation, i.e., the end of primary import substitution, was located at around 1967 for Colombia and somewhat earlier, i.e., 1960, for Mexico – although a slightly different location of the "initial" year would not materially affect things. Deviations from the long-run trend of the terms of trade are plotted for the period 1960–85 for Mexico in figure 3.1(a) and for the years 1967–85 for Colombia in figure 3.1(b).

For Mexico, the period 1960–73 is characterized by a steady improvement in the terms of trade in the sense that the deviations from trend first became progressively less negative and, after 1966, progressively more positive, until a peak was reached in 1973. A trend line fitted to this period has a statistically significant positive slope. The period 1960–73 has, therefore, been identified as the upturn period for Mexico. By contrast, 1974–85 may be designated as the relative "recession" or downturn period. The movement in the terms of trade was in the opposite direction after 1974 and although a trend line fitted to the period 1974–

85 is not statistically significant, Chow tests show that it is significantly different from that in the first period.

It is, however, clear from figure 3.3(a) that this secular relative decline in the terms of trade was punctuated by a brief period of recovery during 1979–81. This is the period of the oil boom in Mexico when export earnings from oil increased tremendously due to an increase in both the price and the volume of oil exports. Since the terms-of-trade movements depicted in figure 3.3(a) capture only the effects of price movements, they do not, in fact, fully reflect the magnitude of this positive external shock.

Thus, in Mexico, we observe a sustained mild recovery in 1960–73 and the "big boom" of 1979–81. Although distinctions according to the strength of the upturn were not explicitly made in our theoretical framework, it is, nonetheless, logical to suggest that the type of behavior posited for government is likely to have its more vivid manifestation during a dramatic boom.

For Colombia also a distinct cyclical pattern emerges that suggests that the whole period 1967–85 may be divided into two subperiods of roughly equal duration, 1967–77 and 1978–85. The first of these is characterized by a more or less steady relative improvement in the terms of trade, the latter by a relative deterioration. Although deviations from trend remained negative until 1975, their magnitude decreased almost continuously, indicating a gradual relative improvement in the external environment during the first subperiod. This improvement was accelerated following the start of the coffee boom in 1976. As is clear from figure 3.2(b), the terms of trade went above trend for the first time in 1976 and improved even more dramatically in 1977 when they reached their peak. The overall trend for this period is statistically significantly positive.

This trend was reversed after 1978 as coffee prices started falling. As is evident from figure 3.3(b), deviations from trend, although continuously positive until 1980, became progressively less so and, in 1981, turned negative. Overall, however, the trend remained significantly negative and Chow tests confirm that the trends are significantly different for the two periods identified.

The external orientation phase of Colombia's economy may thus be divided into two periods, 1967–77, which we identify as the upturn period, and 1978–85, which we identify as the downturn period. Within the upturn or recovery period, we moreover draw a distinction between 1967–75, when the recovery was gradual, and 1976–77, when the improvement in the external terms of trade was dramatic.

Having thus identified the periods of upturn and downturn for each country case, we may now proceed to the analysis of the long-run pattern of policy evolution. We first examine policy behavior during the upturn for both countries, followed by a similar analysis for the downturn. The discussion for each period is organized by the major sets of policy variables and in the sequence set forth in the theoretical discussion of chapter 2.

3.2 Development policy change in Mexico and Colombia: an overview

Mexico

Apart from an initial period of fiscal conservatism, the long-run pattern of policy evolution in Mexico during the external orientation phase, at least until the mid-eighties, resembles a somewhat extreme version of the archetypal pattern of LDC policy evolution described in our theoretical framework. The initially conservative nature of Mexico's macroeconomic policy behavior during the upturn may be summarized by what the government labeled a strategy of *desarrollo estabilizador* or "growth with stability." This strategy, initiated in the early fifties and maintained throughout the sixties, was successful in generating what was then christened the "Mexican miracle" – high rates of growth unaccompanied by serious internal or external imbalances.

This surface stability, however, masked serious weaknesses, notably an inequitable distribution of the fruits of growth and an inadequate development of the system's domestic resource mobilization capacity. Social dissatisfaction resulting from the unequal distribution of income manifested itself explicitly during the late sixties and led to a turnaround in policy at the beginning of the seventies, at a time when the upturn was reaching its peak. Conservatism was abandoned and expansionary fiscal policies were set in motion, financed by money creation and an acceleration of foreign capital inflows. Following a brief respite in 1977, all restraint was abandoned in 1978, after the oil boom hit the economy, with policy excesses becoming even more marked once the temporary boom had given way to renewed recession in the early eighties. We then witness strong attempts at trying to maintain growth and postpone adjustment, until the government finally had to give in, around the mid-eighties, and accept more radical corrections.

Colombia

Colombia's long-run pattern of policy evolution shares with Mexico many elements of the typical LDC pattern, but in a relatively milder form. There is evidence of growth activism and oscillations in policy formation but in a more restrained fashion and occurring against the backdrop of what appears to be a more or less consistent liberalization trend in various markets.

Colombia initiated its external orientation phase with a series of reforms in a number of policy arenas, signaling the beginnings of a process of gradual but steady depoliticization of policy. The most significant reforms were in the area of exchange-rate management, but these were accompanied by substantial changes in the realm of trade and fiscal policy as well. As in Mexico, there was a concern for stability, but, unlike in Mexico, this did not prevent the government from undertaking fundamental reforms.

This initial period of prudence and restraint was followed by a brief period of growth activism initiated in the middle of the upturn, with the government using expansionary policies to boost demand. This first round of growth activism proved, however, a temporary phenomenon and was replaced by relative restraint toward the end of the upturn when the economy was affected by the coffee boom. Moreover, the liberalization trend initiated at the beginning of the upturn was maintained, with further reforms carried out even in the midst of a period of overall growth activism.

Once the coffee boom had subsided and the downturn started, however, Colombia embarked on a strategy of growth activism, on a scale not seen before but, nonetheless, more restrained than its Mexican counterpart. Predictably, the associated expansionary policies led to a balance-of-payments and reserve crisis. The initial response, in "typical" LDC fashion, was to take the politically easier route of adopting quantity rather than price adjustments – such as avoiding devaluations and imposing import controls – thus reversing earlier liberalization trends. As in Mexico, however, adjustments ultimately had to be made, although, unlike in Mexico, this was done relatively faster, before the crisis got out of hand.

This summary overview of policy evolution in Mexico and Colombia brings out the common oscillatory nature of policy behavior as described in our theoretical framework as well as the intercountry differences. Let us now examine the underlying behavior and its causes in greater detail.

3.3 Development policy change during the upturn

Mexico

The overall development strategy of "growth with stability" which was dominant when Mexico entered its external orientation phase emphasized three complementary elements: growth, price and nominal exchange-rate stability, and a dominant role for the private sector. It was believed that stable prices and nominal exchange rates – along with low tax levels – were required to create the appropriate policy environment that would bolster the confidence of the private sector and encourage the generation of adequate savings and investment necessary to maintain high growth rates.

For about a decade – the sixties – this strategy appeared to be successful as it met its major aim: high and stable growth rates at about 6 to 8 percent for most of the decade (see figure 3.4(a)) and inflation at rates generally below 5 percent (see figure 3.12(a)). Performance was, however, poor with respect to exports with the export/GDP ratio, which can be expected to rise with an improvement in the external terms of trade, actually falling throughout the upturn (see figure 3.5(a)). This significantly negative trend occurred despite the adoption of a number of export-promotion measures, superimposed on the inherited strategy of import substitution. While these policies succeeded in diversifying the export structure – the share of manufactured exports in total exports, for example, increased from 20.7 percent in 1960 to 32.5 percent in 1970 – they had little impact on the total volume of exports. The effects of export-promotion measures appear to have been neutralized by the exchange-rate policy followed during this period. Although estimates vary, it is generally agreed that the Mexican peso was substantially overvalued,[1] creating a serious disincentive for exports.[2]

Despite this poor performance of exports, import surpluses were kept low – mostly below 1 percent of GDP (see figure 3.6(a)) – as a result of the absence of any tendency to overheat the economy. There was also no effort to build up reserves, which, in fact, decreased moderately during 1960–70, starting from not very respectable levels in 1960 (see figure 3.7(a)).

The apparent success of the development strategy in terms of achieving high growth with stability, however, masked serious underlying weaknesses, which were potentially destabilizing, and which became more apparent toward the end of the decade. As we shall see below, the concern for stability led to inflexibility in many areas of policy making, which meant that necessary reforms, particularly in the areas of tax, exchange rate, and trade policies, were not undertaken. The complacency induced by the surface stability reinforced such tendencies.

A more fundamental deficiency of the development strategy was its adverse impact on equity. Unlike in East Asia, respectable growth during the sixties was not accompanied by a rapid absorption of unskilled

---

[1] Solis quotes a study by Gerardo Bueno that suggests that the peso was overvalued by 17 to 24 percent during 1960–72. Other estimates placed the degree of overvaluation as high as 30 percent. See Solis (1981).

[2] Solis argues that there was a "growing substitutability between domestic consumption and exports, with a major portion of manufactured goods exported as residuals or surplus after supplying domestic demand" (Solis, 1981, p. 33). This suggests that the incentive effects of export-promotion measures were often offset by the disincentive effects of the overvalued exchange rate.

labor, thus leading to increasing unemployment and a deterioration of the distribution of income (Reynolds, 1978, p. 1007). Rising popular dissatisfaction, most dramatically expressed in the student riots of 1968, made it clear, by the end of the sixties, that the fruits of high growth had not trickled down to substantial segments of the population, and that a change in strategy was viewed as imperative. Policymakers grew increasingly skeptical about the wisdom of continuing with the strategy of *desarrollo estabilizador* and saw the need for "a more active government involvement in the solution of social and economic problems through the expansion of public expenditures."[3] It was in this context that the Echeverría government came to power in 1970, convinced that the "stable growth" regime of the sixties was no longer tenable and committed to more populist, expansionary policies.

Thus, after a prolonged period of pursuing relatively passive macroeconomic policies, Mexican authorities began to show activist tendencies during the late upturn, the seeds of which had been planted earlier. The details of this policy shift, which was sent in motion in earnest after 1972, are discussed below, but its impact on the real variable indicators may be summarized here. The new policies were initially successful in terms of restoring growth to high levels (see figure 3.4(a)) but could make no dent in the poor export performance. With export earnings continuing to stagnate, the adverse impact of the expansionary strategy on the trade balance became transparent by the end of 1973 (see figure 3.6(a)). The heavy recourse to foreign borrowing during this period, however, cushioned the deteriorating foreign exchange reserve situation for a time (see figure 3.7(a)). Let us now discuss these policies during the upturn in greater detail.

Fiscal policy   During the early upturn, i.e., the sixties, the dominant role accorded to the private sector meant that government investment activity was relatively restrained. Government expenditures were kept relatively low, and this, in turn, helped to keep deficits within modest levels – always below 2 percent of GDP during 1960–71 (see figure 3.10(a)), despite a poor tax effort.

Mexico's tax burden was very low to begin with – about 6.5 percent of GDP in 1960 – and increased very slowly, reflecting the failure of the Mexican government to carry out substantial tax reforms despite repeated attempts. The first such attempt, after the shift to external orientation, was made in 1962 when the López Mateos government presented a three-year plan envisaging an increase of the tax/GDP ratio to 12

---

[3] Zedillo (1986, p. 968). The high growth rates also generated increased demand for capital goods and infrastructure beyond what the private sector was thought capable of providing; this also increased the pressures for a greater role for the government.

percent by 1965 and 16 percent by 1970 (Solis, 1981, p. 22). A number of steps were taken to modernize the tax structure, including taxes on rent from dwellings, on capital gains from urban buildings, and on interest from fixed-income securities. These were, however, relatively minor, and a more fundamental tax reform package, although proposed twice during the administration of López Mateos, was not implemented. The package was again proposed at the end of Mateos' tenure and taken up by the new administration of Díaz Ordaz. The proposed reforms included the substitution of the fractionalized (cedular) system by a global income tax that would aggregate all sources of income for purposes of tax estimation. The bill was, however, passed by the Congress in a very diluted form; for example, income from capital was exempted from inclusion in total income. Hence, although there was some increase in direct taxes that helped compensate for the significant decline in international trade taxes during the sixties (see figure 3.9(a)), it was inadequate to generate an increase in the total tax/GDP ratio (figure 3.8(a)).[4]

The change in the stance of government policy behavior from one of conservatism to greater growth activism in the early seventies led to a marked change in the budgetary scenario after 1972. Government expenditures jumped from 10.5 percent of GDP in 1971 to 13.4 percent in 1972 and continued to rise, reaching 17 percent by 1975. Increased expenditures were accompanied by some, but once again inadequate, increases in the tax effort. A tax reform, initiated in 1973, led to an increase in "transactions taxes," but the results were significantly less than planned. Consequently deficits started rising to over 3 percent of GDP during 1972 and 1973 (see figures 3.8(a) and 3.10(a)).

Monetary policy   During the early upturn, modest government deficits were financed mostly by borrowing, both domestically and, albeit on a smaller scale, from abroad, so that recourse to money creation for financing government deficits was negligible. Similarly, the credit needs of the private sector were met through domestic and foreign borrowing. Consequently, the money supply growth rate was slow and pegged to expected output growth (figure 3.11(a)), leading to low rates of inflation (figure 3.12(a)).

The scenario, however, changed in the late upturn as the government expanded its expenditures and, failing to finance them by increased taxes, increased its reliance on covert means of resource transfer domes-

---

[4] Solis (1981, p. 25). Political economy factors played a significant role in the failure of such reforms to be implemented. According to Solis, the friction between the private sector and the government in the early sixties – partly arising from the nationalization of the electric power industry in 1960 – "undoubtedly caused the postponement of the tax reform package of the 1960s and then contributed to its failure in 1964" (Solis, 1981, p. 40).

tically and increased borrowing externally. Money supply (M1) started accelerating after 1972, and, by 1973, its annual growth rate exceeded 20 percent (see figure 3.11(a)). This was accompanied by an increase in the velocity of circulation (see figure 3.13(a)) leading to an acceleration of the rate of inflation, which went into double-digit levels twice, in 1970 and again in 1973 (see figure 3.12(a)).

Rising inflation enabled the government to extract a higher rate of forced savings from the system. As described in chapter 2, the rate of forced savings is a positive function of the rate of growth of the money supply and a negative function of the velocity of circulation, changes in the latter seen as a reflection of the degree to which the public tries to fight off any attempt by the government to extract forced savings. As can be seen from figure 3.14(a), the rate of forced savings was initially moderate, ranging between 1 percent and 2 percent of GDP during the sixties. During the seventies, however, the higher rate of growth of money supply enabled the government to extract higher rates of forced savings despite an increase in velocity, suggesting that Mexico had not yet entered the inflation-sensitive region where the public fights back successfully. This is reflected in the close relationship between changes in the money supply growth rate and changes in the forced savings rate, with increases in the former leading directly to increases in the latter (see figure 3.14(a)).

The initiation of expansionary policies during the late upturn, however, led to a change in the real interest rate regime. During the early upturn, the government had followed a policy of high nominal interest rates that, with low inflation and a stable nominal exchange rate,[5] helped keep the yields of domestic financial assets reasonably attractive relative to those of foreign assets, thus developing the market for such assets and encouraging domestic savings.[6] Real interest rates remained positive throughout the sixties (see figures 3.15(a)), which had a favorable impact on savings. A nearly constant proportion, about 10 percent, of annual savings – itself rising (see figure 3.16(a)) – went into the formal sector (see figure 3.17(a)).

With inflation rising and the nominal interest rate policy remaining rigid, real interest rates, however, started falling after 1970 and finally turned negative in 1973 (see figure 3.15(a)). The trend of modest but steady improvement in the total savings/GDP ratio, which had set in from the mid-sixties, lost momentum, and savings declined (see figure

[5] It may be pointed out that there was full convertibility of the peso during this period so that the nominal exchange rate was an important determinant of the relative yields of domestic financial assets.

[6] An indication of the extent of the development of financial intermediation during this period is provided by the statistics on total assets of financial institutions, which increased from one-third to one-half of GDP during the decade of the sixties. See Solis (1981, p. 14).

3.16(a)), although this was partly compensated for by a surprising increase in the proportion of total savings going into the formal sector (see figure 3.17(a)).

Foreign capital inflows　　The stagnation in domestic savings was accompanied by a resort to increased foreign borrowing to finance the deficits. As can be seen from figure 3.20(a), the net inflow of autonomous foreign capital – defined as total disbursements of public and publicly guaranteed long-term foreign debt minus principal and interest payments – modest up to 1972, started increasing significantly after 1973 and by 1974 amounted to more than 2 percent of GDP. The bulk of this mainly public sector borrowing emanated from private sources as the relative importance of official donors, predominant in the fifties and early sixties, had declined; of the total stock of foreign public debt at the end of 1973, 55 percent was from private intermediaries (Zedillo, 1986). This increase in the reliance on foreign borrowing was certainly encouraged by the low cost of borrowing, i.e., while average annual nominal rates of interest were about 9 percent, real rates were actually negative.

Exchange rate management and trade policy　　As mentioned above, the government maintained a stable nominal exchange rate of the peso vis-a-vis the U.S. dollar throughout the upturn. Such a rigid exchange rate policy led to a steady, albeit modest, real appreciation of the currency (see figure 3.18(a)), which had an adverse impact on exports.[7] The absence of any consistent liberalizing trend is also evident in the case of trade policy. Quantitative restrictions, after steadily increasing over the period 1955–63 – the proportion of import value subject to licenses, for example, jumped from 18 percent in 1955 to above 60 percent in 1963 (Zabludovsky, 1990, p. 177) – remained virtually unchanged for the rest of the upturn (i.e., until the end of 1973), but the level of protection increased with increases in tariff rates after 1965 (see figure 3.19(a)).[8]

Thus, to summarize, policy behavior in Mexico had changed considerably by the end of the upturn, shifting from a regime of restrained fiscal and monetary policy, a reluctance to use covert means of resource transfer, and modest reliance on external borrowing, to one of expansionary growth characterized by an increasing reliance on under-the-table transfers and foreign borrowing. As we shall see below, this shift became even more pronounced after the improvement in the external terms of trade was reversed after 1974 and the downturn started.

---

[7] As mentioned earlier, the exchange rate was probably overvalued by about 20 to 30 percent during this period.
[8] A 6 percent nominal tariff increase was implemented in 1965 (Solis, 1981, p. 5).

Colombia

In Colombia, as we would predict, the exogenously generated upturn was associated with an acceleration in growth, i.e., the real GDP growth rate increased from about 4 percent in 1967 to over 6 percent in 1969 (see figure 3.4(b)). Exports also increased (see figure 3.5(b)), partly due to the favorable external environment but partly also encouraged by exchange rate reforms and export subsidy policies adopted after 1967 (see below). Import surpluses remained modest, at about 1 percent of GDP (figure 3.6(b)), and there was a significant jump in foreign exchange reserves, which increased from a precarious 3.5 weeks' import equivalent in 1967 to a more respectable 2.5 months' import equivalent by the end of 1969 (see figure 3.7(b)).

As we shall see below, the beginning of the external orientation phase in Colombia was associated with a series of fundamental policy reforms in specific areas within an overall pattern of prudence and restraint. However, in the middle of the upturn, Colombia temporarily deviated from this pattern due in part to an enhanced sense of spending power generated by developments in the early upturn as well as by a rising populist threat in the political arena.

Colombia had been governed since 1958 by the so-called National Front formed in 1958 by an agreement between the Liberal and Conservative parties, according to which they were to alternately set candidates for the presidential elections for the next four terms (i.e., until the 1970 elections). The candidates of these parties, however, had to contend with other political groups and parties. Two of these groups – both with strong populist leanings, the MRL of López Michelson and the ANAPO of Rojas – were particularly influential in the political arena. Michelson had captured one-third of the liberal votes in 1966, while four years later, in 1970, Rojas was beaten by the barest of margins – 50,000 votes – by the Conservative candidate Pastrana. The need to neutralize the populist threat was thus seen as paramount at the time Pastrana took over.

The economic basis of the populist threat resided in the high rate of unemployment and underemployment in the country and the rising trend of urbanization, which generated increased demand, not only for jobs, but also for other public services. Thus, although Colombia certainly had a better record than most other Latin American countries with regard to such politically sensitive issues as income inequality and unemployment, these were still at high enough levels to provide the basis for a credible populist threat to the more orthodox National Front politics. The new administration of Pastrana thus felt the need to accord top priority to employment generation and decided that this was to be achieved through the expansion of government economic activity, spearheaded by an expansion of the construction sector.

A combination of political expediency and ideology–the four-year plan of Pastrana was heavily influenced by the views of Lauchlin Currie, an American economist with strong Keynesian leanings – marked the initiation of a phase of expansionary behavior after 1971[9] – very similar to what we observed with Echeverría's accession to the presidency in Mexico. The Colombian government's pursuit of growth activism was, however, relatively mild (see below) and, moreover, of a more temporary nature. Policy became restrained once again in late 1974 and remained so even during the coffee boom of 1976–77.

As can be seen from figure 3.4(b), the active promotion of growth after 1971 permitted growth rates to remain respectable, exceeding 6 percent during 1971–74, but against the backdrop of a modestly declining trend. In 1975, following the reintroduction of some restraint on government expansionary policies, growth rates fell to about 2 percent. The coffee boom, however, arrested this decline, even though recovery was not to the level of the late sixties and early seventies. This relatively modest growth performance of Colombia in the midst of a major boom can be attributed, at least partly, to the restrictive policies, discussed later, that the government initiated in an attempt to counter the inflationary effects of the huge inflow of foreign exchange.

The economy's degree of external orientation continued to rise, although at a moderate pace (see figure 3.5(b)). Thus, while the appreciation of the domestic currency caused by the expansionary policies after 1972 certainly harmed exports, particularly of the nontraditional variety, this was initially compensated, at least partly, by export subsidies, and later by the coffee boom, so that the overall trend in the export/GDP ratio during the entire upturn, i.e., 1967–77, was significantly positive. Foreign exchange reserves, after increasing until 1973, fell in 1974. This was, however, a temporary drop as the coffee boom soon led to a significant build-up of reserves (see figure 3.7(b)). As seen from figure 3.6(b), the trade balance improved significantly during the boom.

Fiscal policy   Colombia's shift to its external orientation phase was accompanied by a number of important reforms in various policy arenas leading to greater price flexibility and an increased reliance on overt means of resource transfer. On the fiscal front, the drive to improve the tax effort, initiated in 1965 with the introduction of the sales tax, was intensified after 1967. A number of tax reforms were carried out during the administration of Carlos Lleras Restrepo (1966–70) involving the introduction of new taxes, raising the rates of existing taxes, and improvements in tax administration. Thus, for example, a withholding tax went

---

[9] See *"Controversias Sobre el Plan,"* which documents some of the debate attending this change in direction.

into effect in January 1967 and levies were imposed on gasoline and diesel oil. In addition, the income tax rate schedule was raised by 0.5 to 3 percentage points for all brackets, and a number of measures were taken to minimize tax evasion and fraud. All this helped raise the tax/GDP ratio, albeit moderately, from about 8.5 percent in 1967 to almost 10 percent in 1969 (see figure 3.9(b)). The proportion of international trade taxes in total taxes (see figure 3.8(b)), however, remained virtually unchanged.

This rising tax effort in the early upturn was accompanied by restraint in expenditures, i.e., whatever increases occurred were matched by increases in revenues. In turn, this helped keep government deficits low, mostly below 1 percent of GDP (see figure 3.10(b)). However, the initiation of growth activism by the Pastrana government after 1971 led to a deterioration in the budgetary situation. Government expenditures increased significantly but were only partially matched by increased taxes, so that deficits increased, exceeding 2 percent during 1972 and 1973, before coming down slightly in 1974 (figure 3.10(b)). In August 1974, the new administration of López Michelson promised a reversal of the inflationary trends generated by the expansionary policies of the Pastrana years. One of the first acts of the new regime was indeed a major tax reform (in 1974), whose purpose was both to raise revenues as well as increase the progressivity of the tax system. Its most important components included raising the proposed rates for the richest 2 percent of the tax-paying population and lowering them for the rest, abolition of most prevailing tax privileges on capital income, a change in the taxation of capital gains, and introduction of a presumptive taxable income defined as 8 percent of net wealth. The impact of these reforms can be seen in the tax/GDP ratio, which jumped in 1975 and remained at around 10 percent of GDP for the rest of the upturn (figure 3.8(b)). Revenue increases were complemented by expenditure reductions so that deficits fell in 1975 and surpluses were achieved with the help of the post-1976 coffee boom (figure 3.10(b)). The proportion of international trade taxes in total taxes remained more or less constant throughout; there was some increase during the coffee boom, but this was marginal since the government made no serious effort to tax away the windfall proceeds of the boom (figure 3.9(b)).

Monetary policy   The relatively restrained nature of government policy in the early upturn was also reflected in the area of monetary policy. Money supply growth rates were relatively modest during 1967–70, ranging between 10 and 22 percent (see figure 3.11(b)). This stability was the result of a number of factors: first, as we saw above, central government deficits were kept low and partly financed by external borrowing, and second, reserve requirements on demand and time deposits were increased. This stability in money growth rates is reflected in the low and stable rates of inflation during the same period (see figure 3.12(b)). Velocity was lower compared to Mexico (see figure 3.13(b)), thus enabling the government to extract higher rates of forced savings on average (see figure 3.14(b)). Real rates of interest hovered around zero, on average, during 1967–69 and became significantly positive only after 1970, following an increase in nominal interest rates (see figure 3.15(b)).[10] The low level of real interest rates had the predictable effect on savings behavior. Thus, although the total savings/GDP ratio was higher than in Mexico (figure 3.16(b)), a smaller proportion of total savings was being channelized through the formal sector (figure 3.17(b)).

This monetary policy stance changed at the beginning of the seventies, when the steep increase in deficits was accompanied by a sharp increase in the rate of growth of the money supply, from about 14 percent in 1971 to over 30 percent in 1973 (figure 3.11(b)). There was a brief reversal in 1974 and 1975 when the new administration of López Michelson, in an attempt to redeem the campaign pledge of reducing inflation, adopted a tight monetary policy and brought money supply growth rates down to below 20 percent. This drop was, however, temporary as the huge build-up of foreign exchange reserves during the coffee boom (figure 3.7(b)) and its monetization led to renewed acceleration of the rate of growth of money supply during 1976 and 1977. Despite the conversion of the government deficits into surpluses, money supply growth rates now exceeded 35 percent (figure 3.11(b)).

Given the extent of the coffee boom and the inflow of foreign capital, however, it is likely that money growth would have been even higher if the government had not actively pursued a policy of sterilization (Kamas, 1985, pp. 313–327). A number of instruments were used. Reserve requirements were raised to 46.5 percent by 1977 and a 100 percent marginal reserve requirement was imposed on short-term deposits. The high reserve requirements effectively reduced the secondary expansion of money (the multiplier fell from 1.56 in 1975 to 1.26 in 1980).[11] The major tool used to offset the build-up of reserves was, however, the decline in net domestic credit issued by the Banco de la Republica – the central bank. Net domestic credit fell so dramatically that it was actually negative – the central bank became a net borrower.[12]

---

[10] In this year, the central bank nominal discount rate was increased from 8 percent to 14 percent.

[11] This, however, also caused large dislocations in financial markets as various ways were found to avoid reserve requirements, including an outflow of funds from the official banking sector into curb markets. Amid growing complaints from the financial sector, the 100 percent reserve requirement was removed in 1980.

[12] One of the means by which net domestic credit was reduced was open market operations where three major instruments were utilized: participation bonds, exchange certificates, and bonds exchangable for exchange certificates. See Kamas (1986, pp. 1191–93).

The acceleration in money growth in the early seventies was accompanied by an increase in the velocity of circulation. To recall, velocity had dropped steadily, if modestly, during 1967–71; now the trend was reversed and there was a moderate increase, which, by 1974, brought it back to the levels prevailing in 1967 (figure 3.13(b)). The combined effect of accelerating money growth and increasing velocity had predictable inflationary effects. The initial price increase was modest, but after 1973 inflation accelerated and by 1974 exceeded 25 percent. With further increases in the money supply growth rate as well as the velocity of circulation, inflation, after a modest dip in 1975, accelerated once again during the coffee boom (figure 3.12(b)). However, Colombia was not in the inflation-sensitive region, so that velocity remained relatively low, although rising, thus permitting the government to extract a higher rate of forced savings from the system compared to Mexico (see figure 3.14(b)).

With rising inflation, real interest rates became negative after 1973 and remained so for the rest of the upturn. Total savings remained stagnant, increasing moderately only after the coffee boom (see figure 3.16(b)). Formal savings, however, got a significant boost during the boom (figure 3.17(b)).

Exchange rate management and trade policy   It was in the area of exchange rate management that the most significant reforms were undertaken after the shift to external orientation. In 1965, Colombia had moved to a system of multiple exchange rates and established two markets for foreign exchange – the preferential market, in which the exchange rate was fixed at 9.00 pesos per dollar, and the intermediate market, in which the rate was 13.5 pesos per dollar. Despite a temporary reversal in late 1966 when, following a current-account crisis, the government decreed total exchange control, further progress with liberalization was made after 1967, with Colombian exchange rate policies becoming more active and moving to a system of crawling pegs. The exchange rate for coffee exports was raised and unified with that for other exports, at 13.50 pesos per dollar, while the crude oil import rate was raised from 7.67 to 9.00 pesos per dollar. With low inflation, the nominal depreciation also meant a gradual depreciation of the real exchange rate until 1970 (see figure 3.18(b)).

The adoption of more realistic exchange rates helped exports, particularly of the nontraditional variety. This was complemented by a variety of export-subsidy measures introduced during this period. The move to a system of crawling pegs was accompanied by the elimination of specific export subsidies and their substitution by a general ad valorem subsidy called CAT (Certificado de Ahorro Tributario) applied to most non-coffee and nonoil exports (Garcia, 1985). In addition, exporters received credit from PROEXPO, an export promotion fund – whose rate of subsidy was determined by the difference between the market rate of interest and PROEXPO's lending rate, and the amount of credit granted per unit of exports-plus a customs rebate on imported inputs under the "Plan Vallejo" system. These measures led to a significant expansion of noncoffee exports, whose share of total exports increased from 37 percent in 1967 to 50 percent in 1970, thus helping to substantially diversify Colombia's exports (Kamas, 1986, pp. 1177–1198).

These trends with regard to exchange-rate management were complemented by steady progress in the area of trade liberalization. Quantitative restrictions were reduced by decreasing the size of the prohibited list until its elimination in 1973, by increasing the rate of approval on prior-licensing imports, and by shifting commodities from the prior-licensing to the free-import list. Thus, along with a depreciating currency, the period 1967–70 was associated with the initiation of trade liberalization, mainly in the form of a substitution of QRs by tariffs. This is reflected in the rise in the average rate of protection, which, we may recall, is defined as import taxes as a percentage of imports, during 1967–72 (see figure 3.19(b)).

The gradual depreciation of the real exchange rate was, however, reversed after 1972 as inflation accelerated. In order to reverse this trend, and also in an attempt to compensate for the reduction in the rate of subsidy for minor exports decreed in late 1974, the government carried out another round of devaluations in late 1974 and early 1975. Although indicative of a degree of flexibility in exchange rate management,[13] these adjustments were, nonetheless, insufficient, given the high rates of inflation prevailing during the mid-seventies, and the real exchange rate continued to appreciate (see figure 3.18(b)).

At the height of the coffee boom in 1976–77, exchange-rate policy changed somewhat; the crawl was initially reduced to moderate the monetary impact of the accumulation of reserves and, in May 1977, a major revaluation of the peso was effected. There was, hence, a substantial real appreciation of the peso during the boom years (see figure 3.18(b)). The government did make an attempt to limit the extent of the real appreciation for a number of reasons. First, since the boom was expected to be transitory, a large appreciation would have necessitated a larger depreciation in the future. Second, since the surplus was viewed as temporary, it was considered desirable to accumulate reserves to cushion the economy when the boom was over. Third, appreciation

---

[13] It should be recalled that 1974 had seen a temporary deterioration in the trade balance in Colombia, so that an element of the "East Asian" type of behavior in terms of reacting to trade imbalances by exchange rate adjustments rather than through increased controls may be discerned here.

could frustrate the efforts to diversify exports without at the same time discouraging imports, because the latter consisted primarily of capital and intermediate goods, not considered very responsive to changes in the exchange rate. Fourth, an appreciation (or even an expected devaluation smaller in magnitude than the interest differential)[14] would induce capital inflows, making it difficult to stabilize the economy.[15] In brief, the authorities decided to avoid the full appreciation of the peso indicated by the current account position and chose instead to accumulate foreign reserves.

The real appreciation that nonetheless occurred after 1975 had predictable effects. The growth rate of noncoffee exports fell from 14.3 percent during 1967–74 to 6.8 percent during 1975–80, while that of manufactured exports fell from 27.1 percent to 10.5 percent (Kamas, 1986, p. 1187). The slower growth in noncoffee exports accompanying the rising value of coffee revenues reversed the decline in dependency on coffee earnings, with the share of coffee in total export proceeds reaching 60 percent by 1980.[16]

Trade liberalization, initiated in the late sixties, continued, with further reductions in the coverage of QRs and a massive reduction in tariffs in 1974 (see figure 3.19(b)). During the coffee boom, as the monetization of the huge inflow of foreign exchange jeopardized the government's anti-inflation program, the need to liberalize imports became more pressing. However, despite the shift of a large number of products from the prior-licensing to the free-import list, progress with regard to trade liberalization slowed down due to the revaluation of the peso and the restrictive monetary policies pursued during this period.

We may now summarize Colombia's policy behavior during the upturn, comparing and contrasting it with that of Mexico. We observed in both countries the initiation of growth activism through expansionary fiscal policies in the midst of an upturn, replacing an earlier period of relative restraint. The phase of expansionary behavior contained many of the hallmarks of the prototypical LDC behavioral model developed in chapter 2, e.g., the use of covert means of resource transfers internally and

[14] Colombian interest rates were higher than world rates.
[15] Although capital movements were controlled in Colombia, evasion was common practice.
[16] Although export subsidies, drastically reduced in 1975, were raised in 1978, they did not regain previous levels. Hence they could not sufficiently offset the adverse effects of the peso appreciation. The Colombian experience thus highlights the problem of adopting a floating exchange rate system when the export basket is not sufficiently diversified. Dependence on one or two major commodities whose prices tend to fluctuate widely implies that real exchange rates are subject to wide fluctuations, so that manufactured exports suffer during booms.

the use of traditional export earnings, augmented by the easy availability of cheap foreign capital, to finance growth. However, we also observed some instructive differences in the manner in which the two governments handled their growth-promotion efforts. Thus, in Colombia the turnaround was milder as the brakes were applied sooner and maintained even in the midst of a coffee bonanza, although, as we shall presently see, this posture could not be sustained once the downturn started. In Mexico, on the other hand, there was no interlude of restraint; and, as we shall see below, with the advent of the downturn, this expansionary behavior and unwillingness to adjust was intensified.

3.4 Development policy change during the downturn

Mexico

According to our theoretical framework, the "typical" natural-resource-rich LDC will try to maintain growth once the downturn starts. Budgetary deficits can thus be expected to increase and to be financed by money creation, leading to an acceleration of inflation, a reduction in real rates of interest, and, hence, reduced incentives for organized (and possibly total) savings. The public response to accelerated inflation is also likely to be more pronounced, reflected in an increase in velocity that may diminish or even completely nullify the government's ability to extract forced savings. As domestic savings fall and the natural resource bonanza terminates there is also likely increased resort to foreign borrowing. Expansionary policies then lead to a further deterioration in the trade balance and a diminution of foreign reserves, although the latter may be partly moderated by foreign borrowing. The initial response to the deteriorating trade balance is usually to impose controls on foreign trade rather than devalue the exchange rate and, more generally, to postpone price adjustments as long as possible. This is likely, however, to prove self-defeating in the end when massive adjustments, including large-scale devaluations, need to be resorted to.

Mexico's behavior during the downturn fits this scenario very closely. Although the expansionary policies initiated in the early seventies had led to a worsening of the current account by 1973, the warning signals were not heeded, and, once the downturn started, the government attempted to maintain growth by an even more vigorous expansion of government expenditures. A brief period of restraint followed a serious balance-of-payments crisis in 1976, but all caution was abandoned as the oil boom hit the country in 1979. Expansionary behavior reached unprecedented levels and was intensified even more once the boom ended in 1981.

The impact of the expansionary behavior on growth can be readily seen from figure 3.4(a). The deterioration in the external environment did lead to some deceleration in growth during 1973–76, but the slowdown was modest as a result of the growth-activist behavior of the government. During the oil boom, however, growth rates were significantly above trend. As predicted, such high growth rates could not be sustained indefinitely: they gave way to an equally dramatic downturn, around 1982, i.e., the time of the debt crisis. Between 1982 and 1985, Mexico, in fact, suffered negative growth rates on average.

The downturn in Mexico was, however, associated with a significantly positive trend in the degree of external orientation. As we can see from figure 3.5(a), the export/GDP ratio increased steadily, from just over 8 percent in 1974 to about 12 percent in 1981, before registering a quantum jump in 1982; between 1982 and 1985, it remained between 16 and 19 percent. While the increase before 1981 was largely due to the increase in oil exports, nonoil exports, induced by various export-promotion measures, combined with a shift to a more realistic exchange rate regime (see below), became more important thereafter. The experience with export orientation in Mexico lends support to the argument that the mere adoption of export-promotion measures is likely to have only a limited impact as long as the exchange rate remains substantially overvalued.

The deterioration in Mexico's trade balance that had started with the initiation of expansionary policies in Echeverría's administration was intensified by the deterioration in the terms of trade and became especially pronounced in 1975, when the import surplus reached almost 3 percent of GDP (see figure 3.6(a)). A devaluation of the peso in 1976 and the adoption of restrictive policies in 1977, discussed in detail below, led to a temporary improvement in the trade balance, but the trends were reversed again with the oil boom. The fact that the import surplus not only remained positive but increased is indicative of the extent to which the economy was overheated during this period. Finally, after a series of adjustment measures were taken, starting in 1982, the trade balance improved dramatically; the import surplus turned into an export surplus in 1982 and further improved in 1983. Although there has been some recent deterioration in the trade balance, export surpluses have since continued to be part of the landscape.

Contrary to what may be expected, foreign exchange reserves did not increase during the oil boom. The explanation for this may be given in terms of the easy availability of long-term foreign finance during that period. This suggests that when a government feels that it can have easy recourse to foreign credit its urgency to accumulate reserves for a "rainy day" will obviously be less pronounced. In the presence of foreign borrowing, reserve behavior may not precisely follow the predicted pattern even if government policy behavior is, in general, "Latin American" in character.[17]

Fiscal policy   The intensification of expansionary fiscal policies after the downturn started is reflected in the budget deficit figures that steadily rose, reaching a level of 5 percent of GDP by 1976, the last year of the Echeverría administration (see figure 3.10(a)). The foremost task of the new López Portillo administration, assuming office in the midst of one of the worst economic crises in Mexican history, was thus to restore fiscal equilibrium.

Initially there was some success; public expenditures were brought down from about 34 percent of GDP in 1976 to 31 percent in 1977, and deficits fell to about 3 percent of GDP (figure 3.10(a)). The improvement was, however, short-lived as fiscal restraint was abandoned after 1978, once it was learned that Mexican oil reserves were substantially higher than had originally been thought. Government expenditures increased, and this was justified by the argument that the successful exploitation of oil reserves required substantial new investment in facilities and that the newfound oil wealth, in turn, would help finance investment in other sectors. A National Development Plan for 1978–82 was announced, under which Mexico was to experience what the president called a period of "administered wealth." The basic strategy was to expand public expenditures between mid-1978 and 1980, giving priority to the petroleum industry, and then consolidating them during 1981 and 1982.[18]

In reality, however, far from creating a phase of "administered wealth," government policies soon led to an overheating of the economy. Government expenditures rose to 36 percent of GDP by 1980 and exploded after 1981 as, with the economic crisis deepening, the government increased its reliance on expansionary fiscal policy to keep the growth momentum going. Expenditures indeed rose to 42 percent of GDP in 1981 and to 49 percent in 1982. Initially, this did not lead to rising deficits – which were kept at roughly the 1977 levels (figure 3.10(a)) – thanks to an increase in taxes, mainly related to international trade (i.e., oil) (figures 3.8(a) and 3.9(a)). After 1981, however, as the tax/GDP ratio stagnated while expenditures shot up, deficits went out of

---

[17] No one, least of all the Mexican government, could have anticipated a reduction in foreign borrowing possibilities in the near-term future during the height of the oil boom, when commercial banks, replete with OPEC deposits, vied with each other to lend to such a prospectively favorable country.

[18] Also to be launched were vast public-sector industrial projects, electric power expansion (including two sizable nuclear plants), port development, urban infrastructure, and so on.

control, rising to a critical 15.4 percent of GDP in 1982 (figure 3.10(a)). Although a series of adjustment measures after 1983 brought the deficits down from these record levels, they remained at above 7 percent of GDP until recent years.

While the stagnation of the tax/GDP ratio after 1981 reflects the failure of the Mexican authorities to take advantage of the boom and effect significant tax reforms,[19] the explosion of expenditures during the oil boom reflects the vulnerability of the typical LDC finance minister to exaggerated demands for funds at a time when it is known that boom-related revenues are accumulating in the treasury. In Mexico, such pressures clearly overwhelmed any restraining forces that might have existed. Thus, although the budget for the fiscal year 1981 explicitly stated that the deficit would not be allowed to rise any further in nominal terms, this turned out, in effect, to be a mere formality as the targeted deficit was revised upward later in the year and the actual deficit at the end of the year was at least double that originally targeted.[20]

Monetary policy   Not only did public expenditures expand during the downturn, so did private expenditures, especially after the oil boom. The increased demand for finance from both sources was met not only by increased foreign borrowing but, in typical LDC fashion, also through money creation by a central bank that increasingly adopted an accommodating posture. Money supply growth rates increased to over 20 percent by 1974 and remained at these levels until 1981. In 1982, with budget deficits at record levels, money supply growth rates reached new highs and, as can be seen from figure 3.11(a), averaged more than 50 percent during 1980–85.

These high rates of money growth, amplified by a rapid increase in velocity (figure 3.13(a)), had a predictable impact on the rate of inflation, which hovered around 20 percent until 1978 and then accelerated, before exploding after 1982 (figure 3.12(a)). The rise in velocity, which until 1981 had remained more or less stable, of course, reflects the inflation sensitivity of the public, which tried to fight back against the government's efforts to compete for resources and extract forced savings. As we can note from figure 3.14(a), the higher money supply growth during the downturn had initially, given the relative stability of

---

[19] Apart from the introduction of a VAT in 1980 to replace turnover taxes.

[20] As Zedillo puts it, "In practice, even a timid gradualistic approach on financial matters and exchange rate policy sounded like heresy – even an insult to the reasoning of the time. The inertia of the public-expenditure-led growth model proved to be overwhelming. The warning voices of the more prudent members of the Cabinet were completely ineffective in provoking a change in course" (Zedillo, 1986, p. 976). Haggard (1990, pp. 186–87) contains a brief discussion of the conflicting political pressures generated by the oil boom for the government's economic policy formation.

velocity, enabled the government to increase the rate of forced savings. However, once inflation crossed the levels considered tolerable by the public, i.e., after 1982, further increases in the money supply became self-defeating and the rate of forced savings fell.

With high inflation, real interest rates remained consistently negative during the downturn and, for a number of years, negative in double figures. What is noteworthy, moreover, is the fact that, although inflation was roughly at the same level as in Colombia (see below) – in fact slightly lower during 1974–81 – real rates of interest were substantially negative compared to the high positive rates in Colombia. This indicates the relative inflexibility of interest rate policy in Mexico. The effects on saving behavior were somewhat paradoxical, however, with the proportion of total savings going into formal savings higher than during the upturn (see figure 3.17(a)), and total savings also higher as a proportion of GDP (see figure 3.16(a)). This can probably be attributed to the complementary domestic effects of the oil bonanza.

Foreign capital inflows   Indeed, increased foreign borrowing was used both by the government as well as the private sector to help finance expanded investment expenditures. Net annual inflows of long-term capital increased to about 4 percent of GDP during 1976–77 (see figure 3.20(a)). There was a reduction in the net inflow of foreign capital in the initial years of the oil boom, but, after 1981, as government deficits reached phenomenal levels, the net inflow of foreign debt jumped once again. The extent to which foreign borrowing was resorted to during the oil boom is, moreover, somewhat understated in figure 3.20(a) by the fact that these figures include only public and publicly guaranteed foreign debt and exclude private nonguaranteed foreign borrowing. Also, the high debt-servicing obligations on previously incurred debt meant that the net inflow was brought down relative to the gross inflow. This drop in net capital inflows reflects the abrupt tightening of external credit after 1982.

The heavy reliance on foreign capital, especially during the oil boom, was undoubtedly encouraged by its easy availability. The creditworthiness of Mexico in international capital markets had increased tremendously following the discovery of oil. There was, in fact, an excess supply of capital and "fierce competition among foreign lenders to grant new loans to the Mexican government and to public enterprises was an every day event during the boom years" (Zedillo, 1986, p. 971). This excess supply also meant that it was quite easy for the private sector as well to obtain external finance.[21] It may be noted that foreign borrowing

---

[21] Unlike in 1972–76, when the bulk of the borrowing was by the public sector, the private sector was now also important. Its foreign debt rose, for example, from $6.8 billion at the end of 1977 to $17 billion at the end of 1980.

was also relatively cheap, given the negative real interest rates then prevailing in world markets. Moreover, Mexican borrowers, taking advantage of the excess supply of credit, could negotiate the best possible terms for their debt.

This scenario, however, changed dramatically after 1981 as Mexico's debt increased tremendously in the course of just one year and the international environment deteriorated. Along with the fall in oil revenues, the sharp increase in the stock of debt reduced Mexico's creditworthiness. New credit lines dried up and interest rates on new loans, now increasingly short-term in nature, soared. As oil revenues fell further in 1982 and interest rates rose, Mexico's ability to service her huge debt was increasingly undermined, culminating in the declaration of "illiquidity" later that year – a dramatic reversal from the situation existing just three to four years prior – and requiring dramatic remedies.

Exchange rate management and trade policy   Dramatic changes were also evident in another realm of Mexico's external economic relations, i.e., that of exchange rate management and trade policy. We may recall from our discussion in chapter 2 that the pursuit of expansionary policies by a typical LDC during the downturn and the resulting acceleration of inflation are likely to lead to an appreciation of the real exchange rate, thus aggravating the adverse effects of such policies on the trade balance. As the trade balance steadily worsens, however, the government becomes increasingly reluctant to let the real exchange rate depreciate, favoring import controls instead until a major devaluation is no longer avoidable. The Mexican experience during the downturn corresponds very closely to this scenario as we observe the expected fluctuations between episodes of liberalization and controls.

In the early stages of the downturn, i.e., during Echeverría's regime, as the trade balance deteriorated (figure 3.6(a)), the government, reluctant to devalue the peso, instead increased its controls on trade, with the percentage of import values subject to import licensing rising to 82 percent in 1974 (Zabludovsky, 1990, p. 177). Although the economic scenario with respect to the trade balance, reserve situation, and capital flight had become quite serious by the end of 1975, the government refused to react with regard to the exchange rate.[22] By mid-1976, however, provoked by expectations about an impending devaluation, capital flight assumed such critical proportions that, with shrinking sources of foreign credit, the government was forced to take drastic action. A 22-year era of fixed parities (1954–76) thus ended, and the peso was allowed to "float" against the dollar. The real rate of exchange conse-

---

[22] See Zedillo (1986, p. 966) for evidence on the extent of capital flight from Mexico during this period.

quently started depreciating (see figure 3.18(a)), an action followed by additional import control coverage in 1977.

These trends were, however, reversed following the onset of the post-1978 oil boom. With inflation accelerating and the nominal exchange rate once again kept virtually fixed, the real exchange rate started appreciating very rapidly; by 1981 the index had fallen to about 90 (1980 = 100) from about 130 in 1977. At the same time the government carried out a brief experiment with trade liberalization, mainly in the form of a reduction of QRs; the percentage of import value subject to licensing dropped to 76 percent in 1978 (from 90 percent in 1977) and further to 60 percent by 1980 (Zabludovsky, 1990, p. 177).

This attempt at liberalization was, however, predictably short-lived, given the complementary expansionary policies followed during the boom. With the deteriorating trade balance and reserve situation, the government, again reluctant to devalue, increased controls once again in 1981. The percentage of import value under licenses reached 85 percent in 1981 and 100 percent in 1982 (Zabludovsky, 1990, p. 177). Although the situation had clearly become precarious by the middle of 1981, little was done on the exchange rate front; the nominal rate continued to depreciate daily but at an annual rate of only 9 percent (Zedillo, 1986, p. 977). It was only in early 1982 that the peso was finally devalued by about 40 percent, resulting in a substantial real depreciation (see figure 3.19(a)). With the situation worsening further, a two-tier foreign exchange rate system was set up in August 1982, and blanket foreign exchange controls were introduced a month later (Zedillo, 1986, p. 978).

The labor market   The efforts of a typical LDC government to impose covert taxation through inflation are likely to be resisted not only indirectly by the public in general as described above but also directly by at least one important group in society, organized labor. The theoretical discussion in chapter 2 indicated a close relationship between cyclical movements in the rate of inflation and the incidence of labor unrest. Organized labor, concerned during the upturn with extracting a larger share of the rents for their members, now faced with rising inflation during the downturn, is likely to protest on behalf of the entire working class. Hence labor disputes can be expected to be higher during the downturn in the presence of union activity. On the other hand, in more atypical (East Asian) LDCs with less distorted labor markets, both the average incidence of labor disputes over the cycle as well as differences within different phases of the cycle can be expected to be less pronounced.

These theoretical predictions are substantially borne out by the observed trends in labor unrest in Mexico and, as we shall see below, in Colombia and in East Asia (in chapter 4). Data constraints have limited our analysis to only the downturn phases in both Latin American countries but the findings nonetheless are illuminating. As we can see in figure 3.21(a), the index of Mexican labor unrest – defined in terms of the total number of workers involved in industrial disputes as a percentage of total industrial employment – already quite high at the beginning of the downturn (relative to, for example, that in the East Asian cases examined in chapter 4) – shot up significantly during the high inflation years of 1983–85.

The dramatic reversal in economic conditions and policies in Mexico within the short span of four to five years (i.e., between the oil boom and the debt crisis), as documented above, has, of course, been the subject of considerable discussion during recent years. It is now generally believed that the Mexican economic crisis of the early eighties was in large measure caused by the manner in which the authorities managed the economy during the prior oil boom. Our empirical analysis lends support to this conclusion, but it also goes a substantial step further by placing this "blip" in historical context. The broad canvas of our study, both in its longitudinal dimension and the consideration of a comprehensive set of macroeconomic policy instruments within a political economy approach, helps us to trace the deeper roots of such crises and of what can only be called the unsatisfactory long-term performance of a system relative to its potential. A satisfactory explanation of the periodic occurrence of crises and associated policy reversals requires consideration of a system's initial conditions as they affect the political economy of response to inevitable shocks from the outside.

Our analysis shows that the roots of the Mexican crisis of the early eighties can be traced back at least to the early sixties when, at the beginning of its external orientation phase, Mexico failed to exploit the opportunities afforded by a favorable external environment to realign relative prices and develop overt methods of resource transfer – both of which could have improved resource allocation and helped increase the degree of external orientation. Instead, Mexico pursued a development strategy the unsustainability of which became clear toward the end of the upturn. However, having "missed the boat" when the external environment was more propitious for reform, the Mexican authorities reacted by taking the politically easier option of promoting growth through expansionary policies. From the late upturn, therefore, the evolution of development policy in Mexico increasingly began to resemble that of the "typical" LDC described in chapter 2, with the process intensifying once the downturn started. Expansionary policies were financed by money creation and external borrowing; this, in turn, led to inflation and balance-of-payments crises that were dealt with by quantity rather than price adjustments. As reforms in major policy areas such as tax policy, interest-rate policy, and exchange-rate policy were slow, modes of resource transfer became once again increasingly covert. The emergence of an oil boom in the midst of the downturn further intensified such tendencies. Viewed in long-run perspective, therefore, the behavior of economic policy in Mexico during the boom years is seen as representing a continuation of what is basically a long-run pattern of policy evolution, the essential features of which are broadly similar to the prototype pattern outlined. Colombia's policy evolution during the downturn, a subject to which we now turn, also exhibits many of these features, albeit in a milder form.

Colombia

Colombia also attempted to maintain growth in the face of a deteriorating external environment, but its growth activism was relatively more moderate. We should recall that Colombia had pursued a strategy of relative restraint during the coffee boom at the end of the upturn. An important component of this strategy was the reduction in government expenditures, particularly investment. We should also recall that these reductions in expenditures had a negative impact on growth, which was relatively modest during the boom years, compared to the late sixties and early seventies. Once the boom was over, i.e., by 1978, fears of further reductions in growth were intensified.

It was under these circumstances that the new administration of Turbay took over and launched a development program that envisaged a reversal of the earlier trends through substantial increases in investment, particularly in infrastructure and projects based on the exploitation of natural resources. A crucial feature of this investment program was that it was to be financed to a large extent by foreign borrowing. The decision to implement a foreign-debt-financed expansionary policy was taken in the light of the expectation that the country's own foreign exchange earnings would be declining following the deterioration in the external environment.

These expansionary policies were temporarily and modestly successful as growth rates were kept at or above 4 percent per annum until 1980 (see figure 3.4(b)). Lower growth rates, however, set in after 1981, with the economy expanding at barely 1 percent in real terms during 1982. The adjustment measures initiated in 1982 and discussed in greater detail below helped to reverse this trend, but growth, nonetheless, remained modest until the mini–coffee boom of 1986. It thus appears that Colombia was approaching a downturn in economic activity in the mid-seventies, as suggested by the deceleration in growth rates during 1974–75, but that this was "postponed" twice – first by an exogenous factor, i.e., the coffee boom of 1976–78, and then by the endogenous growth activism of the government during 1979–80 – before finally materializing in 1981–82.

While the export/GDP ratio had a significantly positive slope during the upturn, during the downturn it exhibited a cyclical pattern (see figure 3.5(b)). A decline in the degree of external orientation set in once the boom was over and became particularly severe during 1981–83 when the export/GDP ratio fell below even its 1967 levels. A number of factors contributed to this decline. Earnings from coffee exports declined due to both a fall in prices – from an index of 103 in 1979 to 74 in 1983–as well as decline in volume. Moreover, nontraditional exports suffered due both to an appreciation in the real exchange rate as well as a recession in world markets, falling by 12 percent in 1982 and stagnating thereafter (Garcia, 1988a, pp. 51–52). Another round of export-promotion measures was initiated as part of the adjustment package introduced in 1984. The success of these measures is reflected in the reversal of the trend in external orientation after 1984. Although not shown in figure 3.5(b), exports got an additional boost in 1986 from the mini–coffee boom of that year. Nonetheless, the overall secular trend during this period is that of a significant decline. The pattern of Colombia's degree of external orientation thus resembles somewhat that predicted by our theoretical framework, i.e., the exports/GDP ratio rises during the recovery phase, but once the economy is hit by a recession, it gradually reverts to a greater degree of internal orientation.

The mild tendency toward growth activism also had its impact on the trade balance as the overheating of the economy led to an increased demand for imports (see figure 3.6(b)). The improvements in the trade balance due to the coffee boom had reached their climax in 1977 when the export surplus was almost 4 percent of GDP. After 1977, however, the trends were reversed and by 1980 the export surplus was below 1 percent of GDP. The real crunch, however, came during 1981–82; as the government persisted with its expansionary policies, even after the worsening trends in the trade balance had become apparent, the relative export surplus finally turned into an import surplus exceeding 3 percent of GDP in 1981 and worsening even further in 1982.

It was at this stage, i.e., in 1982, that the government initiated steps to correct the situation by imposing import restrictions and moderating its expansionary policies. However, it was only after the adoption of a more substantial adjustment package in 1984–85 that a noticeable improvement took place in the trade balance – with import surpluses turned into export surpluses by 1985 and reaching a record 6.5 percent of GDP in 1986 following the mini–coffee boom.

Counter to our predictions, however, the accumulation of foreign exchange reserves noted earlier did not give way to intentional dissipation even after the economy had entered its recessionary post-1978 period and the government embarked on expansionary policies. The accumulation of reserves continued, reaching a peak in 1979 and, moreover, although some reduction started after 1980, reserves remained quite high until the end of 1982 (see figure 3.7(b)). A substantial decline occurred only in 1983 and 1984, by the end of which reserves had fallen to about four months' worth of imports. The reason for this particular pattern of reserve movement during the recessionary period is provided by the significant increase in the government's borrowing from abroad during 1979–84. Consequently, although the trade balance deteriorated, its impact on the reserve situation was moderated by foreign borrowing. It must also be noted that even at their lowest recessionary levels, i.e., in 1984, reserves were not at a very critical level, suggesting that Colombia was relatively prompt in taking corrective measures.

Fiscal policy   The attempts of the Colombian government to promote growth artificially during the downturn are reflected in government expenditures, which zoomed from 11.5 percent of GDP in 1978 to 13.8 percent by 1980, reaching a peak of 16 percent in 1982. There was no effort this time, however, to pay for increased expenditures via increased taxes, since recourse to foreign borrowing was considered an easier option. The tax/GDP ratio, as figure 3.8(b) indicates, in fact decreased continuously during 1979–83, both due to the reduction of earnings from coffee taxes as well as a drop in revenue from import duties following the trade liberalization that accompanied the expansionary policies.[23] The results of these developments are starkly reflected in figure 3.10(b). Deficits reappeared in 1979, when they amounted to 1.0 percent of GDP, soared to 2.0 percent in 1980, and to a record 4.0 percent in 1982. Although there was some reduction after 1983, deficits continued to remain high until 1984, despite the induction into office of a new administration – that of Betancur – in 1982. We have here clear evidence of an effort to maintain growth via domestic expansion, supplemented by foreign lending.

By mid-1984, a new minister of finance was appointed, who immediately initiated a big adjustment program to deal with the worsening macroeconomic situation. The major component of this adjustment effort was the improvement in revenue collection and control of expenditures. On the revenue side, new measures included the establishment of a general 18 percent import duty, an increase in tax rates, an advance payment of income taxes to be credited against future tax liabilities, and an improvement in tax administration. Together these led to an increase in the tax/GDP ratio as seen in figure 3.8(b). At the same time govern-

---

[23] A. Hernández and R. Hommes, "La Bonanza Cafetera: Su Distribución y Manejo"; quoted in Kamas (1986).

ment expenditures were reduced. The combination of these measures led to an improvement in the budgetary position after 1985.

Monetary policy   The expansionary fiscal policies of a government intent on maintaining the growth momentum of the economy by expanding internal demand after the boom was over led to high rates of monetary expansion during the initial years of the downturn. During 1979–82, money supply grew by 25–30 percent annually, resulting in inflation rates of about 25 percent during this period (see figures 3.11(b) and 3.12(b)). After 1985, however, as part of the adjustment package, domestic credit to the public sector and the monetization of government deficits was cut sharply.

Although the rates of money growth were lower than in Mexico, it should be noted that the Colombian government was able to extract comparable rates of forced savings – averaging about 3 percent of GDP (figure 3.14(b)), and, unlike Mexico, to continue to do so almost throughout the downturn. This was possible because velocity increased only modestly (figure 3.13(b)), i.e., while inflation was high, it was not high enough to make the public excessively jittery. Colombia's lower inflation sensitivity is reflected in the much closer correlation observed between money supply growth rates and the rate of forced savings, as compared to Mexico (figure 3.14(b)).

With inflation persisting even after the boom was over, a major interest rate reform was carried out in 1979, with the central bank's discount rate increased from 22 to 30 percent. This pushed real interest rates back to positive levels in 1979; they have remained positive and steady since, in spite of a modest reduction in nominal rates in 1982 (figure 3.15(b)). Neither total savings nor the formal savings rates proportion show any trend during the downturn, although the average levels of the latter were clearly somewhat higher (see figures 3.16(b) and 3.17(b)).

As in Mexico, expansionary policies were fueled partly by the inflow of foreign capital, but, as is clear from figure 3.20(b), Colombia's reliance on external borrowing came considerably later and was substantially less, i.e., the net inflow of public and publicly guaranteed long-term foreign capital never exceeded 2 percent of GDP.

Exchange rate management and trade policy   Once the coffee boom was over, the rate of crawl of the Colombian peso increased after 1978 and accelerated after 1980. Thus, despite the increase in the rate of inflation, this relative price flexibility meant that the peso appreciated relatively little during 1978–82 (figure 3.18(b)). Additional trade liberalization was undertaken in September 1979 and October 1980 against the backdrop of a substantial accumulation of foreign exchange reserves. This persistence of a liberal trade regime during the late seventies and early eighties is reflected in the continued low levels of the average rates of protection seen in figure 3.19(b).

As mentioned above, the trade balance started turning negative after 1981, and foreign exchange reserves, although still at comfortable levels, were falling. These trends warranted a depreciation of the by now somewhat overvalued peso. Instead, the immediate response of the Colombian government was inaction; only at the end of 1982, when the situation had deteriorated, did the authorities respond. That response, moreover, was of the classic type predicted by our framework, i.e., a reluctance to devalue and a preference instead for reimposing quantitative controls. The prolonged period of steady trade liberalization thus came to an end in 1982, as a large number of import items were transferred from the free list to a prior-licensing list and the approval rate of import applications on the prior-licensing list was reduced. By March 1984, 70 percent of the value of imports was again subject to prior licensing and Colombia had joined the circle of Latin American countries in debt crisis.

The massive adjustment package introduced since late 1984, however, included large adjustments of the nominal exchange rate between late 1984 and mid-1986. These adjustments, coupled with a decline in inflation, led to a substantial rise in the real exchange rate in 1984 and 1985 (see figure 3.18(b)). At the same time there was in evidence a trend toward replacing QRs by tariffs. The effects of these actions, taken not only to reduce imports and improve the current account balance but also to reactivate the economy, particularly the industrial sector, are reflected in figure 3.19(b).

The varying speed of trade liberalization in Colombia over the period 1967–82, and its ultimate reversal during 1982–84, can be attributed not only to exogenous shocks but also, as Garcia (1988b, p. 2) argues, to "insufficient commitment on the part of the government, inadequate macroeconomic management and the opposition of vested interests." According to him, the early moves toward liberalization during 1967–74 faced little political opposition, partly due to high growth in the economy as a whole, particularly in the industrial sector, and partly due to the fact that a depreciating currency (at least until 1972) offset to some extent the reduction in protection due to trade liberalization.

Political opposition, however, started brewing after 1975 as growth slowed and it became apparent that expanded imports were likely to become a permanent feature of the economy. The most important parties opposing liberalization were the National Association of Industrialists (ANDI) and bureaucrats responsible for administering import controls. By 1982, with the economy's performance worsening, these groups could create sufficient pressure in favor of reimposing controls. The fact that the new president and new finance minister came from the state of Antioquia, whose textile capital, Medellin, was the main center of opposition to liberalization, may also have contributed to its reversal after 1982 (Garcia, 1988b, p. 110). Since then, however, a new cycle of liberalization has been initiated in the context of the overall Latin American adjustment effort.

The labor market   As in Mexico, we observe a connection between inflationary trends and the incidence of labor unrest (see figure 3.21(b)). We may note an increase in the index during 1982–83 when inflation was high, but a decline later as inflation was brought under control. On average, however, the incidence of labor unrest is lower than in Mexico. This is not only due to the less serious nature of the inflationary phenomenon in Colombia but can also, perhaps, be ascribed to the greater ability of the Colombian polity to resolve disputes, a subject discussed in greater detail below.

3.5 Conclusions

The comparative historical analysis of development policy change in Mexico and Colombia carried out in this chapter suggests that, as far as the broad features of their long-run policy evolution are concerned, both countries represent empirical manifestations of the prototype LDC caricatured in chapter 2. Acting out of political necessity, governments in both countries adopted growth-promoting expansionary policies during the upturn – taking advantage of the natural resource bonanzas and the easy availability of foreign capital – and then desperately tried to maintain these policies in the face of a deteriorating external environment, once again with the help of foreign borrowing. In both countries, this growth activism led to fluctuations in economic performance, a stop-go pattern of liberalization in various markets, and an unsatisfactory performance in terms of sustained growth, employment generation, and the distribution of income.

While these Latin American family commonalities are dominant, significant intrafamily differences in behavior should also be noted, with Colombia representing a milder version of the typical LDC pattern and Mexico (at least until very recently) emerging as a more extreme manifestation of the syndrome. While both countries pursued expansionary policies, these were relatively mild in Colombia as reflected, for example, in lower budget deficit/GDP ratios. There was also in evidence in Colombia a relative preference for explicit over implicit modes of resource transfers as indicated by greater success in implementing tax reform measures, the maintenance of a more realistic exchange rate regime – compared to relative rigidity in Mexico – and the reinstatement of positive real rates of interest even during bad times, contrasted with the persistence of negative interest rates throughout the downturn in Mexico. While growth activism inevitably led to periodic balance-of-payments and reserve crises in both countries, the response in Colombia was consistently faster, with corrective measures taken before the situation became too precarious. Moreover, these corrective measures were usually more price-oriented, e.g., the devaluation in 1974 following a balance-of-payments crisis – while, in Mexico, the tendency was to opt for quantity adjustments as long as possible. This meant that the trend of liberalization initiated relatively early in Colombia was maintained more consistently than in Mexico. Finally, there was less overall resort to foreign borrowing in evidence in Colombia, though we can observe some catch-up in this respect in the late seventies.

Our theoretical framework suggests that the underlying explanation for differential behavior may be found in the initial conditions – in particular, the size and nature of the resource endowments – and the manner in which the political economy consequently plays itself out over time in each case. While Colombia and Mexico are both natural-resource-abundant countries and both experienced natural resource bonanzas during the period covered in our study, there are also noteworthy differences with implications for a government's policy response. In Mexico, for instance, the oil industry is state-owned and operated by PEMEX, a public enterprise. During the oil boom, therefore, oil revenues accrued directly to the government and, in fact, accounted for a very substantial portion of aggregate public revenues. Thus, while in 1978 income from the oil sector accounted for a fifth of total public revenues, by 1982 the share was more than a third and in 1983 almost half (Zedillo, 1986, p. 975). In Colombia, in contrast, coffee is privately produced, mostly by small farmers, and privately exported. The coffee producers' organization, Federación Nacional de Cafeteros (FEDECAFE), stands ready to purchase coffee from producers at an announced price, effectively setting a floor to internal prices. This price is typically below the world price, particularly when the latter is rising rapidly. Coffee is exported by both FEDECAFE and private exporters, the latter's profits depending on the difference between external and internal prices. Part of these profits are taxed away by the government in the form of an ad valorem export tax. In addition, exporters are required to surrender a portion of their coffee exports or the cash equivalent to FEDECAFE (the *retención*), with these funds used to stabilize the internal price when the world price falls. The bulk of the windfall income, however, usually accrues to the private sector.

During the boom years of 1976–77, the internal price rose, but not as much as the world price. A part of the windfall profit to private exporters was then "taxed" away by increasing the *retención* (as high as 85 percent) and by subjecting coffee exports to an effectively lower exchange rate. Despite having at its disposal a wide variety of policy instruments, the government siphoned off a relatively low proportion of the windfall. The *retención* went to FEDECAFE, and the export tax was actually reduced. Hernandez and Hommes estimate that the government received only 11 percent of the boom earnings, while producers earned 34 percent, exporters 30 percent, and FEDECAFE 25 percent.[24] Since such a low proportion of the boom earnings actually accrued to the government, it is likely that the sense of enhanced spending power was relatively moderate, which in turn probably explains the more restrained response on the part of the government.

While differences in the nature and ownership of the two systems' resource endowments thus appear to play a role in explaining differential policy response, the relatively greater degree of consistency and restraint observed in Colombia may also be related to the greater initial homogeneity of the polity in that country, better enabling it to settle disputes between various interest groups before they could have an adverse impact on the process of policy formation. Although Colombia has been in the headlines for its rural and urban violence, it has a multiparty system, with little fundamental difference in the ideology or support base of the two major parties, the Liberals and the Conservatives, who have alternated in power over many years. While diverse interest groups have their representatives within each party, the tradition has been to resolve disputes internally within the parties so that subsequent policy formation could proceed on the basis of an agreed "social contract." Moreover, the potential instability induced by the dependence on coffee, the earnings from which are subject to huge fluctuations due to exogenous factors, has, over the years, taught the Colombians to compromise and evolve a process of policy formation based on consultation, a process that helps reduce oscillations in policy.

In Mexico, on the other hand, despite the existence of a one-party system for many years, it has proved difficult to maintain viable social contracts in a consistent manner. Traditionally, Mexico has been governed by an uneasy three-cornered coalition of established (big) business, organized labor, and the bureaucracy. While the fruits of the respectable growth achieved during this period accrued to these groups, the growth process, as discussed earlier, bypassed important segments of the population, especially Indians, whose dissatisfaction was made explicit toward the end of the decade. The Mexican polity tried to respond to this, but, given the fact that it had already had its social revolution, it proved difficult to find the necessary flexibility for continuous reforms. This is reflected in the frequent conflicts between the government and the established business community during populist episodes, followed

---

[24] See below for a discussion of trade liberalization during this period.

by efforts to placate the capitalist middle classes. One example is the policies that culminated in the massive capital flight of 1976 during the Echeverría administration – a reflection of the private sector's lack of confidence in government policies. The subsequent regime of López Portillo veered to active assistance to established business during the oil boom, both through credit creation as well as public guarantees for private foreign loans, reflecting an attempt to win back the support of this class.

In very recent years, coincident with a weakening of the predominance of the PRI, attempts are being made by the Salinas administration to increase the Mexican polity's ability to resolve social conflicts more consistently. It is too early to evaluate fully the results of these endeavors (also see chapter 6). But it can be concluded from our comparative historical analysis of Latin America's political economy of policy change that the success or failure of these efforts in the political arena is likely to have a strong bearing on the question of whether the recent, apparently more linear, trend toward liberalization in Mexico will indeed be sustained.[25]

[25] For a description of the post–1982 economic liberalization measures in Mexico, see Ghani (1990), van Wijnbergen (1990), and Zabludovsky (1990).

Figure 3.1 External terms of trade (percent deviation from trend)

(a)

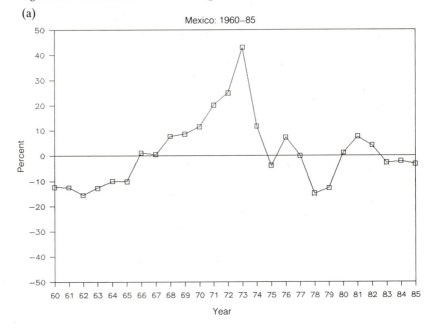

(b)

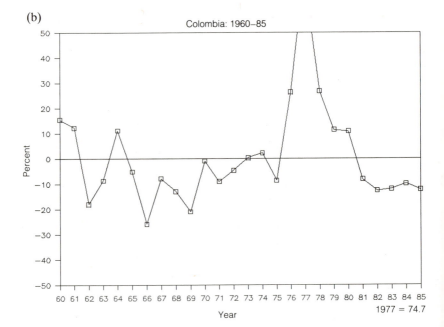

1977 = 74.7

90

Figure 3.2   External terms of trade (percent deviation from trend)

(a)

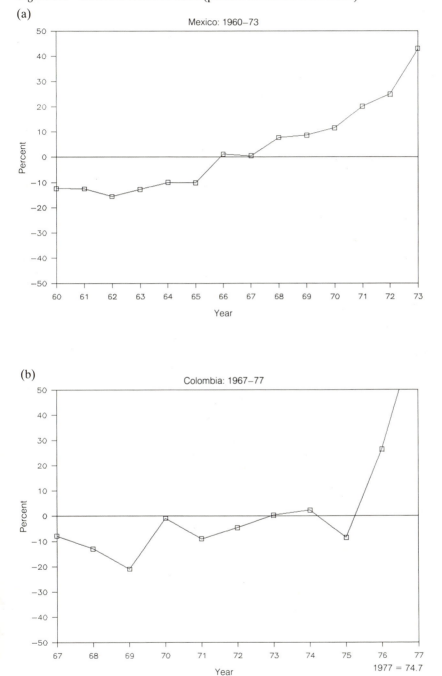

(b)

Figure 3.3   External terms of trade (percent deviation from trend)

(a)

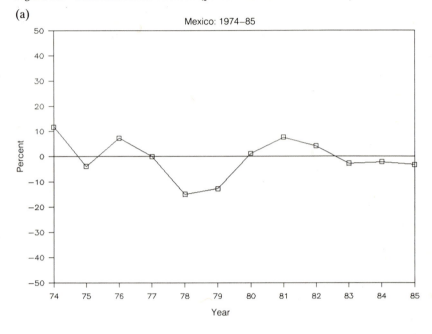

(b)

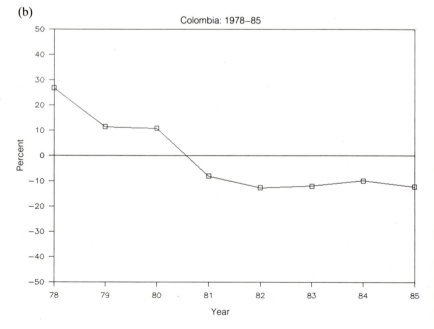

Figure 3.4   Annual rate of growth of real GDP

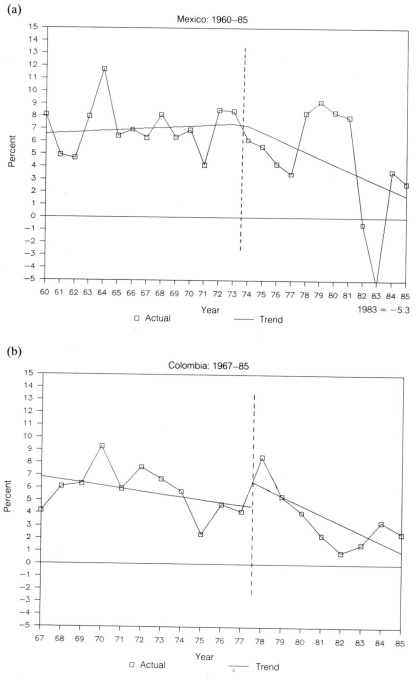

(a)

Mexico: 1960–85

Percent

□ Actual   —— Trend

Year   1983 = −5.3

(b)

Colombia: 1967–85

Percent

□ Actual   —— Trend

Year

Figure 3.5 Exports/GDP

(a)

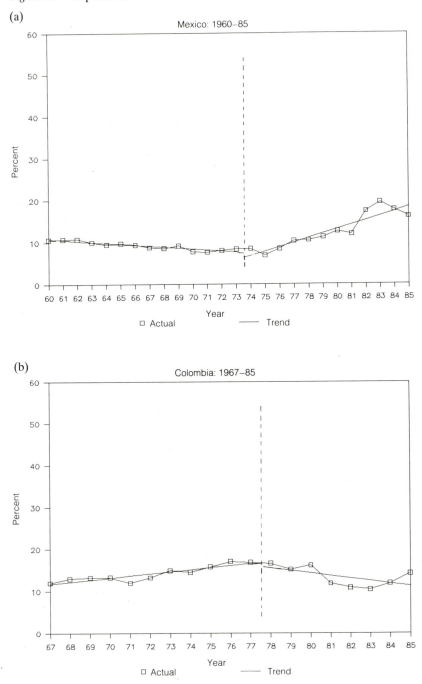

Mexico: 1960–85

(b)

Colombia: 1967–85

Figure 3.6 Trade balance/GDP

(a)

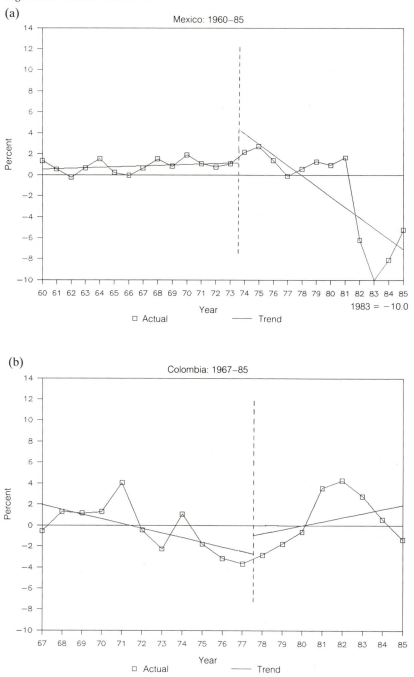

Mexico: 1960–85

1983 = −10.0

□ Actual ——— Trend

(b)

Colombia: 1967–85

□ Actual ——— Trend

Figure 3.7 Foreign exchange reserves/four months' imports

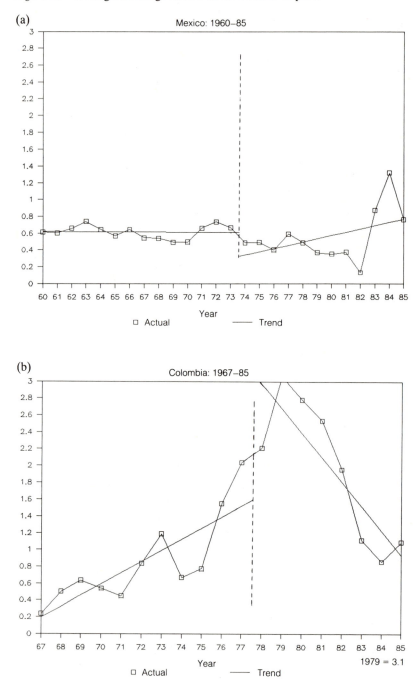

(a)

Mexico: 1960–85

☐ Actual   Year   —— Trend

(b)

Colombia: 1967–85

☐ Actual   Year   —— Trend

1979 = 3.1

Figure 3.8 Total taxes/GDP

(a)

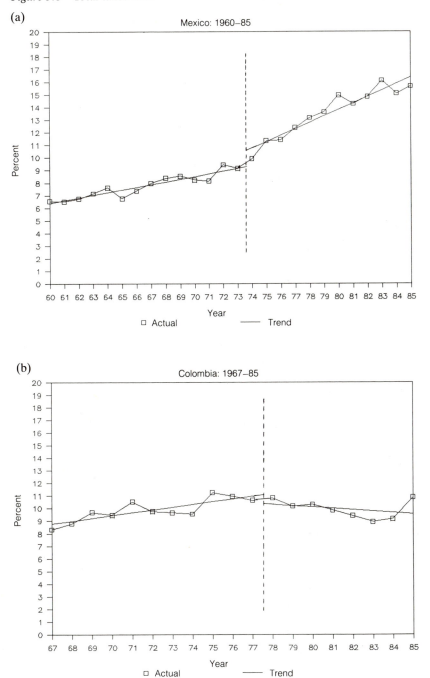

Mexico: 1960–85

Year

□ Actual   —— Trend

(b)

Colombia: 1967–85

Year

□ Actual   —— Trend

97

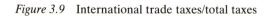

Figure 3.9 International trade taxes/total taxes

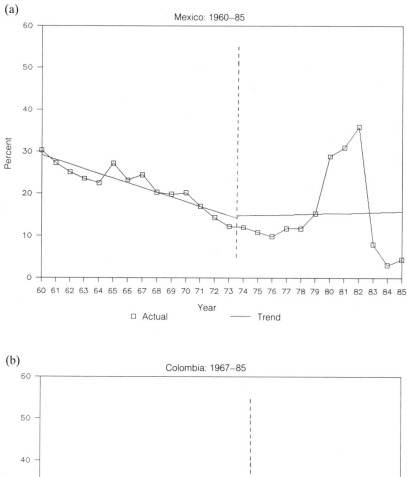

(a)

Mexico: 1960–85

(b)

Colombia: 1967–85

Figure 3.10 Government deficits/GDP

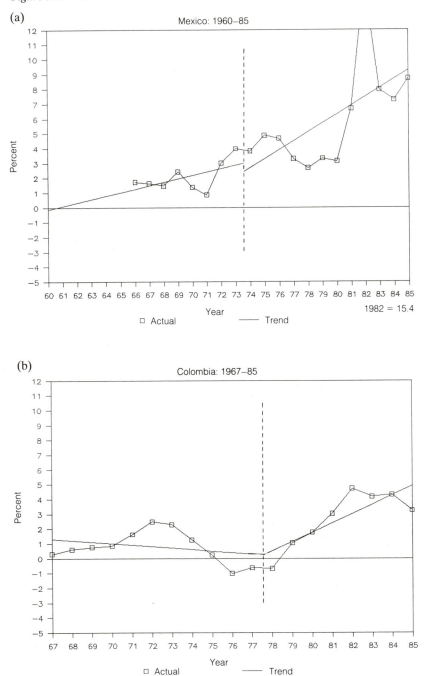

(a)

Mexico: 1960–85

Percent

Year

1982 = 15.4

□ Actual   —— Trend

(b)

Colombia: 1967–85

Percent

Year

□ Actual   —— Trend

99

Figure 3.11   Annual rate of change of money supply

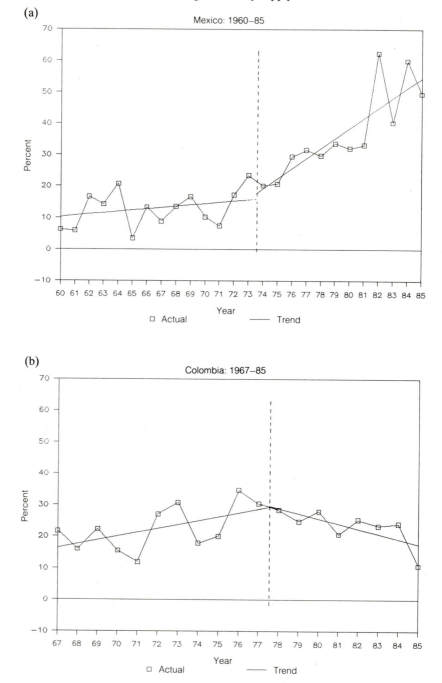

(a)

Mexico: 1960–85

(b)

Colombia: 1967–85

Figure 3.12   Annual rate of inflation

(a)

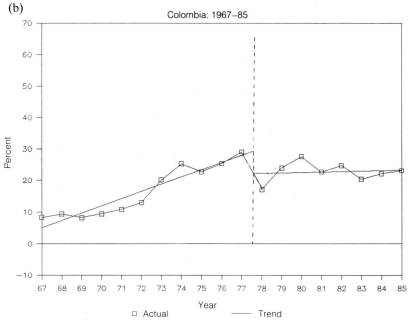

101

Figure 3.13 Income velocity of circulation

(a)

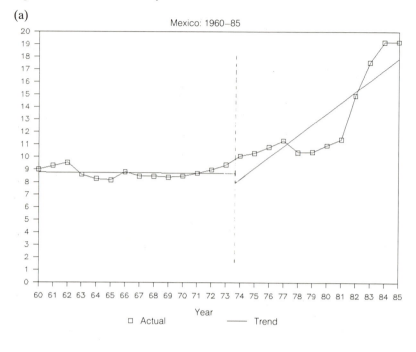

(b)

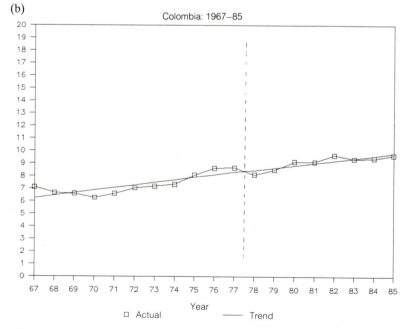

Figure 3.14 Money growth and forced savings rates

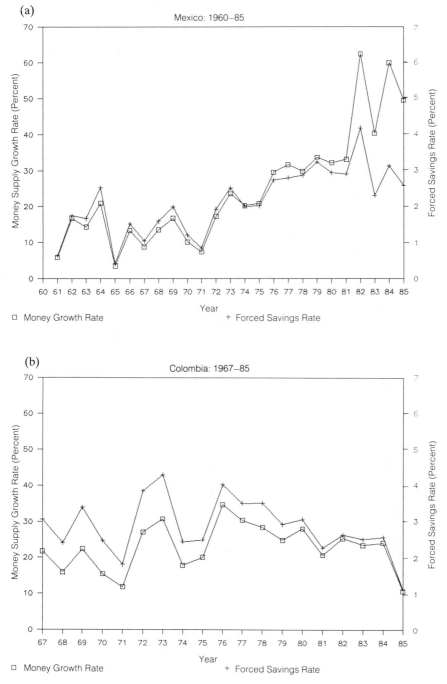

(a)

Mexico: 1960–85

☐ Money Growth Rate   + Forced Savings Rate

(b)

Colombia: 1967–85

☐ Money Growth Rate   + Forced Savings Rate

Figure 3.15   Real rate of interest

(a)

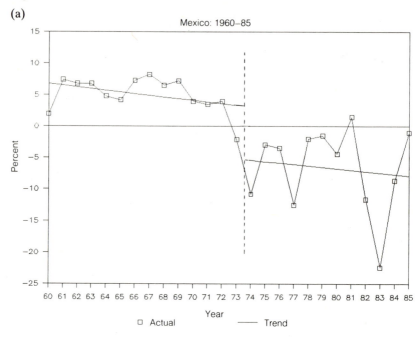

(b)

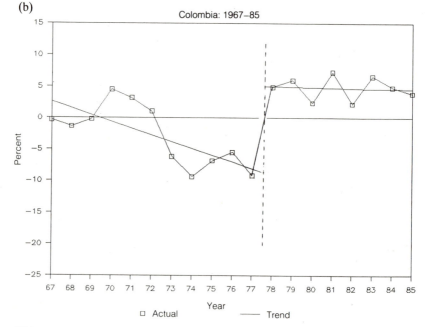

Figure 3.16   Gross domestic savings/GDP

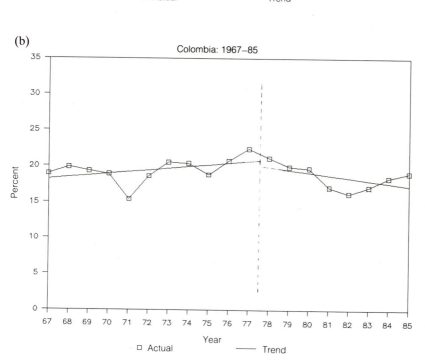

(a)

Mexico: 1960–85

(b)

Colombia: 1967–85

Figure 3.17　　Change in savings deposits/gross savings

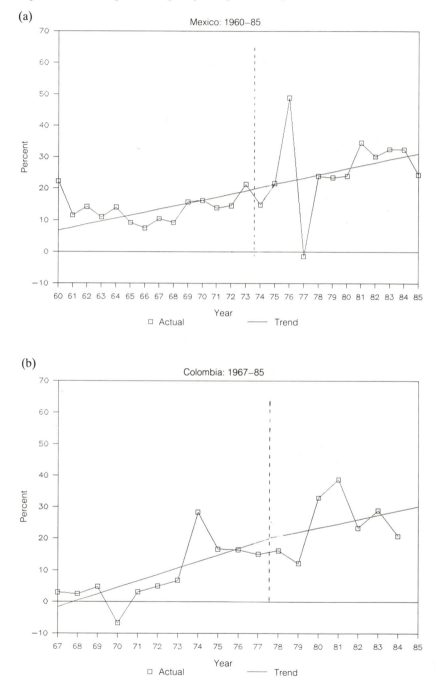

(a)

Mexico: 1960–85

(b)

Colombia: 1967–85

Figure 3.18 Index of real exchange rate (1980 = 100)

(a)

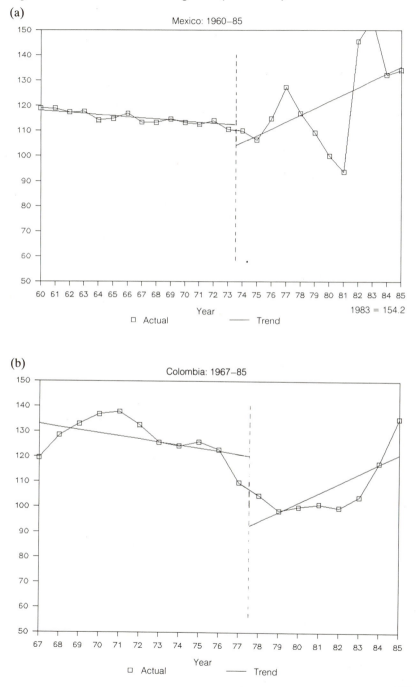

Mexico: 1960–85

□ Actual   ——— Trend

Year

1983 = 154.2

(b)

Colombia: 1967–85

□ Actual   ——— Trend

Year

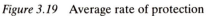

Figure 3.19   Average rate of protection

(a)

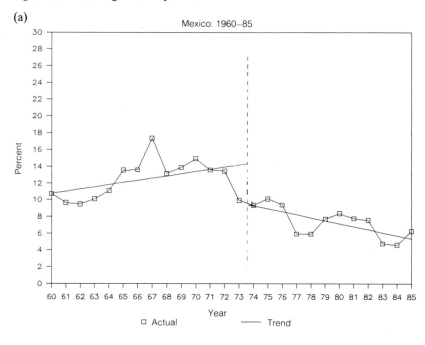

(b)

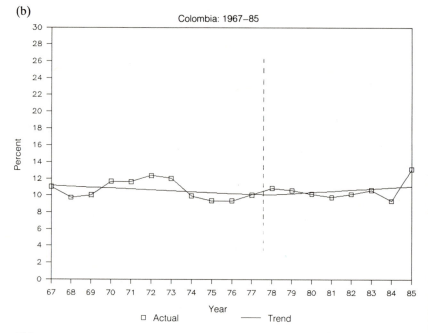

Figure 3.20 Net inflow of long-term foreign capital/GDP

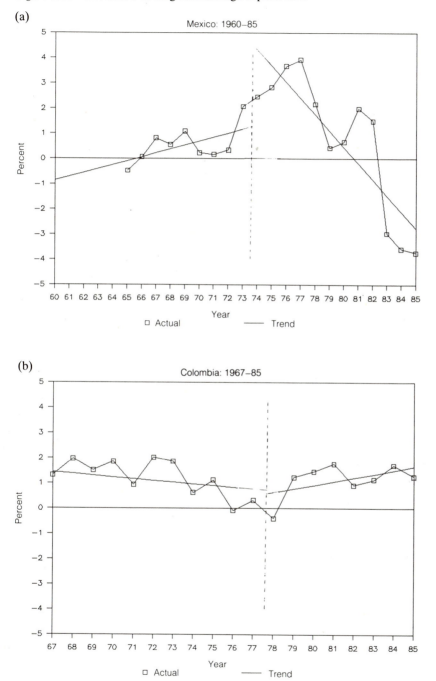

(a)

Mexico: 1960–85

(b)

Colombia: 1967–85

Figure 3.21   Index of labor disputes

(a)

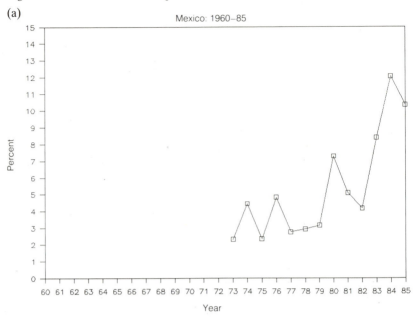

(b)

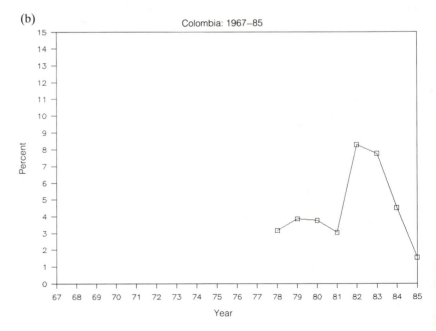

110

Definition of variables

(definitions not spelled out for self-evident variables)

External terms of trade = Unit value of exports divided by unit value of imports

Exports = Exports of goods and services

Imports = Imports of goods and services

Trade balance = Imports minus exports

International trade taxes = Export duties plus import duties

Government deficits = Central government deficits excluding public enterprise accounts

Money supply = M1

Annual rate of inflation = Rate of change in GDP deflator

Income velocity of circulation = $(P_t \cdot Q_{t-1}) / M_{t-1}$, where

P = price level

Q = nominal GDP

M = money supply (M1)

t = time

Forced savings rate = $(dM/dt)/PQ$, where

dM/dt = change in money supply

PQ = nominal GDP

Real rate of interest = Nominal central bank discount rate minus the annual rate of inflation

Savings deposits = Time, savings, and foreign currency deposits

Real exchange rates = Real exchange rates are derived from nominal exchange rates and relative wholesale price ratios of the five major trading partners using trade shares as weights.

Average rate of protection = Import taxes divided by total imports of goods and services

Index of labor disputes = Total number of workers involved in industrial disputes as percentage of total industrial employment

Data sources: Mexico

Variable and source

Unit values of exports and imports: World Bank, *World Tables*, 1976, 1987

Real GDP: IMF, *International Financial Statistics*, Yearbook, 1988

Exports of goods and services: IMF, *International Financial Statistics*, Yearbook, 1988

Imports of goods and services: IMF, *International Financial Statistics*, Yearbook, 1988

Foreign exchange reserves: IMF, *International Financial Statistics*, Yearbook, 1988

Total taxes, import taxes, and export duties: IMF, *Government Finance Statistics*, 1982, 1985, 1988 (for post-1972 data); Nacional Financiera, S.A. *La Economica Mexicana En Cifras*, Mexico, d.f. 1981. (for pre-1972 data)

Government deficits: IMF, *International Financial Statistics*, Yearbook, 1988

Money supply: IMF, *International Financial Statistics*, Yearbook, 1988

GDP deflator: IMF, *International Financial Statistics*, Yearbook, 1988

Nominal rate of interest: Banco de Mexico

Gross domestic savings: Computed from data in IMF, *International Financial Statistics*, Yearbook, 1988

Time, savings, and foreign currency deposits: IMF, *International Financial Statistics*, Yearbook, 1988

Real exchange rate: Computed from data in IMF, *International Financial Statistics*, Yearbook 1988, and IMF, *Direction of Trade Statistics*, various issues

Net inflow of long-term foreign capital: World Bank, *World Debt Tables*, various issues

Number of workers involved in industrial disputes and total industrial employment: ILO, *International Labour Statistics*, various issues

Data sources: Colombia

Variable and Source

Unit values of exports and imports: IMF, *International Financial Statistics*, Yearbook, 1988

Real GDP: IMF, *International Financial Statistics*, Yearbook, 1988

Exports of goods and services: IMF, *International Financial Statistics*, Yearbook, 1988

Imports of goods and services: IMF, *International Financial Statistics*, Yearbook, 1988

Foreign exchange reserves: IMF, *International Financial Statistics*, Yearbook, 1988

Total taxes, import taxes, and export duties: IMF, *Government Finance Statistics*, 1982, 1985, 1988 (for post-1972 data); UN, *Yearbook of Statistics*, various issues, (for pre-1972 data)

Government deficits: IMF, *International Financial Statistics*, Yearbook, 1988

Money supply: IMF, *International Financial Statistics*, Yearbook, 1988

GDP deflator: IMF, *International Financial Statistics*, Yearbook, 1988

Nominal rate of interest: IMF, *International Financial Statistics*, Yearbook, 1988

Gross domestic savings: Computed from data in IMF, *International Financial Statistics*, Yearbook, 1988

Time, savings, and foreign currency deposits: IMF, *International Financial Statistics*, Yearbook, 1988

Real exchange rate: Computed from data in IMF, *International Financial Statistics*, Yearbook 1988, and IMF,

Direction of Trade Statistics, various issues

Net inflow of long-term foreign capital: World Bank, *World Debt Tables*, various issues

Number of workers involved in industrial disputes and total industrial employment: ILO, *International Labour Statistics*, various issues

Significance of trend lines: Mexico

NS	= Not significant
+++	= Significantly positive at the 98 percent level of confidence
++	= Significantly positive at the 95 percent level of confidence
+	= Significantly positive at the 90 percent level of confidence
− − −	= Significantly negative at the 98 percent level of confidence
− −	= Significantly negative at the 95 percent level of confidence
−	= Significantly negative at the 90 percent level of confidence

Variable	1960–73	1974–85
External terms of trade (deviations from trend)	+++	−
Annual rate of growth of real GDP	NS	−
Exports/GDP	− − −	+++
Trade balance/GDP	NS	− − −
Foreign exchange reserves/four months' imports	NS	NS
Total taxes/GDP	+++	+++
International trade taxes/total taxes	− − −	NS
Government deficits/GDP	NS	+++
Annual rate of change of money supply	NS	++
Annual rate of inflation	+++	+++
Income velocity of circulation	NS	+++
Real rate of interest	NS	NS
Gross domestic savings/GDP	++	+++
Change in savings deposits/gross savings	NS	NS
Real exchange rate	− − −	+
Average rate of protection	+	− − −
Net inflow of long-term foreign capital	+	− − −

Significance of trend lines: Colombia

NS	= Not significant
+++	= Significantly positive at the 98 percent level of confidence
++	= Significantly positive at the 95 percent level of confidence
+	= Significantly positive at the 90 percent level of confidence
− − −	= Significantly negative at the 98 percent level of confidence
− −	= Significantly negative at the 95 percent level of confidence
−	= Significantly negative at the 90 percent level of confidence

Variable	1967–77	1978–85
External terms of trade (deviations from trend)	+++	− − −
Annual rate of growth of real GDP	NS	NS
Exports/GDP	+++	NS
Trade balance/GDP	− −	NS
Foreign exchange reserves/four months' imports	+++	− −
Total taxes/GDP	+++	NS
International trade taxes/total taxes	NS	− − −
Government deficits/GDP	NS	++
Annual rate of change of money supply	+++	−
Annual rate of inflation	+++	NS
Income velocity of circulation	+++	+++
Real rate of interest	− − −	NS
Gross domestic savings/GDP	NS	NS
Change in savings deposits/gross savings	+++	NS
Real exchange rate	− − −	+++
Average rate of protection	NS	NS
Net inflow of long-term foreign capital	NS	NS

4

The "Atypical" East Asian Case: Taiwan and South Korea

In this chapter we examine the evolution of development policy in the "atypical" East Asian case exemplified by Taiwan and South Korea. To recall, these systems are small, natural-resource-poor, but human-resource-rich, and followed a pattern of transition growth different from that of the majority of LDCs. At the beginning of the 1960s, they shifted from a strategy of primary import substitution to one of primary export substitution instead of the more typical combination of secondary import substitution and export promotion. As is well known, it is these East Asian "tigers" that have experienced the most dramatic developmental success in the postwar era in terms of growth and equity objectives.

Taiwan initiated her phase of primary export substitution around 1960, while for Korea the shift came a little later, around 1962. Accordingly, as in chapter 3, we first identify the pattern of external shocks once the economy has moved into its external orientation mode and try to determine the periods of relative upturn and downturn. This is followed by an empirically based analysis of the evolution of policy over time in the two cases.

4.1 External shocks

In both Taiwan and South Korea the long-run trend in the actual terms of trade over the entire postwar period is negative, although not significantly so. Yet when we plot the deviations from these trends a distinct cycle emerges in both countries for the post-1960 period, when both shifted out of the IS and into the EO phase of transition growth. These deviations from trend are plotted in figures 4.1(a), 4.2(a), and 4.3(a) for Taiwan and in figures 4.1(b), 4.2(b), and 4.3(b) for South Korea, respectively.[1] In both countries, the sixties represented a period of relatively favorable

[1] Data constraints forced us to fit the long-run trend line to the period 1952–86 for Taiwan and to the period 1957–86 for South Korea.

movements in the terms of trade, while the seventies and eighties were characterized by relatively unfavorable movements. More specifically, we can identify 1960–70 and 1971–85 as representing the upturn and downturn periods, respectively, for Taiwan; the corresponding periods for South Korea are 1962–72 and 1973–85. The trend lines fitted to the deviations show a positive slope for both countries for the upturn – although statistically significant only for South Korea; for the downturn we observe a statistically negative trend for Taiwan and no trend for South Korea. Chow tests, moreover, confirm that in both countries the trends differ significantly as between the two periods. It should also be noted that, within an overall pattern of downturn during the seventies, South Korea experienced a temporary turnaround in the terms of trade during 1977–79.

The cyclical movements in the external terms of trade of Taiwan and South Korea are thus broadly coincident. The two systems' policy responses to these changes in the external environment were also broadly similar but, when viewed more closely, also reveal instructive differences. We examine these issues in the following sections, adopting an approach similar to that of the previous chapter, i.e., we first study the pattern of policy evolution during the upturn for each case, followed by a similar analysis for the downturn.

4.2 Development policy change in Taiwan and South Korea: an overview

Taiwan

Taiwan provides an excellent example of a government that, while active in the creation of conditions conducive to growth, has been remarkably successful in resisting the temptation of artificially pushing it beyond its "natural" levels, especially during difficult times. The long-run pattern of development policy evolution in Taiwan is indeed characterized by restraint in good times and flexibility in bad times – key elements evidence in various areas of policy formation.

During the upturn, Taiwan achieved, as would be expected, high growth rates due to its very successful early pursuit of an "open-economy" export-orientation strategy. This success and the resulting inflow of foreign exchange earnings did not, however, lead to "growth activism" on the part of the government as we have defined it in this volume. Fiscal and monetary policy remained restrained and flexible, with the government resisting the temptation to intervene heavily and, to the extent it did intervene, exhibiting the political courage of relying on overt rather than covert means of transferring resources either to itself or private interest groups. Conservative fiscal and monetary policies were generally adhered to, trade liberalization was slow but steady, and exchange rates were generally kept at realistic levels.

This prudence and flexibility on the part of Taiwanese policymakers became even more evident when put to a stronger test during the downturn. Unlike the typical LDC case, Taiwan accepted lower growth rates in the face of negative external shocks and maintained reforms in various policy arenas, ensuring that resource transfers increasingly took place by overt means and that the trend toward a further depoliticization of policy continued. The end result was not only a consistent increase in the system's external orientation but also much higher average rates of GDP growth and the best distribution of income in the nonsocialist developing world.

South Korea

South Korea's long-run pattern of policy evolution is broadly similar to that of Taiwan, but there are also important differences. During the upturn, South Korea, like Taiwan, achieved high growth rates helped by a successful shift to external orientation. This transition was accompanied by the initiation of a gradual trend of depoliticization of policy formation reflected in a reduction of trade barriers, a move toward more realistic exchange rates and real interest rates, and a broadening of the tax base.

This trend, while generally linear, was less consistently so than that of Taiwan, with deviations emerging during the late upturn and becoming more pronounced in the early downturn. During this brief interlude, South Korea's behavior temporarily came to resemble that of a typical LDC, characterized by growth activism, resort to large-scale foreign borrowing, and use of covert means of resource transfer. However, such deviations were temporary as the South Korean authorities showed a remarkable ability to return to a steady liberalization trend, notwithstanding temporary deviations from it. Consequently her long-run performance with regard to growth and equity remained remarkably different from that of the typical LDCs.

Development policy change during the upturn

Taiwan

Taiwan's upturn was associated with very high rates of growth of real GDP, but this was the natural consequence of a successful external orientation strategy rather than of growth activism on the part of the government. The growth rates of real GDP, after accelerating during the first half of the sixties – from just over 6 percent in 1960 to about 12 percent in 1964 – stabilized within a range of 8 to 10 percent for the rest of the upturn (see figure 4.4(a)). The initial acceleration of growth and its subsequent stability at high levels was undoubtedly related to the significant expansion of exports during this period. As can be seen from figure 4.5(a), the exports/GDP ratio rose from 14 percent in 1961 to 30 percent in 1970, with the trend statistically significant.

This rapid increase in external orientation of course had a major impact on the trade balance. At the beginning of the sixties, Taiwan ran large import surpluses, exceeding 5 percent of GDP, but after 1963 these never exceeded 3 percent of GDP; in fact, export surpluses were earned in four years (figure 4.6(a)). The overall trend for the trade balance/ GDP ratio is significantly negative for the upturn, signifying a steady improvement.

The trend in the trade balance/GDP ratio as well as the movements in the standardized foreign exchange reserves ratio – an initial moderate jump followed by a modest decline later, but more or less hovering around a value of 1 (figure 4.7(a)) – reflects the absence of attempts to promote growth artificially. Although the phenomenal increase in export earnings during the upturn certainly generated opportunities for mercantilist behavior, it is clear that Taiwan did not succumb and instead responded to the positive shocks in a manner quite different from that of the prototypical LDC government described in chapter 2. There was little tendency to use up reserves quickly when times were good and to bring them down rapidly to intolerable levels to finance an ever-expanding import surplus later on. Instead, the reserve ratio followed a path that increasingly recognized the role of reserves for transactions purposes, at least until recently.[2] The steadily declining import surplus/ GDP ratio reflects the success of Taiwan in maintaining prudence in the formulation of fiscal and monetary policy during the upturn – a subject to which we now turn.

Fiscal policy   The improvement in the external environment and the shift to an externally oriented strategy in the early sixties was associated with an expansion of government expenditures. Given a slight decline in the tax/GDP ratio (from 11 percent in 1960 to 9.5 percent in 1962 – see figure 4.8(a)), this initially led to a rise in government deficits.[3] However, as shown in figure 4.10(a), deficits were modest – less than 1 percent of GDP – and, more important, induced the government early enough to correct the situation. The declining trend in the tax effort was

---

[2] In recent years, Taiwan has accumulated the world's second largest foreign exchange reserves and is currently under pressure to liberalize its capital outflows and further appreciate its currency. But this takes us into the post-transition mature economy era and is less relevant to our story.

[3] It should be noted that the "initial" tax/GDP ratio in Taiwan was one of the highest in the developing world at that time. This may be attributed to a series of tax reforms carried out during the 1950s, most notably the establishment of a consolidated income tax in 1955.

arrested, helped partly by an increase in international-trade-related taxes (see figure 4.9(a)), while government expenditures were kept relatively restrained; consequently, budgetary deficits gave way to surpluses after 1964 (figure 4.10(a)). Surpluses were, in fact, maintained throughout the rest of the upturn, helped along by further increases in the tax/GDP ratio after 1968. This improvement in the tax effort, facilitated by additional tax reforms in 1970, also reflects a diversification of the tax base, with international-trade-related taxes falling after 1967 (figure 4.9(a)). In summary, fiscal policy was carried out in Taiwan in a restrained yet flexible manner during the upturn. The government did play a substantial fiscal role, i.e., the expenditure/GDP ratio was quite high, but it was also willing, right from the start, to finance these expenditures by increasingly overt on-the-table means.

Monetary policy   The increased unwillingness of the Taiwanese government to effect resource transfers, either to itself or to favored private entrepreneurs, through under-the-table means is also reflected in the nature of monetary policy pursued. Money supply expansion, for example, was restrained during the upturn. With the exception of four years, the annual growth rate of the money supply remained below 15 percent during the upturn, with no upward trend discernible (see figure 4.11(a)). The relatively low rates of money supply growth, combined with low and declining levels of the income velocity of circulation (see figure 4.13(a)), helped keep inflation down. These consistently declining velocity levels may be attributed to the normal pace of financial innovation in a developing economy successfully transiting to modern growth and stands in sharp contrast to what we observed in Latin America. As figure 4.12(a) shows, inflation was contained below 6 percent in all years except 1968. This association of low inflation with high growth is, in fact, one of the most meaningful aspects of the performance of the Taiwanese economy during the upturn period. It reflects the basic philosophy underlying the evolution of monetary policy in Taiwan, i.e., "the rejection of the insanity of relying on the printing press to create purchasing power for the government to use in an effort to solve socio-economic problems" (Li, 1988, p. 125). Policy makers in Taiwan were consistently haunted by memories of the hyperinflation of the 1940s on the mainland; hence monetary policy has been conducted in a restrained fashion ever since the 1950s.

Taiwan clearly always remained well within the inflation-insensitive region of money growth, permitting the government to extract a respectable, steady rate of forced savings from the system, averaging about 2 percent during this period (figure 4.14(a)). Low inflation, coupled with a flexible nominal interest rate policy, moreover, helped keep real interest rates near a level that equated the demand for investible funds with the

supply of savings. The beginnings of this more or less consistently followed policy indeed go back to the import-substituting 1950s, when
Taiwan broke new ground by adopting high interest rates, primarily to
combat inflation but with many important and beneficial side effects.
For example, in 1961, i.e., at the beginning of the external orientation
phase, the nominal discount rate of the central bank stood at 14.4 percent, with inflation at 5 percent. It was brought down to 11.5 percent in
1963, where it remained until 1967. These downward adjustments were
perhaps not unjustified, given the low levels of inflation persisting during this period; as we can see from figure 4.14(a), real rates of interest
thus remained consistently positive and high.

Turning to the savings behavior of Taiwan, according to our theoretical framework, substantially positive real interest rates are likely to have
a positive effect on total savings, but especially on the relative position
of "organized" savings, i.e., the proportion of total savings put into
savings deposits. Figures 4.16(a) and 4.17(a) depict the trends in the
savings/GDP and the "change in savings deposits/total savings" ratios
respectively. Savings rates are high and rising significantly during the
upturn, jumping from about 12 percent in 1960 to about 26 percent in
1970. However, somewhat paradoxically, the "formal" or "organized"
savings proportion does not show any significant trend, with the average
proportion of savings going into savings deposits remaining somewhere
between 15 and 20 percent.

Exchange rate management and trade policy   The absence of what
we have called growth activism on the part of the Taiwanese government is also reflected in the management of the foreign exchange rate.
During the import-substitution years of the 1950s, Taiwan had a
pegged and increasingly overvalued currency, as did most developing
countries. In 1958, however, as the stage was being set for the transition to a strategy of external orientation, a reform program was started
that involved the abandonment of the system of import quotas accompanied by major exchange rate adjustments. As a first step, a two-tier
exchange rate plus an exchange rate certificate margin determined by
the interplay of market forces was employed. This was followed by the
adoption of a single, devalued exchange rate in November 1958. Further reforms were undertaken in 1960 when, with the certificate margin remaining stable, a further devaluation of the rate, to NT$40 per
U.S. dollars, was announced, a rate that remained in place throughout
the sixties. In combination with modest inflation, this meant only a
modest appreciation of the real exchange rate during the upturn (figure 4.18(a)). The movement of Taiwan's real exchange rate during the
upturn was thus marked by the absence of any tendency to aggressively manipulate the rate for growth purposes, a pattern quite differ-

ent from that observed in the case of more typical growth-activist LDC governments.

While such maintenance of realistic real exchange rates was certainly a major factor underlying Taiwan's remarkable export performance during the 1960s, a series of export-promotion measures also helped. Like most developing countries, Taiwan had instituted extensive quantitative import controls and tariff protection in 1952, i.e., at the beginning of her "easy" import-substitution phase. However, as early as 1956 a step toward partial import liberalization was taken, when a customs rebate system was introduced on imported goods used in export-oriented industries. Further movement toward the partial liberalization of foreign trade took place once the system entered its primary export-substitution phase in the sixties, with one of the major steps being the establishment of export-processing zones, the first in Kaohsiung in 1966. Bonded warehouse arrangements were added during the decade while the duty rebate system was generalized and streamlined. This meant that, while producers facing the domestic market continued to receive protection, exporters increasingly had to face international prices.[4] Such a policy environment certainly generated incentives and pressures for greater competitiveness and efficiency. The fact that Taiwanese entrepreneurs successfully responded to these incentives is, of course, reflected in the export/GDP figures discussed earlier.

The above description of the pattern of policy evolution in Taiwan during the upturn reveals the early beginnings of the depoliticization of policy. In many areas, such as tax reform, interest rates, and exchange rates, the seeds for liberalization were planted even before the start of the transition to the external orientation phase; they were then consolidated during the initial upturn as the government, refusing to be seduced by the rapid growth of the sixties, maintained restraint in fiscal and monetary policy while at the same time introducing sufficient policy flexibility to ensure that resource transfers continued to be effected in an explicit fashion. Underlying all this, moreover, was a development strategy that emphasized the shift from land-intensive activities in the fifties to labor-intensive nonagricultural activities that not only led to high growth and employment but also an increasingly equitable distribution of income.[5] In this Taiwan significantly departed from the typical LDC pattern described in chapter 3. The remarkably equitable record of rapid growth that resulted also meant that the government was under much less pressure to adopt populist expansionary policies during the relative downturn that followed.

---

[4] For a detailed description of export promotion policies in Taiwan, see Wade (1990).
[5] For a detailed analysis of how Taiwan combined high growth with an increasingly equitable distribution of income, see Fei, Ranis, and Kuo (1979).

South Korea

As in Taiwan, the improvement in the external environment and the successful transition to a phase of external orientation led to a respectable growth performance in South Korea during the upturn. While South Korea's average annual real GDP growth rates during the upturn were not significantly different from those of Taiwan, they differed significantly in terms of their greater volatility, often fluctuating by more than 5 percentage points from year to year (see figure 4.4(b)). Like Taiwan, however, South Korea experienced a significant increase in the degree of external orientation during the upturn, with the export/GDP ratio jumping from a little over 8 percent in 1965 to over 24 percent in 1972 (figure 4.5(b)).

The trade balance/GDP ratio, nonetheless, remained very high – without trend – for most of the upturn, usually in double figures (see figure 4.6(b)). The peak was reached in 1968 when the import surplus was almost 13 percent of GDP. The situation, however, improved after 1971 following a significant devaluation leading to a substantial jump in exports and after drastic steps were taken to stabilize the economy as part of a presidential emergency decree in 1972. Reserves show a moderately declining trend but remained at respectable levels throughout the upturn (figure 4.7(b)). Unlike in the typical LDC case, the South Korean authorities were prompt to take corrective actions before reserve depletion became critical.

Fiscal policy   During most of the upturn the conduct of fiscal policy in South Korea was also similar to Taiwan's, i.e., increased expenditures were customarily matched by increased taxes so that deficits were kept low. After the huge fiscal deficits inherited from the 1950s, government expenditures began to shift from reconstruction and the maintenance of minimum consumption standards to long-run economic growth.[6] As a proportion of GDP, government expenditures increased from 11 percent in 1965 to a peak of 19.5 percent in 1968 and remained high until 1973 but were heavily concentrated in the construction of social-overhead capital. Moreover, these increases in government expenditures were accompanied by increases in the tax effort. The tax/GDP ratio increased from 6.5 percent in 1965 to about 13 percent in 1969 before stabilizing at that level over the next few years (see figure 4.8(b)). This increase in the tax/GDP ratio was due to the government's efforts at modernizing the tax system (e.g., an increase in tax rates in 1965) and improving the

---

[6] The Seoul–Inchon highway was opened in 1969, followed by the Seoul–Pusan highway a year later. Large-scale government projects also included the Pohang Steel Company, several harbors, and the construction of export-processing zones.

administrative enforcement process (e.g., the setting up of a new office of national tax administration in 1966). In other words, there was clearly an effort in South Korea, as in Taiwan, to diversify the tax base and gradually to reduce dependence on international trade taxes. In fact, the trend toward a reduction in the relative importance of international-trade-related taxes began earlier here than in Taiwan, i.e., almost at the beginning of the shift to an external orientation (see figure 4.9(b)).

This increase in the tax effort enabled the government to keep budgetary deficits below 1 percent of GDP until 1968 (figure 4.10(b)). Toward the end of the upturn, however, as the tax/GDP ratio stagnated while government expenditures increased even further, budget deficits finally emerged consistently, averaging about 2 to 2.5 percent of GDP during 1969–72 and reaching a record level of 4 percent of GDP in 1972.

Monetary policy   The increase in government deficits after the mid-sixties was accompanied by an acceleration in the rate of growth of the money supply. After remaining below 20 percent until 1964, the annual rate of growth of M1 shot up to 35 percent in 1965 and stayed at exceptionally high levels of 40 to 45 percent at the peak of the boom, i.e., during 1967–69 (see figure 4.11(b)). These high rates of money growth, coupled with high, if declining, levels of velocity (figure 4.13(b)), led to substantial inflation – the annual rates exceeding 15 percent in all but two years – (see figure 4.12(b)). South Korea was thus not able to replicate the Taiwanese scenario of high growth with exceedingly low rates of inflation. Nonetheless, she was able to remain in the inflation-insensitive region, as indicated by the nonbank public's passive reaction to the government's attempts to extract forced savings from the system. With income velocity declining from the initial high levels, the government was able to extract increasing amounts of forced savings during most of the upturn (figure 4.14(b)). This inflation insensitivity during the upturn is reflected in the strong positive relationship between the rate of growth of the money supply and the forced savings rate revealed in figure 4.14(b).

Interest rate policy is another policy arena in which significant reforms were carried out. After remaining negative in the early sixties, real interest rates became significantly positive in 1965 when a major interest rate reform was carried out in an effort to promote the mobilization of domestic savings and improve investment allocation (see figure 4.15(b)).[7] Despite higher inflation, real rates indeed remained positive for almost all of the upturn. By the end of the 1960s, however, these high interest rates were being viewed as threatening to undermine the price competitiveness of exports and the profitability of favored firms. This prompted the gov-

---

[7] The reforms raised nominal rates to unprecedented levels; the central bank discount rate, for example, went from 10.5 percent to 28 percent.

ernment to reverse itself and gradually bring down the level of nominal interest rates. The central bank discount rate was reduced to 23 percent in 1968 and further to 16 percent by 1971. Finally, in 1972, the year of the Presidential Emergency Decree for Economic Stability and Growth, nominal interest rates were brought down to 11 percent, i.e., roughly the same level that had prevailed prior to the reforms of 1965. This brought the real interest rate, which, although declining, had managed to remain positive until 1971, back to negative levels.

The dramatic adjustment of real interest rates in the mid-sixties clearly had a favorable effect on savings. As seen from figure 4.16(b), the savings rate surged from approximately 8 percent in 1965 to approximately 18 percent in 1969. The relative growth of the more interest-rate-elastic formal savings was even more dramatic. Until 1964, only about 5 percent of total savings had found their way into additional savings deposits; in 1965, following the dramatic rise in interest rates, this proportion rose to nearly 27 percent (figure 4.17(b)). This rapid growth in the relative size of the formal money market continued until 1968, by which time more than half of total savings was moving into official channels. Subsequent reductions in real rates of interest at the turn of the decade, by the same token, had a restraining effect on the growth of savings, especially formal savings. Savings as a percentage of GDP fell during 1970–71 and only about 30 percent of annual savings was being channeled formally during 1970–72, compared to an average of 50 percent during 1968–69.

Exchange rate management and trade policy   In contrast to Taiwan, where we observed only a modest appreciation of the real exchange rate during the upturn, in South Korea real exchange rates were more volatile and followed a path similar to the one predicted for a more typical LDC. Prior to 1964, the exchange rate (often multiple) was continuously overvalued, accompanied by extensive exchange controls and tariffs. In 1964, soon after the economy started its external orientation phase, a major exchange rate reform was undertaken with the introduction of a unitary currency system under which the won was fixed at 256 to the dollar, representing an almost 100 percent devaluation and a significant depreciation of the real exchange rate (figure 4.18(b)). The period between 1964 and 1972 witnessed a number of further discrete devaluations of the currency, notably in 1965, 1969, 1971, and 1972, but, given the high rates of inflation prevailing in South Korea during this period relative to her trading partners, these could not prevent a substantial appreciation of the real exchange rate between 1965 and 1970 (figure 4.18(b)).

The harmful impact of an appreciating currency on exports was, however, moderated by a number of reforms in the trade regime that increased direct incentives for exports. Some of these steps were undertaken even before the exchange rate reforms of 1964, e.g., raw materials directly used for export production could be imported duty-free after 1961. Imports of machinery for export production received a tariff exemption from 1964 until 1974, when the tariff exemption system was changed into deferred payments on an installment basis. As in Taiwan, a system of export-processing zones in port areas and bonded factories in the interior areas was established.[8]

South Korea also proceeded with import liberalization and at a pace somewhat faster than in Taiwan. As can be seen from figure 4.19(b), the rate of protection declined significantly during the upturn. Quantitative import controls were reduced after the 1964 devaluation and further relaxed in 1967 when a switch was made from a positive list of items that could be imported, with or without authorization, to a negative list that could not be imported without specific government authorization. The import deposit scheme, with its tariff-equivalent effects, was, however, continued.

To summarize, although some real differences can be noted, South Korea's policies during the upturn were broadly similar to those of Taiwan over the same period. In South Korea, as in Taiwan, the shift from a PIS to a PES strategy was associated with conscious efforts to steadily liberalize various markets. This is reflected in the fiscal reforms intended to increase and diversify the tax base, interest rate changes to ensure significantly positive returns to savers, and the movement toward more realistic exchange rates and lower trade barriers. Thus, as in Taiwan, we witness a secular tendency to liberalize markets, make price rather than quantity adjustments, and ensure that an increasing volume of inter–interest group transfers take place on the table rather than covertly.

It is, nonetheless, true that, within this broadly similar East Asian scenario, some differences in behavior did emerge during the upturn. Apart from the higher rates of South Korean inflation we also notice some moderate deviation, during the late upturn, i.e., about 1968, from the trends established earlier. These include a moderate rise in government deficits, a reduction in real rates of interest following downward revisions in nominal rates, and a modest appreciation of the currency. However, one can also note attempts, exemplified by repeated devaluations, to maintain flexibility and moderate reversals. Thus, while differences emerged between our two East Asian cases, during the upturn they remained modest. Once the downturn started, however, they became more pronounced, as we shall see next.

---

[8] For a description of export promotion policies in South Korea, see Westphal and Kim (1977) and Rhee, Ross-Larson, and Pursell (1984).

4.4 Development policy change during the downturn

Taiwan

As we noted earlier, Taiwan suffered negative external shocks during the seventies, with the external terms of trade deteriorating after 1971. In this respect, the situation is not very different from that of most other developing countries, which also faced a deteriorating external environment during the seventies and early eighties. Taiwan stands out, however, in its response to these shocks. This is reflected in the approach to growth management in general as well as in specific policy areas. While the more "typical" interventionist LDC government caricatured in chapter 2 and described in chapter 3 can be expected to make desperate attempts to maintain growth in the face of a deteriorating external environment, Taiwan's response once the downturn started was to allow growth rates to follow a more "natural" path. The average growth rate for the period 1972–85 was about 8.5 percent, only marginally below that achieved during the upturn. This average figure, however, hides an important fact revealed in figure 4.4(a), i.e., Taiwan's willingness to accommodate and accept lower growth in the face of negative external shocks. This is demonstrated by the experience following each of the two oil shocks: growth rates were temporarily brought down to below 5 percent in 1974 and 1975 and fell steadily from about 13 percent in 1978 to about 4 percent in 1982. In both cases the economy recovered after the shock had receded.

Despite the worsening external terms of trade, Taiwan maintained a significantly positive trend in the degree of external orientation initiated during the upturn although, understandably, moderate fluctuations can be observed. The export/GDP ratio continued to rise dramatically from 35 percent in 1971 to 55 percent in 1985 (figure 4.5(a)). This remarkable export performance, coupled with the government's continued unwillingness to overheat the economy (see our discussion on fiscal and monetary policy below), meant that relative import surpluses followed by crisis did not characterize the downturn, as in most LDCs. Export surpluses were indeed earned in most years (see figure 4.6(a)), and, while there were modest declines in foreign exchange reserves during the seventies, these rose significantly during the eighties (see figure 4.7(a)).

Fiscal policy   The unwillingness of Taiwanese authorities to use macroeconomic policy instruments to maintain growth artificially during the downturn is manifested vividly in its exercise of fiscal policy. Fiscal prudence, achieved during the upturn, was maintained. Except for one year, surpluses were earned during the downturn of 1971–85 (figure 4.10(a)). In 1981, however, the government was close to incurring a deficit, and in 1982 a deficit actually occurred before the budget was once again brought under control.

The temporary tendency toward deficits in the early eighties may have been caused partly by a reduction in the tax/GDP ratio after 1979. As can be noted from figure 4.8(a), that ratio had steadily increased over the period 1971–79, until a remarkable peak of about 17 percent was reached in 1979. However, as soon as the tax/GDP ratio started falling in the wake of the second oil shock (figure 4.8(a)), the government responded by initiating a second round of tax reforms. Thus, legislation was introduced in 1983 to establish a VAT, which was put into full operation in April 1986, replacing the sales tax and intended as complementary to the reduction of tariffs carried out during the same period. In this fashion import liberalization could proceed without occasioning major fiscal problems.

In brief, therefore, one can observe a consistent tendency to maintain a conservative and flexible stance in fiscal policy. Moreover, the policy of increasing reliance on overt means of resource transfers, instituted during the upturn, continued to be pursued in the more difficult environment of the seventies and eighties.

Monetary policy   Such relative consistency and prudence in the area of fiscal policy was also reflected in the conduct of monetary policy. The relative restraint with regard to the expansion of the money supply noted during the upturn was maintained during the downturn. Indeed, as seen in figure 4.11(a), there was a decline over time. Except for 1972, 1973, and 1978, the rate of M1 growth remained well below 30 percent. This, coupled with a low and further declining income velocity (figure 4.13(a)), meant that, although Taiwan in the 1970s was not an exception to the worldwide phenomenon of inflation, it occurred here in short spurts, interspersed with much longer periods of relative price stability (see figure 4.12(a)). It also meant that with moderate rates of money creation the government was able to avoid inflation and extract considerable amounts of forced savings from the system, the forced savings rate exceeding 3.5 percent in most years (figure 4.14(a)).

Given low inflation and a flexible nominal interest rate policy, real interest rates remained largely positive and high during 1971–85 (figure 4.15(a)); the only significant exceptions were the three years following the two oil shocks, i.e., 1974, 1979, and 1980, when real interest rates were significantly negative. However, in both 1974 and 1979 the nominal interest rate was immediately raised by at least 2 percentage points in an effort to contain inflationary trends. A number of specific steps were also taken to allow the market to play a larger role in the determination of interest rates. These included the establishment of a market for loanable funds in 1976 independent of the largely government-controlled commercial banking system; the partial decontrol of bank rates in 1980, allowing banks more flexibility in determining interest rates when lending to bank customers; and, finally, the introduction of the prime rate system in 1985, which gave bankers greater flexibility in assessing risk premia on top of the prime rate. This step moved the financial system one step closer to the free-market end of the spectrum, with borrowers stratified by credit-worthiness rather than political connection. These developments reflect a linear trend toward the gradual depoliticization of the financial system, characterized by a higher degree of central bank independence from government political pressure and greater reliance on market adjustment mechanisms.[9]

The maintenance of significantly positive real interest rates had the expected effect on savings behavior. Although the total savings/GDP ratio showed no trend, it remained high (see figure 4.16(a)). The proportion of savings going into the formal sector, which can be expected to be more interest elastic than total savings, was not only much higher than during the upturn, but also rose steadily over the period (see figure 4.17(a)).

Exchange rate management and trade policy   As in other policy arenas, Taiwan's policymakers exhibited continued flexibility in exchange rate management. In response to the export surpluses that started appearing in the late sixties, the exchange rate was appreciated in 1973 and fixed at NT$38 to the dollar. The rate remained at that level until 1978, when another moderate revaluation was carried out. Once the impact of the second oil crisis had ended, the government once again pushed ahead with the liberalization and internationalization of the economy and the pursuit of an active exchange rate policy. As can be seen from figure 4.18(a), the real exchange rate consequently experienced mostly moderate upward movements.

The process of trade liberalization, relatively slow during the upturn, accelerated during the downturn. The 1971 devaluation was accompanied by the additional easing of quantitative controls on imports. Moreover, the executive branch was given the authority to adjust tariffs by 50 percent without additional legislative approval. The most substantial steps toward liberalization of the trade regime were, however, taken only more recently. Average nominal tariff rates were reduced from 31 percent in 1984 to 23 percent in 1986 and the maximum tariff rate was reduced from 75 percent to 67.5 percent in January 1986 and to 58

[9] Earlier, in 1974, the commercial banks were exempted from the requirement of encashing government bonds held by the nonbank public prior to maturity and thus, by implication, the requirement to support the price of government bonds. This step gave an important boost to the movement toward greater autonomy for the central bank.

percent in 1987. The number of items exempt from tariffs has also been increased. Capital transactions were decontrolled in July 1987.

It is thus seen that trade liberalization in Taiwan once QRs were converted to tariffs took the form of very gradual tariff reductions, with most of the substantial steps of relatively recent vintage. This observation is confirmed by the trend in the "average rate of protection," defined as import taxes as a proportion of total imports. While there is no trend during the first period there is a moderate – albeit statistically insignificant – declining trend in the second period (figure 4.19(a)).

In summary, in Taiwan we may observe the consistent maintenance of restraint and flexibility in macroeconomic policy even during the relatively difficult times of the post-1973 downturn. This achievement is exceptional since, as the theoretical discussion of chapter 2 suggests and the empirical analysis of chapter 3 confirms, it is during the downturn that LDC governments are most subject to pressures to adopt countercyclical expansionary policies to be financed via budgetary and monetary expansion and/or increased foreign borrowing. Moreover, such a policy stance almost invariably leads, with a time lag, to balance-of-payments crises and a reversal of the depoliticization of policy trend.

In Taiwan, by contrast, we observe that the process of gradual liberalization continued and, in some cases, even accelerated during the downturn. The flexibility of policy, e.g., the rapid advent of tax reforms once deficits appeared, the raising of nominal interest rates once inflation threatened, quick adjustments in nominal exchange rates to keep real exchange rates at realistic levels, institutional reforms in financial markets, and continuous reductions in trade restrictions all attest to this. This remarkable linearity of policy evolution in Taiwan even during the difficult times of the downturn resulted from a stance of persistently refusing to resort to quantity adjustments in a vain effort to maintain growth artificially, which was characteristic of the more typical LDC case.

South Korea

As noted above (see figure 4.1(b)), the improvement in South Korea's terms of trade lasted until 1972, with a downturn ensuing thereafter. Our theoretical framework predicts that a growth-activist government would respond to such a deterioration in the external environment by desperately trying to maintain growth, mostly with the help of increased domestic expenditures and partly via foreign borrowing. We have just seen that Taiwan resisted such temptations and allowed growth rates to fall whenever the economy was hit by negative shocks. South Korea, however, proved more prone to succumb to these temptations, if briefly, i.e., it was more likely to attempt to maintain growth artificially in the face of adverse circumstances.

South Korea's economy grew at an average rate of 6.5 percent during 1974–75. While this was substantially lower than the exceptional 14 percent rate of growth attained in 1973, just before the first oil shock, it was only moderately lower than the average 8 percent achieved during 1970–72, and higher than growth rates in Taiwan over the same years. This modest slowdown in growth was, in any case, a temporary phenomenon; by 1976, growth exceeded double-digit levels and, in fact, during 1976–78, South Korea achieved one of the highest growth rates in its history, an average of 12 percent.

The causes of this pattern of growth in South Korea can be traced to an element of growth activism that came to characterize government behavior during the 1973–79 period. The reflection of this behavior in various policy variables is discussed in detail below; some of its salient features may, however, be noted here. At the beginning of the seventies, just before the downturn began, South Korea shifted to a growth strategy based on the development of heavy industries. South Korea's Third Five-Year Plan, launched in 1972, gave priority to the development of chemical industries; this emphasis was intensified with the announcement of the Heavy and Chemical Industry Development Plan (HCIDP) in 1973, which called for an accelerated schedule for developing technologically sophisticated industries. An enormous volume of investment in these industries followed, with large-scale projects encouraged through special tax incentives, preferential credit allocations and negative real interest rates, often on an individual firm basis, in a system dominated by widespread credit rationing.[10]

Two of the important assumptions on which the HCIDP was based was that economies of scale would dominate and that world trade would continue to expand at a very rapid rate. The validity of both assumptions started looking very doubtful after the first oil shock, but this did not induce the government to slow down its promotion of investment. On the contrary, the original investment plans laid down in the Fourth Five-Year Plan (1977–81) were revised by crowding into three years (1977–79) 80 percent of the total investment originally planned over five years and by increasing the share of heavy industries in total investment beyond the levels originally envisaged (Scitovsky, 1985).[11]

This restructuring of the manufacturing sector in South Korea, of course, reflected the shift from a strategy of PES to one of SIS/SES.

---

[10] A national investment fund was set up that channeled a substantial proportion of private savings at regular banking institutions into these projects at below market rates. Banks were pushed to provide additional loans on a preferential basis when these funds were not adequate. See Corbo and Nam (1987).

[11] The share of investment in GNP rose from 29.4 percent in 1975 to 36.9 percent in 1977–79, and the combined share of metals, chemicals, intermediate products, machinery, transport equipment, and electronics in total investment rose from 48 percent to 79 percent.

Such a shift also occurred in Taiwan at roughly the same time. However, South Korea's restructuring differed from that of Taiwan not only in the aggressive manner in which it was carried out, as reflected in the volume and speed of investment, but also in the much more interventionist role played by the government in carrying out the investment program. In Taiwan, except for the development of the steel, shipbuilding, and petrochemical industries, all of which were state-owned, the shift to the SIS/SES path was largely spearheaded by private investors responding to changing market signals and market conditions. On the other hand, in South Korea, the government, besides investing on its own, also made extensive use of firm-specific directional policies – such as differential terms of credit and tax rates mentioned above – in order to influence the direction of investment.

We would argue that an important part of the explanation for the different behavior of South Korea during this period is likely to reside in the easy availability of foreign capital, which impacted in a fashion similar to that of natural resource abundance in our theoretical model. South Korea's relative failure to have her agricultural sector generate adequate savings led to a significantly greater dependence on foreign capital to finance development even during the early PES phase of export orientation. This dependence continued during the seventies, as is shown in figure 4.20(b), which indicates a sharp contrast between the two countries.

As can be seen from these data, capital inflows played an important role in South Korea's economy throughout the seventies, in contrast to Taiwan, where foreign capital inflows were much lower as a proportion of GDP (figure 4.20(a)). This continued greater South Korean dependence on external finance can be traced to both demand- and supply-side factors. The demand-side factors have been identified above, i.e., they essentially relate to South Korea's desire to maintain, if not accelerate, growth by means of an expanding investment program, which necessitated a substantial dependence on external finance. However, supply-side factors were also important. First, given South Korea's past track record on growth, it is understandable that foreign investors were keen to invest in the country. This tendency was perhaps intensified following the political uncertainties generated in Taiwan after its ouster from the United Nations in 1971.

As we might have predicted, South Korea's relatively more activist growth strategy ultimately proved to be self-defeating. The growth rate started falling after 1979 and in 1980 became negative (minus 3 percent) for the first time in at least two decades. The government's response to these developments was, however, prompt. Starting in 1979, a series of measures, discussed in detail below, was taken to deal with the problems of decelerating growth and the relatively high inflation that had accompanied the high growth of the seventies. As figure 4.4(b) shows, growth recovered after 1981, with real GDP expanding at a fairly respectable average rate of 7 to 8 percent per annum during 1981–85.

The exports/GDP ratio continued to rise during the downturn, although not as spectacularly as in Taiwan. The trend is significantly positive, with the ratio rising from 35 percent in 1973 to 40 percent in 1986 (see figure 4.5(b)). As in Taiwan, the trade balance/GDP ratio shows a significant decline, but there are some important differences with regard to year-to-year fluctuations between the two countries that are reflective of the broad tone of government policy followed during the downturn. In South Korea, the trade balance exceeded 8 percent during the very bad years of 1974 and 1975. This was, however, followed by a sharp improvement during 1976–77, caused to a significant extent by an increase in remittances from the Middle East. This improvement was, however, temporary; the expansionary strategy introduced in the late seventies resulted in another deterioration of the trade balance during 1978–80. A series of stabilization measures adopted in the beginning of the eighties, however, reversed these trends and brought down the trade balance during the eighties. Thus, although the overall trend during this period is that of a significant decline in the trade balance/GDP ratio, we may also note some significant fluctuations around this trend (see figure 4.6(b)).

With the deterioration in the trade balance after the downturn, the dissipation of foreign exchange reserves that had begun toward the end of the upturn worsened. A crisis was reached in 1974 when, following the first oil shock, reserves fell to a level equivalent to just two weeks of imports (figure 4.7(b)). In 1974 there was a major devaluation of the South Korean won (see below); the subsequent improvement in the trade balance as chronicled above led to a recovery in the reserve position, but only temporarily. The deterioration in the trade balance consequent to the adoption of expansionary policies in the late seventies led to another round of reserve dissipation and, by 1981, reserves had once again dropped to crisis levels (figure 4.7(b)). Although the array of stabilization measures adopted after 1979 arrested the further dissipation of reserves, the latter had not, even by 1985, returned to relatively "safe" levels.

Fiscal policy   As would be expected from the above discussion about the government's active promotion of investment during 1973–79, expansionary fiscal behavior, incipient during the later stages of the upturn, became pronounced during the downturn. Government expenditures increased, particularly in the area of infrastructural construction and direct investment in various large-scale public sector industrial projects.[12] At the same time, however, the government carried out a series of tax reforms. These included the introduction of several indirect taxes – a defense tax in 1975, a value-added tax in 1977, and an education tax in 1977.[13] These reforms helped raise the tax/GDP ratio, which maintained the significant upward trend observed in the earlier period (see figure 4.8(b)). The increase in taxes was, however, not sufficient to offset the increased expenditures of the government. Consequently, deficits remained high, at around 2 percent of GDP during 1974–78 and, with growth decelerating, rose sharply during 1979–81 to reach a peak of about 3.5 percent in 1981 (see figure 4.10(b)).

A series of stabilization measures was taken beginning in 1978 to deal with, among other things, the worsening fiscal situation. The most substantive measures were, however, introduced as part of a major stabilization program announced in April 1979, just before the second oil shock hit the world economy. The measures adopted during 1978–79 included a cut in current expenditures, an increase in public utility tariffs, a postponement of construction projects, and a decline of investment in heavy industry.[14] After a temporary relaxation, following the deceleration of growth in 1980, the government reverted to a restrictive fiscal stance in 1982. Deficits were brought down from about 3.5 percent of GDP in 1981 to about 1 percent by 1983. Further reforms of the tax system were also carried out during the eighties. The corporate tax structure was simplified and the VAT was extended in 1981. More sweeping reforms were introduced in 1982 with the aim of both increasing the tax effort as well as rendering the system more neutral with respect to resource allocation.[15] It is thus seen that although South Korean authori-

---

[12] These included the Changwan machinery complex, the Ulsan petrochemical complex, shipyards, drydocks, atomic power stations, etc. In addition, the Seoul subway was opened in 1973, the same year in which the Honam and Namhae highways were opened. The Yungdung and Danghae highways were opened in 1975, and the Guma highway in 1977. Certain other actions of the government also led to increased social expenditures. In 1977, medical insurance was introduced as a first step toward a system of social security and welfare. During 1975–78, the government extended its price support program for rice, with a resulting deficit in the Government Grain Management Fund. According to Corbo and Nam (1987), the deficits in the Grain Management Fund and the Fertilizer Account were jointly responsible for 37 percent of the total growth of the money supply during 1976–78.

[13] As mentioned above, tax policy was used not only to raise revenue but also to discriminate among economic activities. Various industries received preferential tax treatment. For example, selected petrochemical industries, machine industries, and shipbuilding firms were given five-year tax holidays.

[14] These took the form of "postponement, cancellation or scaling down of some excessive and duplicative investment plans" (Corbo and Nam, 1986).

[15] The new tax measures changed the tax status of corporations, modified certain deductions and tax incentives to reduce the discrimination against small and medium-sized firms, introduced tax credits to promote R & D, reduced the number of industries that received tax advantages, and set a minimal tax on public corporations.

ties were induced by a number of factors, including the easy availability of foreign capital, to expand government expenditures during the downturn, leading to deficits, the latter were relatively moderate – thanks to simultaneous efforts to raise taxes – and temporary because of the promptness with which the authorities took corrective action.

Monetary policy   The expansionary policy of 1973–79 was also fueled by domestic money creation. Expansionary monetary policy, initiated during the upturn, continued in the initial stages of the downturn, with the annual growth rate of the money supply exceeding 25 percent before 1977 (see figure 4.11(b)). This trend was reversed, however, after 1978 with policies that included controls on credit expansion, an upward revision of interest rates (in 1978), and a quantitative reduction of subsidized lending (in 1979). The growth rate of the money supply fell from over 40 percent in 1977 to about 5 percent in 1980 and, except for a one-shot increase in 1982, was subsequently kept below 20 percent (figure 4.11(b)).

The South Korean pattern here may thus be seen as a very mild version of the typical LDC pattern predicted by our theoretical framework. During the relative upturn, the money supply is allowed to expand faster, with the growth rate accelerating even after the downturn sets in, as the government attempts to prop up growth through expansionary fiscal and monetary policies. As the relative boom decelerates and the government's capacity to fight inflation by drawing down reserves or by relying on foreign borrowing is diminished, a drastic contraction in the growth of M1 is effected.

The high rates of money growth in the initial phase of the downturn indeed meant that, unlike Taiwan, South Korea experienced a sustained period of high inflation between the two oil shocks, with the annual inflation rate ranging between 20 and 25 percent for most of the 1974–80 period (figure 4.12(b)). However, unlike many Latin American and other more "typical" developing countries, South Korea reacted promptly before inflation could become a chronic or "runaway" phenomenon. The array of stabilization measures, some of which have been discussed above, initiated as early as 1978 and intensified in 1979, were continuously implemented all through the eighties so that inflation was first brought down, i.e., to about 5 percent by 1982, and then contained at even lower levels for the rest of the period, i.e., 1983–85 (figure 4.12(b)).[16] The overall trend for this period describes a significant decline.

The relatively higher rates of inflation during 1974–80 did have some

---

[16] As Corbo and Nam (1986) show, a decline in import prices also helped in the containment of inflationary pressures.

effect on the public, which started showing increased signs of inflation sensitivity. In contrast to the upturn, income velocity now increased slightly before 1978 but rapidly during 1979–80 (see figure 4.13(b)). Nonetheless, the public's reaction was relatively mild compared to that observed in the Latin American cases. Moreover, as policies were relatively quickly reversed, confidence was restored; this is reflected in the substantial drop in velocity after 1983. The relatively lower degree of inflation sensitivity of the public enabled the government to extract relatively high rates of forced savings from the system until 1978 (see figure 4.14(b)), the subsequent drop being caused more by the government's monetary restraint rather than the public's reaction. Unlike in the Latin American cases, the relationship between the money supply growth rates and the rate of forced savings remained significantly positive throughout the downturn (figure 4.14(b)).

We had noted earlier that the real rates of interest, positive for many years after the 1965 reforms, finally turned negative in the last year of the upturn. In contrast to Taiwan, a regime of negative real rates of interest was maintained during the subsequent downturn due to the pursuit of a relatively inflexible nominal interest rate policy in the face of rising inflation (see figure 4.15(b)), i.e., despite rising inflation the central bank discount rate was kept fixed at 11 percent between 1972 and 1975. Real interest rates consequently turned significantly negative, reaching about −20 percent in 1974 (see figure 4.15(b)). This, in turn, clearly had a negative impact on the efficiency of the credit system. The excess demand for credit generated forced banks to follow a selective loan policy, which, as mentioned above, was used to encourage the growth of particular industries, i.e., the heavy industry and chemical sector, and extended to individual *chaebol* firms. The preferential allocation of subsidized loans to such large firms increased and, as might be expected under a system where credit rationing is carried out by administrative decision rather than price, the efficiency of the allocation decision declined.

Nominal interest rates were finally raised to 14 percent in 1975. This was, however, insufficient given the high rates of inflation. Consequently, real rates remained negative all through the seventies and became positive again only after the dramatic decline in inflation rates following the stabilization measures of the early eighties. Since then lower inflation has helped keep real rates positive despite the fact that nominal rates were, in fact, reduced further in 1981 and 1982.

Although real interest rates were thus negative during most of the seventies, their overall trend during the upturn, as is evident from figure 4.15(b), was significantly positive, i.e., there was an almost continuous reduction in the extent of negativity. Nevertheless, in terms of a comparison of the average real rates, the overall behavior of South Korea over the two periods conforms somewhat to the predictions of the typical or Latin American LDC model, i.e., positive in the upturn and negative in the downturn. The aforementioned trend toward a reversal in the latter period is, however, testimony to the fact that the South Korean government did finally make attempts, through increases in nominal interest rates as well as by containing inflation, to redress the damage of the early eighties and bring real rates back to levels where savers earn a positive return.

The government also took steps to improve the credit allocation system in the second half of the seventies. In 1977, the ministry of finance announced its intention to change what might be called a "positive" system of credit allocation to a "negative" system, i.e., one that lists industries and types of businesses that should not (rather than should) receive loans. This policy change, however, appears to have had limited effectiveness. More significant reforms were initiated after 1982 to liberalize the banking sector and let market forces become a more important factor in the credit market. As a first step, the ceiling on interbank call rates was lifted. Direct credit controls via credit ceilings on individual banks were replaced by indirect controls operating through the management of bank reserves. Furthermore, between 1981 and 1983, the government handed over the ownership of four nationwide commercial banks to the private sector. This completed the denationalization of the five leading commercial banks, the Commercial Bank of Korea having been privatized in 1972. The General Banking Act was also revised in 1982 in order to give banks a freer hand in dealing with their own managerial affairs while boosting their public accountability by setting upper limits on stockholder ownership of bank stocks.

Notwithstanding these developments in the financial markets, which in any case came late in the downturn, savings behavior was adversely affected by the prolonged existence of negative interest rates. Although the savings/GDP ratio continued to rise, it did not do so as consistently as in the previous period (figure 4.16(b)). The growth in the relative size of formal savings appears to show even more sensitivity to real interest rates. Its overall trend was negative for this period, and movements in individual years also reflected changes in interest rate policy. Thus the rise in nominal rates in 1980 was associated with an increase in the ratio and, more convincingly, the quantum drops in nominal rates in 1981 and 1982 were followed by a dramatic drop in the ratio (figure 4.17(b)).

Exchange rate management and trade policy   In the area of external monetary management as well, the pattern of policy in South Korea during the downturn exhibited elements of both the atypical East Asian and the more typical Latin American pattern. The appreciation of the South Korean won that had occurred during the last years of the upturn was corrected in 1974, following a balance-of-payments crisis, by a massive devaluation that fixed the exchange rate at 484 won per U.S. dollar. This correction was, however, temporary as the nominal exchange rate was kept fixed at this level until 1980 despite the very high rates of inflation prevailing during 1974–79, thus leading to another round of significant appreciation of the real rate during this period (figure 4.17(b)). These trends were, however, once again reversed after 1980 as significant exchange rate changes were instituted as part of the broader stabilization program initiated toward the end of the 1970s. A large devaluation – of about 33 percent – was carried out in 1980, with the exchange rate adjusted from 484 won to 650 won per dollar. This move was accompanied by a switch from a single to a basket currency peg and signaled the transition to a flexible exchange rate system. As can be seen from figure 4.18(b), real rates came back to more realistic levels following these reforms. Thus, twice during the downturn, i.e., 1974 and 1980, the South Korean authorities, faced with balance-of-payments crises, responded relatively promptly by correcting the exchange rate immediately rather than first imposing trade controls in the vain hope of postponing the day of reckoning.

Thus, although no major movement toward further import liberalization took place in South Korea during 1972–79, there was no reversal either. Moreover, at the beginning of the eighties, as part of comprehensive efforts at structural change, the South Korean government announced a five-year plan of import liberalization according to which the proportion of free items was to be raised to 85 percent by 1984. Steps were also taken to liberalize capital flows. In 1980 the government adopted the "Measures for the Inducement of Foreign Investment," relaxing a number of restrictions on capital movement. In 1982 South Korean residents were for the first time allowed to open foreign currency accounts without restriction and, in 1988, restrictions on the autonomous outflow of capital were further eased.

The labor market   We may, finally, have a quick look at the labor market in both countries. As predicted, the incidence of labor unrest is much lower in East Asia than Latin America, with little difference between the two parts of the cycle (see figures 4.21(a) and (b)). However, even here, some sensitivity, albeit moderate, of labor unrest to inflationary trends can be observed, as in Taiwan during 1973–74 – which, we may recall, is one of the few times when Taiwan experienced significant inflation – and in South Korea during 1980–81. The increased labor unrest in very recent years, especially in South Korea, can be attributed more to these economies' graduation to full employment, mature economy status, as well as to gradual democratization of their political systems.

In summary, in East Asia we witness differences even within this deviant subfamily of LDCs, with the South Korean government more likely to react to negative shocks by trying to promote growth artificially. Such growth activisim was partly financed by foreign borrowing, the easy availability of which can impact on policy in a fashion similar to that of an ample natural resource endowment. In South Korea, the government felt the political pressure to make use of foreign capital as a way of maintaining artificially high rates of growth. What marks off South Korea from the more typical LDC case, however, is the remarkable ability of the authorities to recognize mistakes and relatively quickly take appropriate corrective action and thus prevent temporary excesses from blowing up into a crisis that might ultimately lead to the total abandonment of the liberalization trend.

4.5 Conclusions

Our empirical analysis of the history of policy evolution in the two East Asian cases thus reveals that, while there exist behavioral differences within the family, the differences that mark them off from the typical LDC cases are indeed more pronounced. The central feature of long-run policy evolution in our two East Asian systems is represented both by the more pronounced trend toward depoliticization of the economic system and much greater linearity, or fewer oscillations, along that trend. Early liberalization, which was an integral component of the transition from PIS to PES, enabled these systems to exploit successfully the opportunities provided by international trade and diversify their production and exports, leading not only to high growth, but also to reduced dependence on agricultural rents and lower vulnerability to terms-of-trade fluctuations – and, over time, even the international business cycle and neoprotectionism abroad. Consequently, they found it easier – relative to, for example, the Latin American cases – to maintain a more or less steady policy course.

Underlying all this was the willingness of the governments of both countries – albeit somewhat less so in South Korea – to allow growth to proceed along a "natural" path and an aversion to the use of covert means of resource transfers in order to promote growth artificially. This is reflected, among other things, in relatively low government deficits – helped by an almost linear trend toward increased tax efforts – relatively low rates of money growth and inflation, positive real rates of interest, more or less flexible and realistic exchange rates, and a gradual but steady trend toward trade liberalization.

The steady process of tax reforms leading to ever-increasing tax ratios reflects the fact that pragmatic governments in these countries never had the illusion that a fiscally responsible treasury could avoid the unpleasantness of having to confront the pain of political compromise. The relatively low rates of money supply growth rates reflected the basic philosophy of rejecting the printing press as a solution to socioeconomic problems. The notion had taken hold relatively early in East Asia that money creation is not to be consistently used as a way to force savings and shift profits to favored private parties or state enterprises.

Thus, in neither of these NIE cases did governments try to suppress the interest rate consistently by sustained monetary expansion but permitted the rate to move upward toward equilibrium values. Even in the somewhat deviant South Korean case, real rates of interest became progressively less negative over time during the downturn, thus avoiding increases in velocity, resulting from the nonbank public's reaction of "fighting back" to avoid resources being snatched away by the government, that signifies a critical difference between the East Asian and the more typical LDC cases.

The relatively lower degree of repression in the money market does not mean that there wasn't a good deal of direct credit allocation in both Taiwan and South Korea throughout; in fact, the so-called commercial banking system in both these countries is very much misnomered, i.e., it is a part of the public sector, and allocations continue to be directed toward particular industries and firms, especially in the case of South Korea, although there appears to be a movement away from such firm-specific support in recent years.

The early abandonment of the idea of using covert means to transfer resources was partly caused by the fact that natural resources, often used to continue fueling increasingly inefficient industrialization processes, were basically scarce in East Asia, and that foreign aid, which can be important in keeping the process going, was officially announced to be terminated in the early sixties, in the case of Taiwan, and to be substantially reduced in the case of South Korea. In other words, neither natural-resource-based rents nor the equivalent flow of foreign aid to fuel the continuing expansion of noncompetitive industries could continue to be counted on; a change in the policy mix was forced, in the national interest, in the early sixties. Private foreign capital inflows assumed importance only after these systems had already determined their outer-oriented industrial export-substitution paths.

The East Asian, and especially the Taiwanese experience, also shows that a country can put up with some discretionary controls for a long while and still be quite successful in its transition growth effort. In Taiwan, for example, only small steps in the direction of tariff reduction and import liberalization were taken in the 1960s and 1970s as a prelude to a major push in 1983. Although effective rates of protection were relatively low by LDC standards, there has been no radical reduction in tariffs, such as occurred in Chile, until this day. The message from Taiwan thus is that monetary restraint and a realistic exchange rate are more important than the elimination of discretionary trade controls that can be tackled at a later point in this evolutionary policy perspective.

Finally, it may be suggested that in both countries the liberalization movement generally maintained a linear course over a long period of time because the process of depoliticization gained momentum in small cumulative steps rather than by the large leaps and bounds that often imply reversal and policy fluctuation. Policymakers in both countries recognized that for any particular macroeconomic policy, such as a devaluation, to take root, it must be a "step" in the "life" of the total policy adjustment process. In a successful policy reform process, an ad hoc first small step is usually followed by a bigger step a few years later, one that has more popular appeal. A good example is provided by the evolution of fiscal policy in Taiwan, in particular the sequence of tax reform measures: income tax reform (1955), overall tax reform (1970), and ultimately the introduction of the value-added tax (1983). To cite another example, the ad hoc liberalization of import controls via several small steps by 1971 subsequently gained momentum so that, by 1983, it could take on an entirely new and unprecedentedly ideological appeal, that of accepting the principle of the "survival of the fittest" via the discipline of international competition even in the domestic market, leading to substantial tariff reforms. The East Asian experience in sum demonstrates that a realistic, pragmatic liberalization effort, resolutely maintained, is much superior to the frequently encountered fluctuating policy patterns that alternate between periods of doctrinaire interventionism and equally doctrinaire laissez-faire. Such an approach is more likely to be successful because it recognizes the realities of political economy in terms of who is helped and who is hurt by various policy changes over time and how, in recognition of all this, the required consensus for action can be established and sustained. The sustained gradualism of East Asian policy reforms, assisted by the timely ballooning of foreign aid, as well as its later withdrawal, stands in contrast to the stop-go oscillations of the more typical Latin American cases. Its success may also be relevant to the current debate over the advantages of gradual versus "cold turkey" reforms in the contemporary East European context.

Figure 4.1 External terms of trade (percent deviation from trend)

(a)

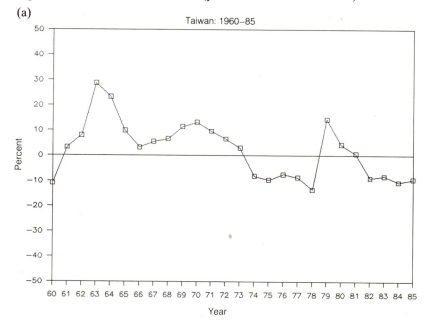

Taiwan: 1960–85

(b)

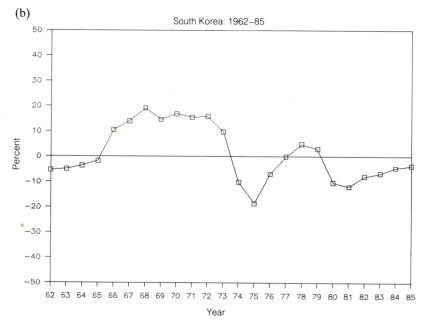

South Korea: 1962–85

141

Figure 4.2 External terms of trade (percent deviation from trend)

(a)

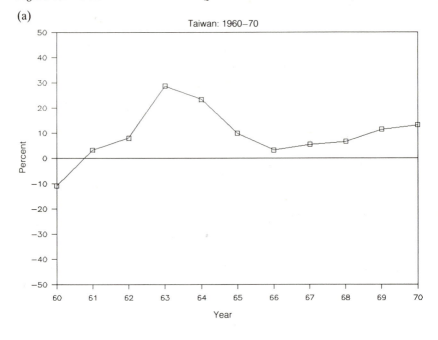

(b)

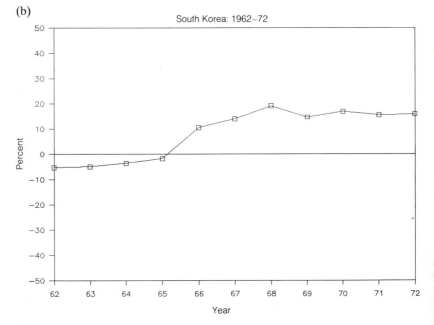

Figure 4.3 External terms of trade (percent deviation from trend)

(a)

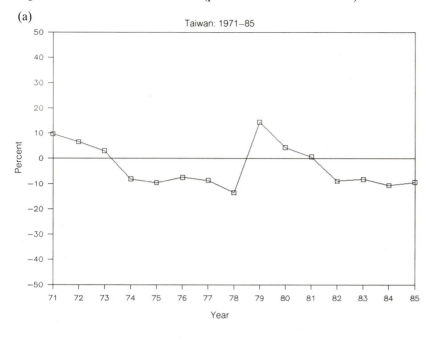

Taiwan: 1971–85

(b)

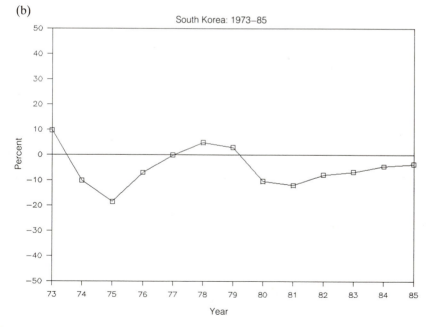

South Korea: 1973–85

Figure 4.4   Annual rate of growth of real GDP

(a)

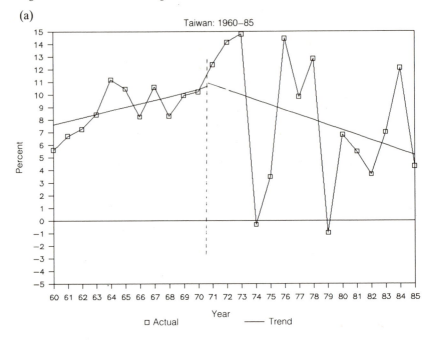

(b)

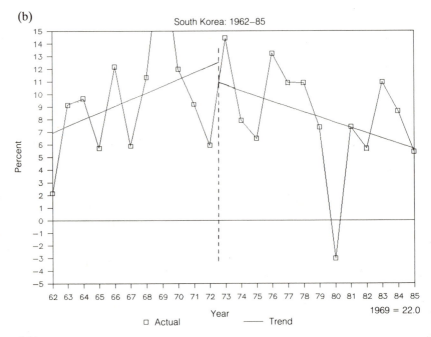

Figure 4.5   Exports/GDP

(a)

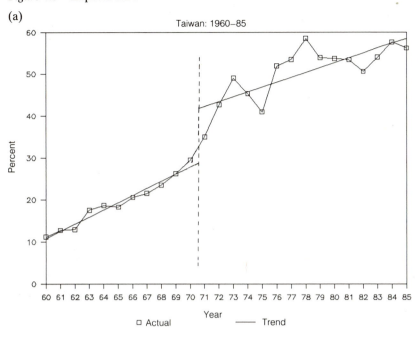

Taiwan: 1960–85

(b)

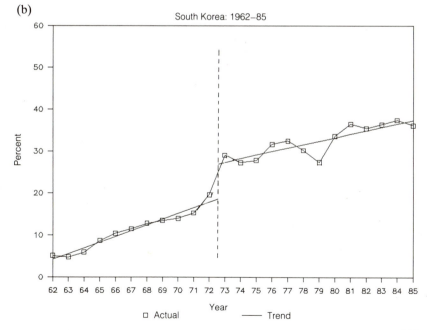

South Korea: 1962–85

145

Figure 4.6   Trade balance/GDP

(a)

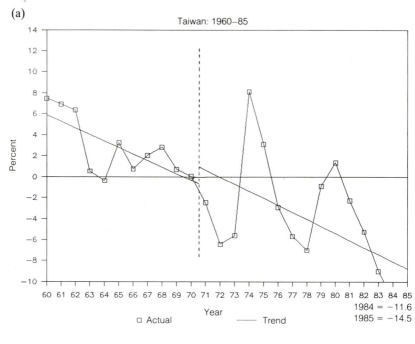

(b)

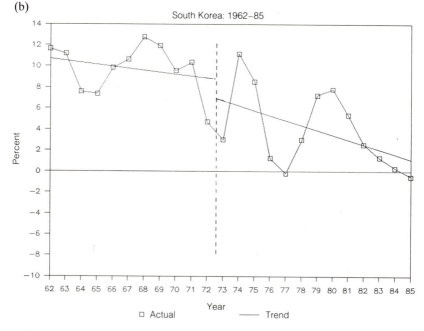

146

Figure 4.7 Foreign exchange reserves/four months' imports

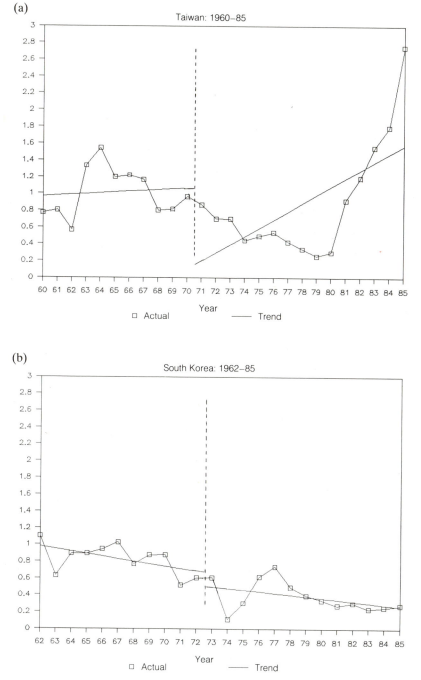

(a)

(b)

Figure 4.8 Total taxes/GDP

(a)

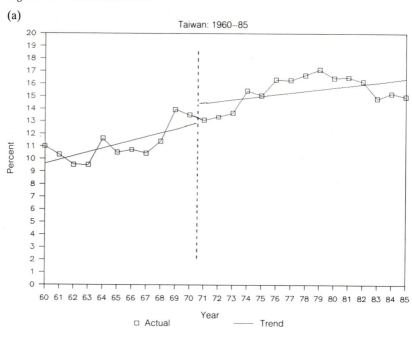

(b)

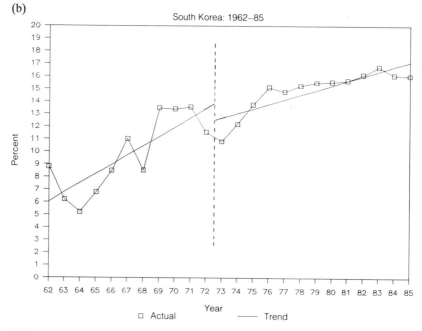

148

Figure 4.9 International trade taxes/total taxes

(a)

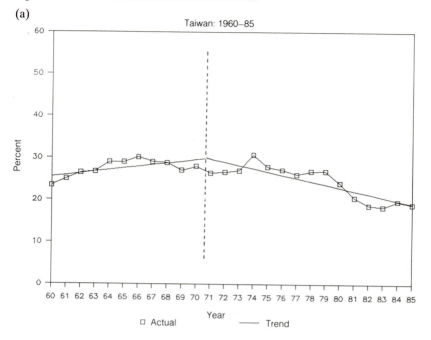

Taiwan: 1960–85

(b)

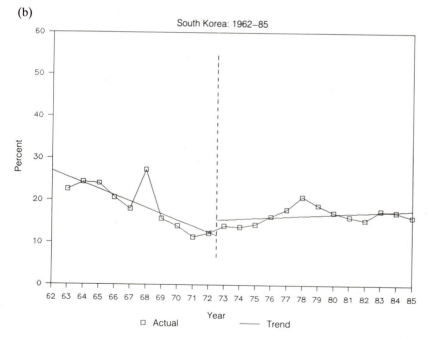

South Korea: 1962–85

Figure 4.10 Government deficits/GDP

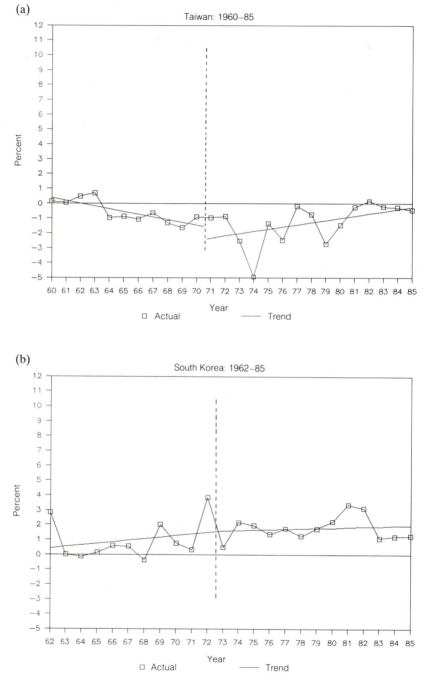

Figure 4.11   Annual rate of change of money supply

(a)

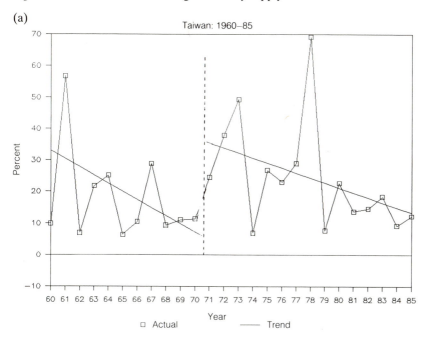

(b)

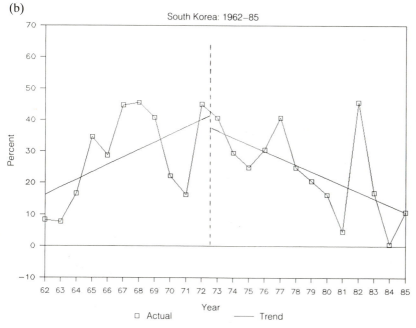

151

Figure 4.12   Annual rate of inflation

(a)

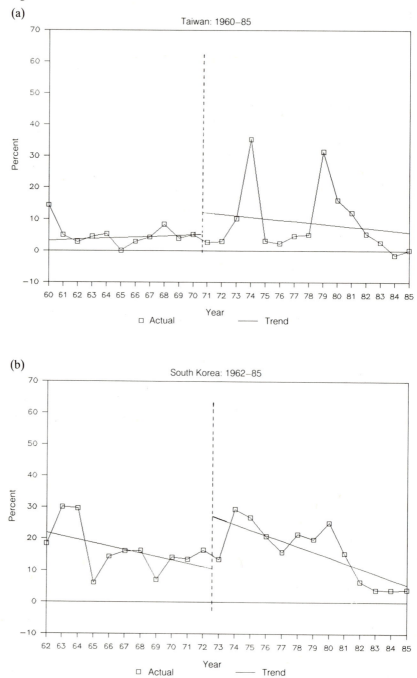

(b)

Figure 4.13 Income velocity of circulation

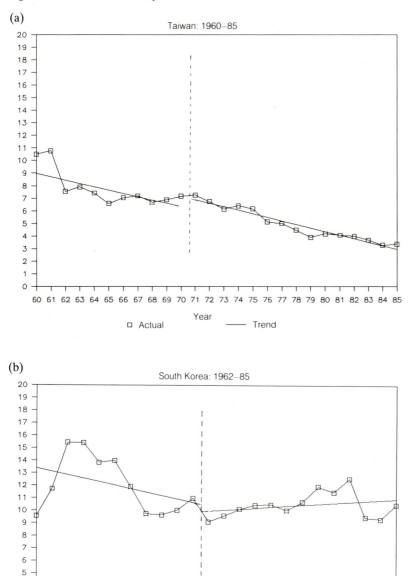

(a)

Taiwan: 1960–85

□ Actual   —— Trend

(b)

South Korea: 1962–85

□ Actual   —— Trend

153

Figure 4.14 Money growth and forced savings rates

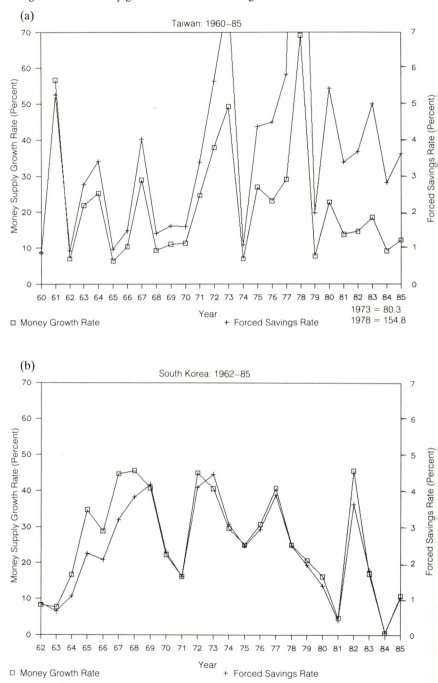

(a)

Taiwan: 1960–85

1973 = 80.3
1978 = 154.8

□ Money Growth Rate   + Forced Savings Rate

(b)

South Korea: 1962–85

□ Money Growth Rate   + Forced Savings Rate

154

Figure 4.15   Real rate of interest

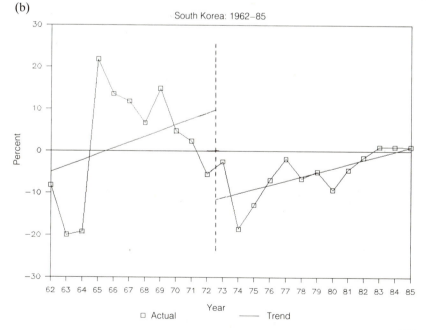

155

Figure 4.16　Gross domestic savings/GDP

(a)

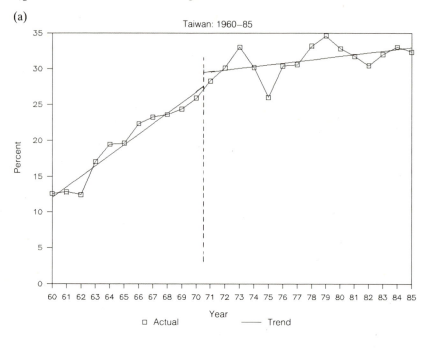

(b)

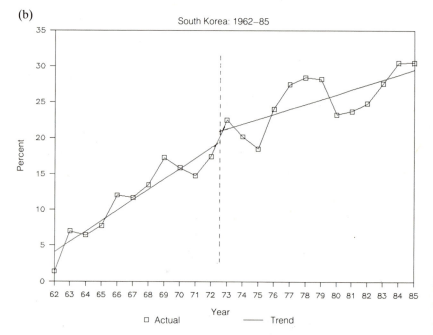

Figure 4.17 Change in savings deposits/gross savings

(a)

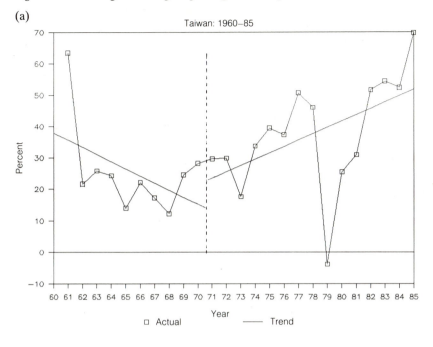

(b)

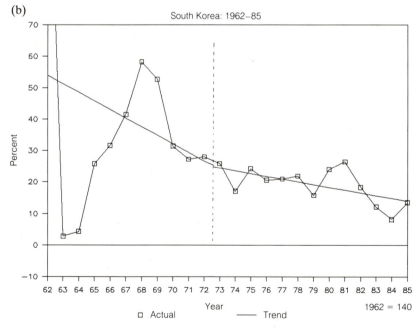

157

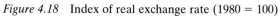

Figure 4.18 Index of real exchange rate (1980 = 100)

(a)

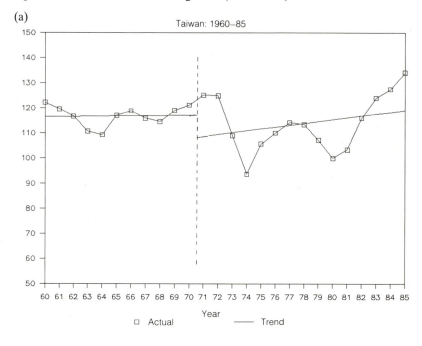

(b)

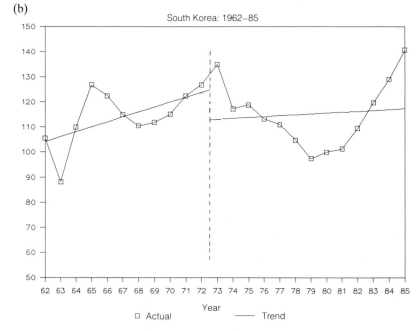

Figure 4.19 Average rate of protection

(a)

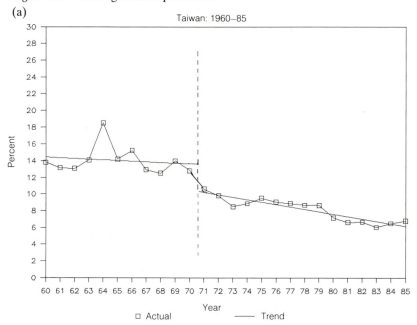

(b)

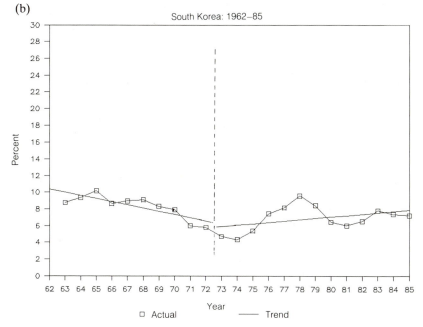

Figure 4.20 Net inflow of long-term foreign capital/GDP

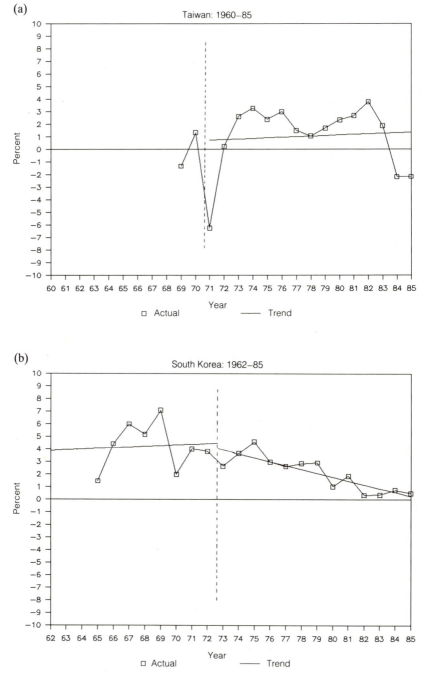

(a)

Taiwan: 1960–85

□ Actual ——— Trend

(b)

South Korea: 1962–85

□ Actual ——— Trend

160

Figure 4.21 Index of labor disputes

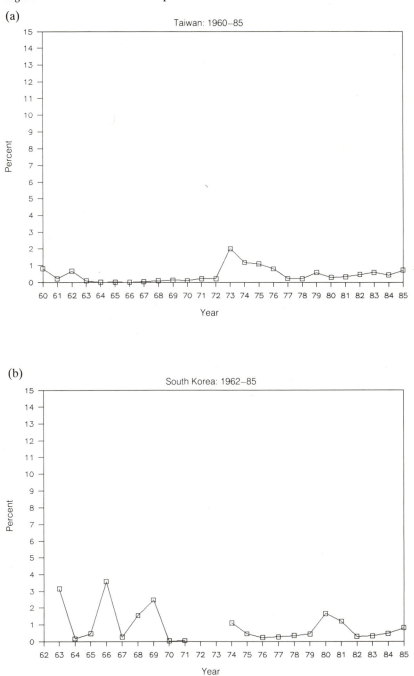

(a)
Taiwan: 1960–85

(b)
South Korea: 1962–85

Appendix

Definition of variables

(definitions not spelled out for self-evident variables)

External terms of trade = Unit value of exports divided by unit value of imports
Exports = Exports of goods and services
Imports = Imports of goods and services
Trade balance = Imports minus exports
International trade taxes = Export duties plus import duties
Government deficits = Central government deficits excluding public enterprise
accounts
Money supply = M1
Annual rate of inflation = Rate of change in GDP deflator
Income velocity of circulation = $(P_t \cdot Q_{t-1}) / M_{t-1}$, where
P = price level
Q = nominal GDP
M = money supply (M1)
t = time
Forced savings rate = $(dM/dt)/PQ$, where
dM/dt = change in money supply
PQ = nominal GDP
Real rate of interest = Nominal central bank discount rate minus the annual
rate of inflation
Savings deposits = Time, savings, and foreign currency deposits
Real exchange rates = Real exchange rates are derived from nominal
exchange rates and relative wholesale price ratios of
the five major trading partners using trade shares as
weights.
Average rate of protection = Import taxes divided by total imports of goods
and services
Index of labor disputes = Total number of workers involved in industrial
disputes as percentage of total industrial
employment

Data sources: Taiwan

Variable and Source

Unit values of exports and imports:
The Central Bank of China, *Financial Statistics,* various issues (post-
1978 data); IMF, *International Financial Statistics,* Yearbook, 1979
(pre-1978 data)
Real GDP: as above
Exports of goods and services: as
above

Imports of goods and services: as
above
Foreign exchange reserves: as above
Total taxes, import taxes, and export
duties: *Statistical Yearbook of the
Republic of China,* various issues
Government deficits: The Central
Bank of China, *Financial Statistics,*
various issues (post-1978 data);

IMF, *International Financial Statistics*, Yearbook, 1979 (pre-1978 data)

Money supply: as above

GDP deflator: as above

Nominal rate of interest: as above

Gross domestic savings: Computed from data in The Central Bank of China, *Financial Statistics*, various issues, (post-1978 data) and IMF, *International Financial Statistics*, Yearbook, 1979 (pre-1978 data)

Time, savings, and foreign currency deposits: The Central Bank of China, *Financial Statistics*, various issues (post-1978 data); IMF, *International Financial Statistics*, Yearbook, 1979 (pre-1978 data)

Real exchange rate: Computed from data in The Central Bank of China, *Financial Statistics*, various issues; IMF, *International Financial Statistics*, Yearbook, 1979; and *Statistical Yearbook of the Republic of China*, various issues

Net inflow of long-term foreign capital: World Bank, *World Debt Tables*, various issues, and *Statistical Yearbook of the Republic of China*, various issues

Number of workers involved in industrial disputes and total industrial employment: Republic of China, Directorate General of Budget, Accounting and Statistics, *Yearbook of Labour Statistics*, various issues

Data sources: South Korea

Variable and Source

Unit values of exports and imports: IMF, *International Financial Statistics*, Yearbook, 1988

Real GDP: IMF, *International Financial Statistics*, Yearbook, 1988

Exports of goods and services: IMF, *International Financial Statistics*, Yearbook, 1988

Imports of goods and services: IMF, *International Financial Statistics*, Yearbook, 1988

Foreign exchange reserves: IMF, *International Financial Statistics*, Yearbook, 1988

Total taxes, import taxes, and export duties: IMF, *Government Finance Statistics*, 1982, 1985, 1988 (for post-1972 data); Bank of Korea, *Economic Statistics Yearbook*, various issues (for pre-1972 data)

Government deficits: IMF, *International Financial Statistics*, Yearbook, 1988

Money supply: IMF, *International Financial Statistics*, Yearbook, 1988

GDP deflator: IMF, *International Financial Statistics*, Yearbook, 1988

Nominal rate of interest: IMF, *International Financial Statistics*, Yearbook, 1988

Gross domestic savings: Computed from data in IMF, *International Financial Statistics*, Yearbook, 1988

Time, savings, and foreign currency deposits: IMF, *International Financial Statistics*, Yearbook, 1988

Real exchange rate: Computed from data in IMF, *International Financial Statistics*, Yearbook 1988, and IMF, *Direction of Trade Statistics*, various issues

Net inflow of long-term foreign capital: World Bank, *World Debt Tables*, various issues

Number of workers involved in industrial disputes and total industrial employment: ILO, *International Labour Statistics*, various issues

Significance of trend lines: Taiwan

NS   = not significant
+++ = significantly positive at the 98 percent level of confidence
++   = significantly positive at the 95 percent level of confidence
+   = significantly positive at the 90 percent level of confidence
−−− = significantly negative at the 98 percent level of confidence
−−   = significantly negative at the 95 percent level of confidence
−   = significantly negative at the 90 percent level of confidence

Variable	1960–70	1971–85
External terms of trade (deviations from trend)	NS	−−
Annual rate of growth of real GDP	++	NS
Exports/GDP	+++	+++
Trade balance/GDP	−−	−−−
Foreign exchange reserves/four months' imports	NS	+++
Total taxes/GDP	+++	+
International trade taxes/total taxes	++	−−−
Government deficits/GDP	−−−	+
Annual rate of change of money supply	NS	NS
Annual rate of inflation	NS	NS
Income velocity of circulation	−−	−−−
Real rate of interest	NS	NS
Gross domestic savings/GDP	+++	+++
Change in savings deposits/gross savings	NS	++
Real exchange rate	NS	NS
Average rate of protection	NS	−−−
Net inflow of long-term foreign capital		NS

Significance of trend lines: South Korea

NS   = Not significant
+++ = Significantly positive at the 98 percent level of confidence
++   = Significantly positive at the 95 percent level of confidence
+   = Significantly positive at the 90 percent level of confidence
−−− = Significantly negative at the 98 percent level of confidence
−−   = Significantly negative at the 95 percent level of confidence
−   = Significantly negative at the 90 percent level of confidence

Variable	1962–72	1973–85
External terms of trade (deviations from trend)	++	NS
Annual rate of growth of real GDP	NS	NS
Exports/GDP	+++	+++
Trade balance/GDP	NS	−−−

Foreign exchange reserves/four months' imports	−	−
Total taxes/GDP	+++	+++
International trade taxes/total taxes	− − −	NS
Government deficits/GDP	NS	NS
Annual rate of change of money supply	NS	− − −
Annual rate of inflation	NS	− − −
Income velocity of circulation	NS	NS
Real rate of interest	NS	+++
Gross domestic savings/GDP	+++	+++
Change in savings deposits/gross savings	NS	− − −
Real exchange rate	+	NS
Average rate of protection	− − −	NS
Net inflow of long-term foreign capital	NS	+++

5

The "Intermediate" Southeast Asian Case: The Philippines and Thailand

The Philippines and Thailand represent two neighboring Southeast Asian countries that, at first sight, seem not so radically different from one another, either in terms of initial conditions, historical background, or geographic location; and yet, as demonstrated in chapter 1, their performance during the postwar era has been radically different. If our theoretical framework proves sufficiently sensitive to shed some light on the differential performance of these two initially not-so-startlingly-different systems, this would indeed provide encouraging support of its more general usefulness. It would certainly provide a more robust test of its relevance than a comparison between the most extreme representative of natural-resources-poor East Asia, on the one hand, and the most extreme representative of natural-resources-rich Latin America, on the other.

We have already presented detailed information on the initial conditions of our country cases in chapter 1. It is especially important to recall that Thailand was more land abundant or less labor surplus, with its natural resource abundance focused heavily on staples production (rice and maize), while the Philippines was relatively more abundant in tropical food, raw materials, and minerals. It should also be recalled that, during the primary-import-substituting 1950s, the Philippines grew somewhat faster than Thailand, but that this situation has reversed itself rather dramatically since. Moreover, the income distribution and poverty alleviation record has been substantially better in Thailand throughout the period for which data are available. It is, finally, necessary to recall that the overall extent of participation in the world economy as measured by the export-orientation ratios of the two economies has not differed markedly over time, though the composition of exports, and the way it was achieved – as between more export substitution, as in the case of Thailand, and more export promotion, as in the case of the Philippines – is relevant and important to our story.

5.1 External shocks

As in the earlier case studies, we set the stage for our empirical analysis of development policy change in the Philippines and Thailand by first examining the long-run movements in the external terms of trade and identifying the periods of "upturn" and "downturn." Both the Philippines and Thailand experienced a long-term deterioration of their terms of trade during the postwar period taken as a whole, with the deterioration more severe in the case of the Philippines. Yet, when we plot the deviations from these linear trends a distinct cycle emerges in both countries for the post-1960 period, when both countries shifted out of the IS and into the EO phase of transition growth (see figures 5.1(a) and (b)). When we examine the full cycle more carefully we find that, in both countries, the sixties and early seventies represented a period of relatively favorable movements in the terms of trade, while the late seventies and early eighties were characterized by relatively unfavorable movements. These deviations from trend have been plotted in figures 5.2(a) and 5.3(a) for the Philippines and in 5.2(b) and 5.3(b) for Thailand. For the Philippines, the periods 1961–74 and 1975–85 mark the upturn and the downturn phases, respectively, while, for Thailand, the corresponding periods are roughly similar, i.e., 1961–73 and 1974–85 respectively. The Chow tests, moreover, indicate that the slopes of the trend lines fitted to the two subperiods are significantly different from each other in both countries – the trend lines being significantly positive during the upturn and significantly negative during the downturn in both cases. This means that we have, for both countries, a confirmed period of a relatively improving external environment followed, at roughly the same time, by a period of a relatively worsening external environment.

We will now proceed to a comparative examination of the response of government policy in the two country cases under consideration as a way of further testing the theoretical framework advanced in chapter 2. The same approach as in the previous empirical chapters is taken, and we look first at the pattern of policy change during the upturn, followed by a similar analysis for the downturn. For each period the various policy parameters affected by the shocks to the system are scrutinized empirically, one by one, in the light of the comparative political economy response mechanisms we have been hypothesizing about.

5.2 Development policy change in the Philippines and Thailand: an overview

The Philippines

In the Philippines, development policy formation during the upturn was initially restrained and flexible, with a number of reforms carried out in various policy areas. By the mid-sixties, however, the government, proceeding in a typically growth-activist fashion, embarked on an expansionary path, financed by covert means of resource transfers, which, by the end of the decade, led to serious balance-of-payments problems. The resulting crisis was initially dealt with by reversing earlier trends toward liberalization in various markets; ultimately, however, external pressures forced a major devaluation and a renewed, if short-lived, import liberalization effort.

Once the external environment began to deteriorate consistently, in the mid-seventies, the government clearly reverted to growth-activist policies but with even greater intensity, using both expansionary monetary and fiscal policies and increased borrowing abroad. As the inevitable resulting crisis eventually hit the economy in the late seventies the government responded in typical Latin American fashion by postponing required adjustments until these could no longer be avoided and ultimately had to be carried out on a much larger scale. Overall, the movement in both the macroeconomic performance indicators as well as the policy variables exhibits a substantial degree of oscillation around a somewhat uncertain trend.

Thailand

While the long-run pattern of policy evolution in the Philippines appears to resemble the typical LDC or Latin American pattern, that in Thailand is closer to the East Asian case. Although, like the Philippines, Thailand also initially indulged in government-sponsored expansionary behavior, there was a much greater effort in evidence to develop a domestic resource mobilization capability and to use overt rather than covert means of resource transfer. In particular, there was an effort to encourage domestic savings by keeping real rates of interest high and foreign borrowing within manageable limits. In general, policy was characterized by a blend of stability and flexibility necessary to maintain a more or less linear trend of depoliticization of the system.

5.3 Development policy change during the upturn

The Philippines

To recall, our overall theoretical framework suggests that an improvement in the external environment would, by accelerating the rate of growth of GDP and by increasing the degree of external orientation as well as the level of foreign exchange reserves and tax revenues, create the underpinnings for a policy response whereby an interventionist government is induced to promote further growth by means of expansionary policies. Thus, one may expect the growth rate to accelerate before stabilizing at a high rate toward the end of the upturn, the degree of external orientation to accelerate as government promotes exports further via export-promotion measures, but to slow down later as the expansion becomes artificial and is "overdone," the trade balance worsens, and reserves start dissipating.

The movements in the real variable indicators in the Philippines during the upturn appear to match this scenario quite closely. The improvement in the terms of trade was initially associated with an acceleration in the GDP growth rate (see figure 5.4(a)), a jump in the exports/GDP ratio, from about 11 percent in 1961 to more than 18 percent in 1966 (see figure 5.5(a)) and an accumulation of foreign exchange reserves, as the standardized foreign exchange reserves ratio increased from a precarious ten days of imports at the end of 1961 to about two months of imports by 1965 (see figure 5.7(a)). As we shall see below, reforms in exchange rate management involving a substantial devaluation of the currency as well as export-promotion measures were adopted during the first half of the sixties; these undoubtedly contributed to increasing exports and enhanced reserve accumulation. As predicted, the trade balance/GDP ratio also improved in the first few years of the upturn; in fact, export surpluses were achieved in three years during the 1961–66 period (see figure 5.6(a)).

The enhanced sense of growth promotion as well as spending power unleashed by these positive developments, coupled with a change in government (the assumption of power by Marcos) in 1966, created the underpinnings for additional government-sponsored expansionary policies that were set in motion in the second half of the sixties. The reflection of this in various policy arenas is the subject of discussion in subsequent sections; but first we may note the effects on the real variable indicators.

Growth rates continued to be respectable, ranging between 5 and 6 percent, although there is no overall trend for the upturn as a whole (figure 5.4(a)). Exports, however, suffered, predictably, as artificially expansionary policies led to inflation and an appreciation of the currency, which was not corrected before the end of the decade (see below). The acceleration in the exports/GDP ratio was stopped and the degree of external orientation actually fell in the second half of the sixties until a major devaluation in 1970 helped push it up again (see Figure 5.5(a)). In the four years following the 1970 devaluation, substantial growth took place in the volume of exports. Some of this growth, however, represented the gestation of large investments made in the late sixties, particularly in copper mining, banana plantations, and sugar milling, and cannot really be ascribed to the 1970 devaluation.

With falling exports and rising imports, the trade balance deteriorated, with the trade balance/GDP ratio rising to 3.5 percent in 1969.

Consequently, foreign exchange reserves fell at a fast rate and, by the end of 1969, had reached an alarmingly low level – equal to only three weeks of imports (figure 5.7(a)). At the end of the sixties, therefore, the Philippines found itself facing a serious balance-of-payments crisis – as it had done exactly a decade earlier. Adjustment measures taken in response and discussed in detail below, however, led to an improvement in the situation, with the trade balance/GDP ratio brought down to below 1 percent during 1972–74 and an export surplus being earned in 1973 following a commodity boom (figure 5.6(a)). Reserves improved significantly, reaching a respectable level by 1972 (figure 5.7(a)).

The evolution of development policy in the Philippines during the upturn thus appears to have all the hallmarks of the pattern expected of a typical interventionist LDC government. A detailed analysis of each of the major policy arenas confirms this.

Fiscal policy   The Philippines entered her external orientation phase with a rather low tax effort. The tax/GDP ratio was only 6 percent in 1961 (figure 5.8(a)), comparable to that of Mexico and less than half that of Thailand. Despite an improvement in the terms of trade, the tax effort remained modest for a decade, with the tax/GDP ratio remaining below 7 percent until 1971 (figure 5.8(a)). This was partly due to a modest fall in the relative importance of international-trade-related taxes over the same period (figure 5.9(a)).

Initially this low tax effort did not lead to serious budgetary problems since expenditures were relatively restrained. In the first half of the sixties, government deficits were modest, averaging only about 0.5 percent of GDP (figure 5.10(a)). This situation began to change after the Marcos administration took over in 1966 and immediately embarked on an expansionary path. Vigorous programs of infrastructural construction were initiated in order to accelerate both agricultural and industrial growth. Consequently, total government expenditures increased quite rapidly in the second half of the sixties, increasing as a proportion of GDP from 12 percent in 1965 to a peak of almost 16 percent in 1969. Although expenditures were brought down after this, they nonetheless remained high for the rest of the upturn. As a result, with taxes remaining low, government deficits increased and by 1969 exceeded 3 percent of GDP. During the rest of the upturn, however, deficits were, on average, lower, i.e., less than 1 percent of GDP. This was due to a significant increase in tax revenues after 1972 – the tax/GDP ratio rose from about 7 percent in 1971 to about 10 percent in 1974 (figure 5.8(a)) following the imposition of martial law in 1972 and the announcement of a tax amnesty. This was accompanied by an increase in the proportion of international trade taxes in total taxes (figure 5.9(a)). Temporary export taxes of 8 or 10 percent on major products, legislated in 1970, were made permanent in 1972, and some new products were added; in February 1974, an additional premium duty was introduced for 15 products. This dramatic increase in the tax effort was, however, of the one-shot variety, related to the imposition of martial law. As we shall see below, the tax effort in the Philippines has subsequently consistently deteriorated.

Monetary policy   The expansionary fiscal policies adopted after 1966 were accompanied by a loosening of monetary policy that had been relatively restrictive in the initial years of the upturn. The decontrol measures of 1962 were accompanied by a tightening of monetary policy (see figure 5.10(a)); the central bank discount rate was raised from 3 percent to 6 percent and the reserve requirement from 15 percent to 19 percent. However, after 1966 the monetary authorities initiated a policy that they described as one of "massive credit relaxation" (Baldwin, 1975, p. 65). In 1966, the basic rediscount rate of 6 percent was lowered to 4.75 percent, rediscount ceilings on commercial banks were raised, and reserve requirements against savings and time deposits reduced. Although the central bank once again began to reverse these easy credit policies following the mid-1967 worsening of the trade balance and increase in inflation,[1] the rate of money growth remained high during the second half of the sixties, and accelerated further in the early seventies.

In combination with a high and moderately rising velocity of circulation (figure 5.13(a)), such high rates of money supply growth eventually led to substantial inflation. The rate of inflation, after remaining around 5 percent for most of the sixties, reached double-digit levels in the early seventies (see figure 5.12(a)). It enabled the government to extract somewhat higher amounts of forced savings from the public, the forced savings rate jumping from an average of 0.5 percent during 1963–66 to 1.5 percent during the rest of the upturn (see figure 5.14(a)).

Due to these rising rates of inflation in the later stage of the upturn, it was also not possible to maintain a positive real interest rate policy despite a series of reforms in nominal interest rates. The nominal central bank discount rate was doubled in 1962 – from 3 to 6 percent – and kept at that level until 1967 (except for a temporary reduction in 1966) before being increased, in two steps, to reach 10 percent in 1969. It remained at that level until 1974 when it was drastically brought down to 6 percent once again. These increases in nominal rates were, however, clearly inadequate so that, even with moderate inflation, real rates of interest were very low, on average only about one-third of 1 percent during most of the decade (figure 5.14(a)). The persistence of such negative real

---

[1] The steps taken included the raising of the reserve requirement for commercial banks from 12 to 16 percent and an increase in the basic discount rate from 4.75 percent to 6 percent and, further, to 7.5 percent in 1968.

interest rates clearly had an adverse impact at least on the composition of domestic savings. Although total gross savings exhibited a significantly positive trend during the upturn, rising from about 17 percent of GDP in 1961 to about 22 percent in 1974 (figure 5.16(a)), the formal savings ratio was low and showed no improvement (figure 5.17(a)).

Exchange rate management and trade policy   Policy evolution in the area of exchange rate management followed a path similar to that of fiscal and monetary policy, i.e., an initially conservative phase quickly giving way to a more interventionist posture. Like most LDCs, the Philippines had, in the early postindependence period (i.e., in 1949), imposed a regime of exchange controls as part of her overall strategy of primary import substitution started in response to an emerging foreign exchange crisis; this was intensified over the next decade.[2] However, by the end of the fifties, there was growing dissatisfaction about the manner in which exchange controls were being administered. Pressure from exporters, especially the powerful sugar lobby, which was well represented in the Congress, for the adoption of a more realistic exchange rate and the decontrol of foreign exchange markets steadily increased. The Garcia administration, which emphasized the role of controls in promoting industrialization, initially resisted these pressures but ultimately gave in following a serious balance-of-payments crisis in 1959 when reserves were severely depleted, leaving little room for further cuts in imports.

Starting in 1960 and coinciding with the beginnings of the Philippines' external orientation phase, the government initiated a number of measures to gradually decontrol the foreign exchange market. In April 1960, the central bank introduced a two-tier exchange rate system: an "official" rate that was equal to the current rate of 2 pesos per dollar and a "free market" rate of 3.2 pesos per dollar.[3] The proportion of foreign exchange transacted at the free market rate increased from about 25 percent during April 1960–November 1960 to about 75 percent during March 1961–January 1962. This liberalization process got a big boost in 1962 when the new government of Macapagal completely decontrolled imports and temporarily allowed the peso to float. By mid-1967, the exchange rate had settled at 3.9 pesos per dollar, where it was held until 1970.[4] The decontrol of imports was accompanied by increases in some tariffs. In addition, it rendered the tariff increases carried out earlier operative for the first time.

[2] See Baldwin (1975), chapter 2, for a detailed description of the nature of exchange controls during this period.
[3] This was not strictly a free market rate, as it was set by the central bank.
[4] Exporters were, however, required to surrender 20 percent of their earnings at the old exchange rate of two pesos per dollar. This requirement was abolished in 1965, thus unifying the exchange rate.

The floating of the peso resulted in a significant real depreciation of the currency (see figure 5.18(a)). This had a beneficial impact on exports. However, until about 1966, most of the recorded increases were in the traditional product groups – sugar, cement, logs, and mining. Manufactured exports also grew but at a much slower pace, accelerating only after 1966. Manufacturing as a whole suffered; the growth rate of manufacturing GDP dropped from about 7.7 percent in 1957–59 to 3.7 percent in 1960–65, as primary import substitution had come to an end and the existing policy regime did not permit a further sustained increase in industrial exports.

The slow growth of manufacturing generated significant political pressure from the industrial class in favor of a reimposition of controls. The initial response of the government was to take a number of steps to assist industry and exports, the most visible of which was the Investment Incentives Act of 1967, which provided important fiscal incentives. While the official intention was one of export promotion the system in fact made benefits available only to large-scale Manila-based firms. Eventually in the face of the growing balance-of-payments crisis of 1967–70 already referred to, the government gradually reversed earlier moves toward trade liberalization and reimposed controls. The first steps in this direction consisted of the reintroduction of foreign exchange controls in March 1968. In June 1969, the importation of various categories classified as "semiessential" and "nonessential" – by and large the very goods that domestic manufacturers tended to produce – were, once again, i.e., for the first time since 1962, subject to central bank approval. All these controls, nevertheless, proved insufficient to deal with the mounting foreign exchange crisis. Consequently, in February 1970, faced with a serious balance-of-payments situation and under pressure from the IMF, the government was forced to float the peso and eliminate many of the exchange controls. The exchange rate immediately rose from 3.9 pesos to 5.5 pesos per dollar and, by the end of the year, to 6.4 pesos per dollar. Discrimination against certain types of transactions, notably traditional exports, however, remained for some time.[5] Moreover, additional controls were placed on imports in the form of prior-deposit requirements and import permits for certain types of goods.[6]

The fairly substantial level of liberalization of the foreign exchange market in the early upturn thus proved to be a short-lived phenomenon. Although the immediate cause of this reversal was the balance-of-payments crisis, the underlying political pressures for a reimposition of protection

[5] Until May 1970, 80 percent of all receipts from the leading traditional exports such as sugar, copra, logs, etc., had to be surrendered to the central bank at the old rate of 3.9 pesos to the dollar. This was replaced, in May 1970, by the aforementioned special export taxes varying between 8 and 10 percent.

[6] A detailed description of these policy reversals is contained in Baldwin (1975, chapter 4).

emanating from the manufacturing sector partly explain why quantity rather than price adjustments were resorted to in order to deal with the balance-of-payments problems. In the Philippines the government clearly succumbed to political pressures against liberalization, unlike its East Asian counterparts, which were more likely to help firms to survive in a more competitive environment or, failing that, to let them wither away.

Attempts were made, however, toward the end of the upturn and under the political shelter against vested interest groups the early martial law years provided, to carry out some tariff reforms. One of the first economic acts of the new government was a thorough rationalization of the tariff structure in January 1973. With regard to the average rate of protection, however, no trend could be observed for this period (figure 5.19(a)).

Notwithstanding the initial decontrol and devaluation as the Philippines entered its external orientation period, the exchange rate remained generally overvalued almost throughout the ensuing upturn. Although the initial devaluation of the currency in 1962 brought the nominal rate temporarily back in line with the real rate, the fact that the rate of inflation in the sixties was generally higher in the Philippines, compared to her major trading partners, meant that the real exchange rate appreciated during the sixties. This is seen in figure 5.18(a), which indicates that, sandwiched between the initial devaluation of 1962, which signaled the end of the import-substitution subphase, and the second major devaluation in 1970, the real rate was appreciating slightly during the sixties. Various studies suggest that the degree of overvaluation throughout this period was about 15–20 percent (Intal, Jr., and Power, 1990; Torigoe, 1986).

In order to compensate for this overvaluation a number of export-promotion measures were taken during the upturn. The aforementioned Investment Incentives Act of 1967 had legislated fiscal incentives for the export of nontraditional goods for the first time. It enabled exporters to acquire imported inputs at world prices (through a tax credit on import duties) and provided for some modest subsidy for the use of local raw materials (via tax credits) and export-related marketing and shipping expenses (via tax deductions). These measures were augmented by the Export Incentives Act of 1970, which legislated additional incentives for nontraditional exports, extending some of the incentives to export traders, for firms exporting in excess of 50 percent of their output. In addition a direct subsidy to value added was provided. In November 1972, provisions to create the first export-processing zone in Bataan were announced. More incentives were added in January 1973.[7] In combina-

---

[7] Although tax deductions for export-related marketing and shipping expenses introduced in 1967 were removed, these were replaced by stronger tax deduction incentives for using local raw materials and labor. In addition, the inclusion of bonded warehouses was permitted for larger firms exporting at least 70 percent of their output.

tion with the export taxes described earlier, mostly on traditional exports, this array of export-promotion measures created a distinct bias against traditional exports (mostly agricultural and mining) and in favor of nontraditional exports (mostly manufacturing). In brief, this was a clear use of export promotion, i.e., as the exchange rate became increasingly overvalued, exports were increasingly subsidized directly or indirectly, possibly in excess of what was required to restore equilibrium.

The evolution of exchange rate management, trade policy, as well as of fiscal and monetary policy during the upturn thus appears to have followed a path similar to the one predicted in chapter 2. We notice that the transition to the external orientation phase was initially accompanied by a certain measure of policy caution, e.g., a relatively restrained fiscal and monetary policy, plus some bold policy reforms intended to liberalize the economy, e.g., with regard to exchange rate management and, albeit inadequately, interest rate reforms. As predicted, however, such caution, largely a reaction to the balance-of-payments crisis at the end of the primary import-substitution era, soon gave way to a more flamboyant type of policy as the external environment improved and the crisis seemed to fade. This change in course, which also involved the return to an increased reliance on covert means of resource transfers, led to a reversal of the liberalizing trends even before the economy was hit by negative external shocks, as the government, faced with the results of its expansionary policies, opted for quantity rather than price adjustments. Moreover, as is usually the case, once the government had succumbed to such temptations it became increasingly difficult for it to apply the brakes and reverse the expansionary trend during the ensuing downturn. As we shall see below, the interventionist nature of Philippine government policy became more pronounced once the external environment started deteriorating after the first oil shock.

Thailand

The upturn in Thailand was associated with very respectable growth rates ranging between 7 and 8 percent for most of the period (figure 5.4(b)), better than in the Philippines. However, Thailand's performance with respect to the degree of external orientation was relatively less impressive; although the export/GDP ratio was higher to start with, there is no trend (figure 5.5(b)), unlike in the Philippines where the degree of external orientation rose steadily. We may attribute this to the fact that the shift out of Thailand's (relatively mild) import-substitution phase was more gradual, signaling a more sustained and gradual increase in participation in the world economy over the entire period. As we shall see below, export orientation increased substantially during the downturn.

As would be expected, the improvement in the terms of trade was initially associated, as in the Philippines, with an improvement in the trade balance. During 1961–66, an export surplus was earned in one year, and in all but one of the five remaining years the import surplus was kept below 2.5 percent of GDP (see figure 5.6(b)). Reserves, already at a high level to start with – i.e., equivalent to eight months of imports in 1961 – increased even further, enough to finance more than ten months of imports, by the end of 1966 (figure 5.7(b)).

As in the Philippines, therefore, the underpinnings for growth activism were being generated once the upturn had started. The Thai government responded, as did its Philippines counterpart, and embarked on expansionary policies after the mid-sixties. The nature of these policies and the manner in which they differed from that in the Philippines is described in detail below, but the effects on real variable indicators for the rest of the upturn may be quickly summarized. Growth continued to be high although, as noted above, there was no significant change in the degree of external orientation (figures 5.4(b) and 5.5(b)). The trade balance deteriorated but much less severely than in the Philippines (figure 5.6(b)). Reserves diminished, as expected, but always remained at respectable levels (figure 5.7(b)).

Fiscal policy   As mentioned earlier, Thailand started her external orientation phase with a respectable level of tax effort. The tax/GDP ratio was 11.5 percent in 1961, almost double that of the Philippines (figure 5.8(b)), reflecting the greater relative willingness of the Thai government to rely on overt means of resource transfers. A dominant feature of the tax structure was the reliance on international trade taxes, which, in 1961, accounted for more than half of total tax revenues (figure 5.9(b)), a significant proportion consisting of export taxes on rice. During the upturn, however, Thailand steadily lowered its dependence on international trade taxes and by 1973 had brought their share in total taxes down to about one-third (figure 5.9(b)). Initially, this reduction in international trade taxes was more than offset by increases in other taxes so that the tax/GDP ratio rose moderately, reaching about 13 percent by 1969. Subsequently, however, it fell slightly as the continuing decline in international trade taxes was no longer offset in this fashion (figure 5.8(b)). This situation was, however, reversed as a result of major tax reforms in 1974.

The overall relatively high tax rates, coupled with restrained expenditure policies, helped keep government deficits below 1 percent of GDP until 1966 (figure 5.10(b)). From the mid-sixties, however, with expanding expenditures, such deficits started increasing and had reached almost 5 percent of GDP by 1972. Given the aforementioned decline in tax revenues, deficits were relatively high during the early seventies, averaging about 3.5 of GDP during 1970–73 (figure 5.10(b)).

Monetary policy   Judged solely in terms of the size of budgetary deficits, Thailand's fiscal policy during the upturn would thus not appear to have been more orthodox than that of the Philippines. However, as the discussion in chapter 2 indicated, it is the manner in which the fiscal deficit is financed, rather than simply its size, which may be the more relevant indicator, i.e., a growth-activist government is more likely to resort to simple money printing rather than borrowing from the non-bank public. Thailand was clearly more reluctant to use monetary policy to fully accommodate all the budgetary demands of the government.[8] The strong link between government deficits and financing by the central bank was broken as early as 1955, i.e., even during the IS phase, at the same time as the multiple exchange rate system was abolished. A series of interest rate reforms was undertaken during 1953–55, which stimulated private bond sales and helped to reduce the pure "money printing" nature of government finance. These reforms included income tax exemption for interest income derived from government bonds (1953) and a substantial increase in interest rates on these bonds (1955) (Trescott, 1971, ch. 6). This break between Thailand's budget deficits and central bank financing is reflected in the reduction of the relative share of government debt held by the central bank, from 94 percent in 1954 to 80 percent in 1960, and further to only 20 percent by 1968–69. Overall money supply growth rates were consequently substantially lower in Thailand (see figure 5.11(b)).

The relatively greater independence of the central bank, however, came to a temporary halt in 1969 when, given falling interest rates and private sector saturation with government bonds, budget deficits had to be financed once again in large part by the central bank – the first major instance of domestic "money printing" since the late 1950s. As can be seen from figure 5.11(b), this was reflected in a rise in the rate of money supply growth during the later portion of the upturn. Nonetheless, money growth rates were, on average, slightly lower in Thailand than in the Philippines. Moreover, there was much greater year-to-year stability.

The difference between these two "neighbors" is even more striking with respect to their inflationary experience. The degree of price stability in Thailand during the high growth period of the upturn was indeed remarkable; in fact, in a number of years, inflation was actually negative (figure 5.12(b)). This was partly due to the fact that, while velocity steadily increased during the upturn, its levels were always lower (see

---

[8] A number of commentators have noted the insistence by a succession of central bank governors, even during the import-substituting fifties and early sixties, that their responsibilities must not primarily reside in rendering "residual," after-the-fact accommodation for fiscal decisions already made, but must instead include strong "ground-floor" independent inputs into such decisions. See Silcock (1967, pp. 177–80) and Ingram (1971).

figure 5.13(b)), indicating the lower degree of inflation sensitivity of the public, itself a reflection of the greater degree of confidence in the consistency of government policy. Because of the lower level of velocity, the Thai government was able to extract, on average, similar rates of forced savings as in the Philippines but in the presence of a much lower rate of money creation and a much lower rate of inflation (figure 5.14(b)).

The sharpest contrast in the area of monetary policy between the two countries is, however, in the realm of interest rate policy. Low inflation in combination with high nominal interest rates helped keep real rates substantially positive throughout the upturn, in contrast to the low and often negative rates experienced in the Philippines (figure 5.15(b)). Year-to-year adjustments in the nominal rates were also more frequent during the upturn, with a consistent effort in evidence to keep real rates significantly positive. The savings/GDP ratio increased persistently during the upturn (see figure 5.16(b)), with a larger proportion of savings going into formal channels, certainly as compared to the Philippines (figure 5.17(b)).

Exchange rate management and trade policy   Exchange rate management in Thailand also tells a somewhat different story from that in the Philippines. Thailand abolished her multiple exchange rate system in 1955, with the baht pegged to the U.S. dollar at a rate of about 20.8 per dollar from 1957 to 1972. The price level in Thailand, as already noted, was relatively stable during the sixties, so that no pronounced divergence resulted between real and nominal rates; if anything, the real exchange rate, as we can see from figure 5.18(b), actually depreciated slightly in the second half of the sixties as inflation in Thailand fell below that of her trading partners.

Import restrictions had traditionally been relatively mild in Thailand. QRs had played a very minor role in Thailand's overall policy package since the mid-fifties, with most of the protection being in the form of tariffs. Some changes in the tariff structure occurred during the upturn; in 1959–60, for example, the system of tariffs was changed to a value-added basis and rates were raised by an average of 10 percent across the board. There was a further increase in 1964 and again in 1969 following a balance-of-payments crisis. Nonetheless, the overall trend was that of a steady decline in the average rate of protection during the upturn (see figure 5.19(b)).

The evolution of exchange rate and trade policy in Thailand during the upturn thus followed a path of gradual but steady liberalization, in contrast to that in the Philippines where dramatic steps toward liberalization were taken early on, only to be reversed. Thailand, like the Philippines, was encouraged by improvements in the external environment to initiate expansionary fiscal policies in the middle of the upturn. This led to increases in government deficits – even larger than those in the Philippines – but there was clearly a greater tendency to finance them by borrowing from the nonbank public and to reduce them over time by increased resort to taxation. As we shall see below, these differences in the two countries' behavior became more pronounced once the external environment had deteriorated.

5.4 Development policy change during the downturn

The Philippines

The theoretical discussion in chapter 2 suggested that in the "typical" LDC, growth activism, incipient during the upturn, is likely to emerge full-blown during the downturn when the external environment deteriorates, as the government uses expansionary policy even more vigorously in a desperate, but ultimately self-defeating, attempt to maintain growth. The Philippines story fits this scenario very closely. Once the negative shocks hit the economy, the government made an attempt not only to maintain, but, in fact, to actively accelerate growth beyond the levels achieved during good times. For the period 1974–77, for example, the target annual rate of growth was set at 7.0 percent; this was increased to 7.6 percent for the period 1978–82 (Remolona et al., 1986, pp. 993–1018). While these were higher than the actual rates achieved, it is clear that the Philippine government endeavored to carry out these intentions as reflected in the actual growth rates for 1975–79 (see figure 5.4(a)). These growth rates were, on average, about 1 percent higher than those achieved during the upturn. The self-defeating nature of this strategy of artificially propping up growth, however, became apparent after 1980 when growth started decelerating and actually turned negative.[9]

This promotion of growth during the downturn led, among other things, to an appreciation of the currency (see below), which had an adverse impact on exports. The export/GDP ratio, which had risen to just under 20 percent following the massive devaluations of 1970, remained at that level until a fresh round of devaluations and export-promotion measures were implemented as part of the post-1983 adjustment to the debt crisis (see figure 5.5(a)). There was, however, a change in the composition of exports. Between 1974 and 1980, for example, the share of the top four export groups (coconut, sugar, wood, and copper concentrates) fell from 77 percent to 43 percent, while the share of

---

[9] A study found that the Philippines adjusted to external shocks during the downturn in such a manner as to accommodate only one-fourth of these shocks. Moreover, the output growth rate had a negative adjustment effect, i.e., it took the form of an internal shock that exacerbated the imbalances created by the external shocks. See Power (1983).

manufactured exports rose from 16 percent to 39 percent. We have real evidence of export promotion at work here.

As expected, the overall stagnation in export earnings, coupled with the increased demand for imports generated by the government's efforts to maintain growth artificially, led to a deterioration of the trade balance. The average level of the import surplus/GDP ratio during the downturn period was substantially higher than in even the worst years of the upturn (figure 5.6(a)) and declined only after 1983.

As the trade balance continued to decline during the downturn, the Philippines utilized more and more foreign bank borrowings to keep the reserve position at about four months of imports.[10] The hazard of relying on temporary inflows of foreign capital to maintain a reserve position was, however, soon exposed when, in the later years of the downturn, and in the absence of continued OPEC recycling flows, reserves started falling dramatically, reaching a crisis level of one month's imports in 1982 (see figure 5.7(a)).

Fiscal policy   As the government tried to accelerate growth by raising expenditures but was unwilling to raise taxes, budget deficits were on the increase and by 1981 exceeded 2 percent of GDP (see figure 5.10(a)). The rise in the tax effort recorded after the imposition of martial law in 1972 proved to be a one-shot measure. The government found it politically difficult to carry out further tax reforms and to diversify the tax base in order to compensate for the decline in international trade taxes during the seventies; consequently a modest drop in the tax/GDP ratio could not be avoided (see figures 5.8(a) and 5.9(a)). The major cause of the increase in deficits was, however, the expansion in government expenditures. Public sector resource management became increasingly inefficient – encouraged in part by easy access to foreign capital – and a large number of projects of doubtful economic value was undertaken.[11]

Monetary policy   In "typical" LDC fashion, given a more expansionary fiscal policy with the onset of the downturn, monetary policy once again assumed an accommodating role in the Philippines. The annual rate of money supply growth accelerated rapidly after 1974 and by 1977 had reached almost 25 percent (see figure 5.11(a)). It was subsequently brought down to below 15 percent by 1979 and, under IMF pressure, kept there during most of the eighties.

[10] See below for a discussion of foreign capital inflows during this period.

[11] These include the reclamation schemes along Manila Bay, the spate of luxury hotel construction and other tourism-related expenditures in the mid-1970s, the Bataan nuclear power reactor, eleven major industrial projects (later shelved), and a variety of large construction projects ranging from Mrs. Marcos' University of Life to her Cultural Center complex.

At the same time, continued increases in velocity (figure 5.13(a)) now led to higher average rates of inflation. With the public "fighting back," especially after 1978, the government's ability to extract forced savings from the system through money creation was being increasingly compromised. Thus, in contrast to the rising trend observed during the upturn, the forced savings rate now fell steadily and by the 1980s had declined to below 0.5 percent (see figure 5.14(a)). Inflationary expectations seem to have shifted, with the same rate of growth of the money supply now unable to elicit the same response as before.

Voluntary savings, certainly in terms of its composition, also suffered as a consequence of the government's failure to raise nominal interest rates in line with accelerating inflation. Real interest rates were not only negative virtually throughout the downturn but became increasingly more so over time. Although total savings continued to rise in the second half of the seventies, the trend was reversed during the eighties. By 1985, the savings/GDP ratio had fallen to a level only marginally higher than that in 1961 (see figure 5.16(a)). Formal savings as a percent of the total remained low by international LDC standards throughout the period (see figure 5.17(a)).

Foreign capital inflows   With domestic savings low and a substantial appetite for investment, there was large-scale resort to foreign borrowing during the downturn. While dependence on long-term foreign borrowing had been fairly modest during the upturn, it increased significantly during the downturn (see figure 5.20(a)); net inflows of public and publicly guaranteed long-term foreign capital increased to over 3 percent of GDP by 1976 and stayed there until 1983. As in the Latin American cases, especially Mexico, the growth activism in the Philippines during the downturn was thus fueled in substantial part by inflows of foreign capital, public and private.

Exchange rate management and trade policy   Rising inflation during the downturn led to an appreciation of the peso. This happened despite the fact that the stated adoption of a "more flexible" exchange rate system in 1970 had given monetary authorities a greater degree of potential power to adjust the exchange rate as they saw fit in response to imbalances in the external accounts. It is clear, however, that this announced "flexibility" was never fully exploited and that heavy central bank intervention continued. Although the nominal exchange rate depreciated, it did so at a very slow rate of 1.5 percent per annum, not adequate to prevent the real rate from continuously appreciating (see figure 5.18(a)).

The continuous appreciation of the currency was temporarily reversed only in 1983 with a two-part major (16 percent) devaluation. This was followed by a further devaluation of 28.6 percent in June 1984 and the continuation of a substantially "dirty" float later that year (World Bank, 1987, p. 5). Nevertheless, though the Philippines exchange rate policy, partly under IMF pressure, had become somewhat more flexible by the mid-eighties, the degree of overvaluation remained high. Estimates suggests that the nominal exchange rate continued to be overvalued by at least 25 percent (Intal, Jr., and Power, 1990; Torigoe, 1986).

In spite of continuous World Bank structural-adjustment-loan-related commitments, little progress with regard to trade liberalization was made before 1980; in fact, in certain ways there had been major retrogression in the sense that between 1974 and 1976 many ad hoc (i.e., individual-firm-related) tariff exemptions (i.e., those broadly outside the overall fiscal incentive legislation) were introduced; the ratio of estimated duty exemptions to actual duties paid on all imports rose from 9 percent in 1973 to a level of at least 22 percent after 1976. Such "directed" interventionism is characteristic of "crony capitalism" at its worst.

It was in 1980 that the most substantial effort at trade liberalization was initiated as a consequence of the country's newly acquired membership in GATT as well as the availability of additional financing coupled with conditionality, mainly from the World Bank, to support some basic structural adjustments. The 1981 liberalization package indeed had two main components: the reduction of quantitative import restrictions and a general tariff reform that was to include a reduction in maximum nominal tariffs from 100 percent to 50 percent, the reduction in the degree of tariff escalation, and the lowering of the average rate of protection from 45 percent to 28 percent by 1985. Some progress was made in implementing this program, but much of the effort was reversed during the 1983 crisis and has still not been fully restored.[12] In general, the average rate of protection has indeed been higher during the downturn as compared to the upturn (figure 5.19(a)).

In summary, the evolution of development policy in the Philippines during the downturn thus contains all the hallmarks of the typical LDC scenario described in chapter 2. As predicted, the government used expansionary fiscal and monetary policies to maintain growth artificially in the face of a deteriorating external environment. This trend was accentuated by the response of the public, which raised velocity in an attempt to fight back the government's efforts to extract forced savings. By forcing real interest rates to become negative, the government helped transfer incomes to industrialists, the famous "crony capitalists," as well as to itself,

---

[12] The most recent reversal of liberalization proposals made by the economics team in the cabinet occurred in September 1990.

but in the process adversely affected domestic savings. This, coupled with the fall in export earnings caused by the rapid appreciation of the currency, increased the recourse to foreign borrowing. As predicted, this stance was self-defeating as a balance-of-payments crisis inevitably occurred, responded to by quantity rather than price adjustments until a major adjustment effort had to be undertaken.

Thailand

In contrast to the Philippines, which made a major, if self-destructive, effort to maintain growth after the downturn had started, Thailand responded to the negative shocks in a more East Asian-like fashion, i.e., it allowed growth to decline in the short-run, benefiting growth over the longer term. Indeed, growth rates declined modestly, especially after 1979, but always remained positive, dipping below 4 percent only twice (see figure 5.4(b)). The more price-flexible policy choices made by Thailand meant that, when the environment deteriorated, the ultimate adjustment that had to be made was relatively less severe. This is in sharp contrast to the Philippines, where negative growth eventually occurred and which today still finds itself in deep difficulties. In Thailand, the temptation to borrow extensively abroad during the seventies was, moreover, resisted much more forcefully than in the Philippines; indeed the inflow of long-term foreign capital increased significantly only in the aftermath of the second oil shock of 1979 (see figure 5.20(b)).

There was also much greater success recorded in Thailand with respect to the pursuit of external orientation during the downturn. The export/GDP ratio, which had had no trend during the upturn, rose significantly during the downturn (figure 5.5(b)). The lack of pronounced efforts to promote growth artificially thus had its long-term favorable impact on the trade balance. In Thailand, the import surplus as a percentage of GDP was only marginally higher during the downturn, compared to the worst years of the upturn (1968–70), and always lower than in the Philippines during the downturn (see figure 5.6(b)). We may observe a continuous gradual reduction in reserves, as in the upturn (figure 5.7(b)). This gradual monotonic diminution of the reserve position across both periods indicates that, in contrast to the Philippines, Thailand viewed reserves from the long-term needs for international transactions point of view and was much less buffeted by the perception of the changing needs of growth under the impact of cyclical shocks from the outside. The standardized foreign exchange reserve ratio consequently exhibits a significantly secular negative trend over both periods, whereas in the Philippines we observe a significantly positive trend during the upturn and a significantly negative trend during the downturn – precisely the pattern corresponding to the case of the hypothetical interventionist government depicted in chapter 2.

Fiscal policy   Thai government deficits were, on the average, higher during the downturn than the upturn, but stabilized after 1976 (figure 5.10(b)). The share of international-trade-related taxes in total taxes continued to fall, the trend significantly negative in both periods of the cycle (see figure 5.9(b)). It is important to note in this context that the total tax/GDP ratio, which had remained stable at relatively respectable levels of more than 11 percent for most of the upturn, actually showed a significantly positive trend during the downturn, reaching almost 14 percent of GDP by 1984 (figure 5.8(b)). It is thus clear that Thailand was substantially more successful than the Philippines in diversifying her product mix and revenue base and managing a reasonably respectable overt resource transfer mechanism in place.

An examination of the levels and trends with regard to the government's budgetary deficit might at first glance suggest a larger degree of fiscal profligacy on the part of the Thai government. However, as suggested in our theoretical framework, it is the manner in which such deficits are financed and the extent to which they lead to attempts at forced saving that determines the character of a government's pursuit of growth activism. It is to these issues that we now turn.

Monetary policy   The downturn in Thailand was initially associated with an acceleration of money supply growth rates, which rose from just under 10 percent in 1974 to 20 percent in 1978 but were then swiftly brought down and – except for a temporary rise in 1984 – remained below 5 percent duirng the eighties (figure 5.11(b)). In contrast to the upturn, when there was a significantly positive trend, there is no trend discernible for the downturn.

Although the money supply growth rate was not much higher, on average, during the downturn as compared to the upturn, the continued increase in velocity – which shows a significantly positive slope during the downturn as well (figure 5.13(b)) – led to higher average rates of inflation relative to the upturn (figure 5.12(b)). However, one may once again note a contrast between Thailand and the Philippines; not only were the levels, on average, lower than in the Philippines, but there was no trend, compared to the significantly positive trend in the Philippines. In fact, in Thailand once inflation threatened to get out of hand, as it did in 1980, it was immediately brought under control and kept below 5 percent during the 1982–85 period (figure 5.12(b)). In the Philippines, as we may recall, while similar levels of inflation were experienced in 1980, the subsequent efforts to control it were much less successful. As in the Philippines, the rate of forced savings extracted by the government – reasonably high at the beginning of the downturn – fell during the eighties and amounted to less than 1 percent after 1981 (see figure 5.14(b)). But, while in the Philippines this reduction was caused largely by the public's response in the form of a rapidly rising velocity, in Thailand it happened because the government was able to rely relatively more on its fiscal resources and borrowing from the nonbank public (see below) and less on deficit financing.

With low rates of inflation, real rates of interest continued to remain positive for most of the downturn. The inflationary shock of the immediate post-1974 period did reduce real rates for a few years initially, but it is especially noteworthy that for the downturn phase as a whole we see a significant increase in the real rate of interest, back to the 7–8 percent level by the early eighties (figure 5.15(b)). Note the sharp contrast with the Philippines.

The gross savings rate held steady during the downturn at an average respectable level of 22–23 percent (figure 5.16(b)). The significantly positive trend of formal savings was, moreover, maintained so that during the eighties, on average, more than one-third of total savings was channeled officially (figure 5.17(b)). This meant that, although total savings did not increase during the downturn, formal savings did, making it easier for the government to finance its deficits via internal debt rather than money creation. This again is in contrast to what was experienced in the Philippines. The differential ability of the monetary authorities to maintain positive and high real interest rates in the two countries thus appears to be reflected in the differential ability to generate formal sector savings.

Exchange rate management and trade policy   In the initial stages of the downturn the Thai currency appreciated as the nominal exchange rate was kept fixed, with inflation exceeding that of Thailand's major trading partners (figure 5.18(b)). The Thai authorities were, however, relatively quick to react and adjusted the baht by 10 percent in 1982.

Thus, while in the Philippines a more or less overvalued exchange rate was consistently used to transfer rents from natural-resource-oriented exporters to others, notably the government and import-substituting industrialists, in Thailand the government seems to have refrained from extensive use of this particular tool of covert income transfers – even though the (albeit milder) primary import-substitution subphase of transition probably extended well into the sixties here. Moreover, the levels of protection as measured here were higher than in the Philippines initially, but there was also a significantly negative trend in evidence during the downturn (figure 5.19(b)). Between 1974 and 1978 effective protection rates probably increased as tariff rates on capital and intermediate goods were reduced while those on finished consumer goods were not affected. Nevertheless, the tariff system was better harmonized than in the Philippines; de Rosa's (1986) findings that Thailand's overall average effective tariff rates of 26 percent in 1983 compared favorably not only with 30 percent for the Philippines, but also, and perhaps surprisingly, with 33 percent for South Korea, remain significant for our comparative purposes.

The labor market   As can be seen from figures 5.21(a) and (b), there is a difference in the degree of incidence of labor unrest between the two countries, with that phenomenon much less pronounced in Thailand, apart from a brief period in the early seventies, than in the Philippines. However, the Philippines, in turn, does better than most Latin American countries, reflecting the relatively lower levels of inflation experienced there.

To summarize, we observe significant differences in policy behavior between Thailand and the Philippines, with the differences most pronounced during the downturn. In contrast to the Philippines, where the government indulged in a self-defeating countercyclical effort to maintain growth, the Thai government responded to similar external shocks in a more pragmatic manner. Consequently, growth rates were permitted to fall, but moderately, compared to their ultimately drastic decline in the Philippines. Such a policy stance enabled Thailand to weather the external shocks without interrupting the course of a relatively steady liberalization in various markets. Although government deficits were higher, there was greater monetary restraint and less external borrowing. Consequently, inflation was low and confidence in the continuity of government policies high.

More specifically, in contrast to the Philippines, the Thai government clearly showed a greater willingness to effect resource transfers through overt means – the tax/GDP ratio continued to rise, the real rate of interest remained positive, and the exchange rate was not allowed to deviate too much from competitive levels. Such pragmatism and flexibility enabled Thailand to remain on a clear external orientation and competitive markets trend, instead of encountering stop-go fluctuations around an uncertain trend as in the Philippines. Consequently, despite its relatively late start, Thailand has been substantially outpacing the Philippines in terms of overall development performance, with the result that it is now considered to be the next NIE to share the international spotlight with the "four tigers" while the Philippines has been left in the dust – both in terms of levels of achievement to date in the growth-cum-equity arena as well as prospects for change in the years ahead.

5.5 Conclusions

The comparative empirical analysis of these two Southeast Asian countries thus indicates that, although they are geographic neighbors, the pattern of their policy evolution and their responses to similar shocks has been markedly different. There was a relatively more "steady-as-you-go" aspect to Thailand's policies over time, with substantially more oscillations in evidence in the Philippines. Moreover, there was clearly a pronounced tendency on the part of the government in the Philippines to use covert means of resource transfers while its counterpart in Thailand did not shy away as much from the politically difficult task of transferring resources through "on-the-table" policy measures. The explanation for these differences in behavior can be undoubtedly traced in part to the different composition and distribution of their natural resource endowments, i.e., more equally distributed rice land in Thailand versus more concentrated traditional crops in the Philippines.

Moreover, while their relative importance cannot be parsed econometrically, the differing degrees of initial organic nationalism undoubtedly also played an important role. As Oshima (1983) has pointed out, "despite frequent military coups, the strength of the Thai monarchy . . . served as the rallying point for national unity and social cohesion." The stable monarchy that reigned and a core of technocrats that ruled under a military umbrella imparted a degree of continuity and consistency for both the political and economic spheres, which was often obscured by frequent changes in the composition of the cabinet at the political level. Indeed, the very frequency of these changes may have inhibited the development of the very kind of "crony capitalism" that has constituted a particularly poignant feature of the Philippine landscape. One reason why Thailand has been less subjected to oscillations in policy around an uncertain trend has been the very ability of government to be less influenced by the need to cater to the immediate economic interests of politically influential groups or individuals. The synthetic nationalism of the Philippines, in contrast, resulting from its substantial geographic, cultural, religious, and language diversity, resulted in a more oscillatory path with lower growth and much less equity. As in the Latin American countries studied in chapter 3, considerable pressure has existed for adopting populist expansionary slogans and political maneuverings in place of long-term steady-as-you-go policies. Here technocrats were more likely to be used by rent-seeking politicians for purposes of international "cover" and continuity. Given Philippine diversity it has proven consistently difficult to formulate and adhere to a national social contract enabling the system to mobilize its considerable human and natural resources in the service of some agreed set of development objectives.

Figure 5.1 External terms of trade (percent deviation from trend)

(a)

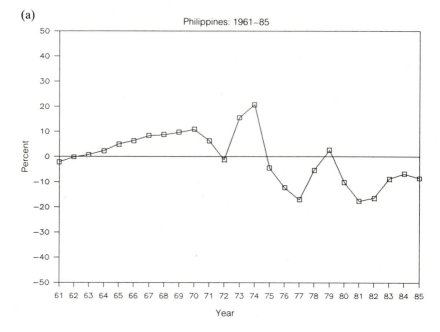

Philippines: 1961–85

(b)

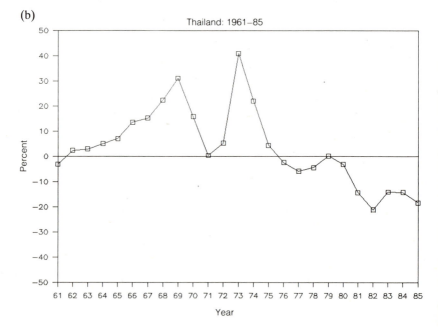

Thailand: 1961–85

Figure 5.2   External terms of trade (percent deviation from trend)

(a)

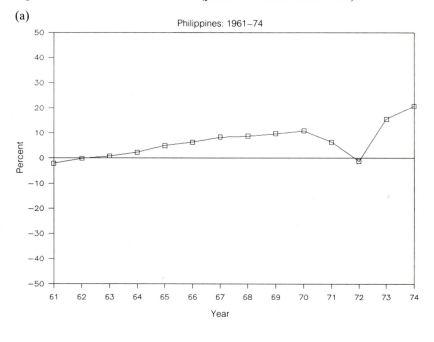

Philippines: 1961–74

(b)

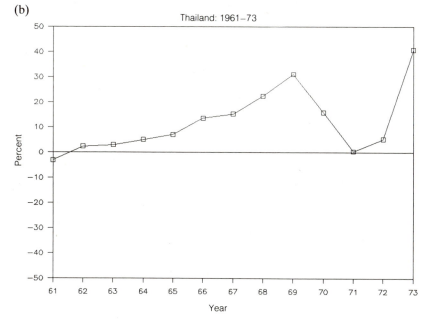

Thailand: 1961–73

Figure 5.3 External terms of trade (percent deviation from trend)

(a)

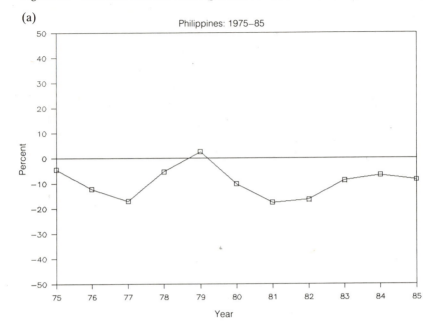

Philippines: 1975–85

(b)

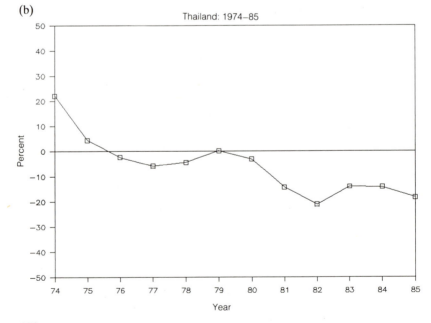

Thailand: 1974–85

190

Figure 5.4 Annual rate of growth of real GDP

(a)

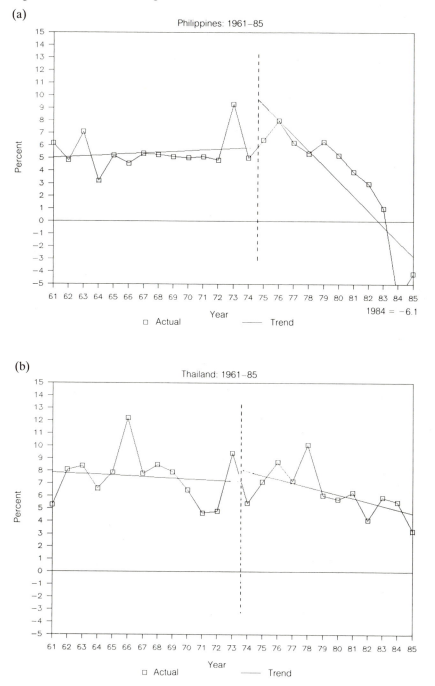

Philippines: 1961–85

1984 = −6.1

Year

□ Actual ——— Trend

(b)

Thailand: 1961–85

Year

□ Actual ——— Trend

Figure 5.5   Exports/GDP

(a)

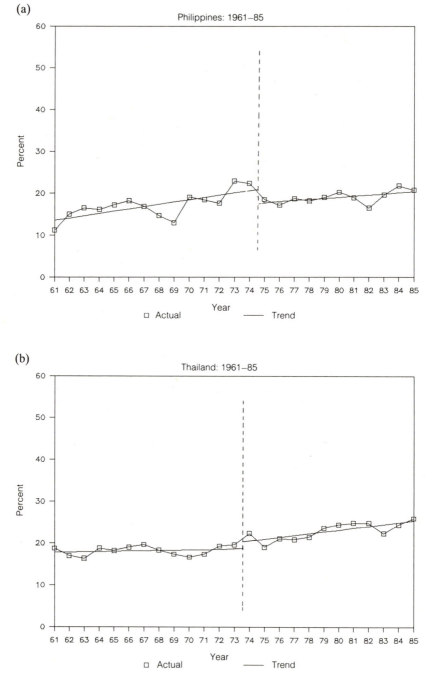

Philippines: 1961–85

(b)

Thailand: 1961–85

192

Figure 5.6   Trade balance/GDP

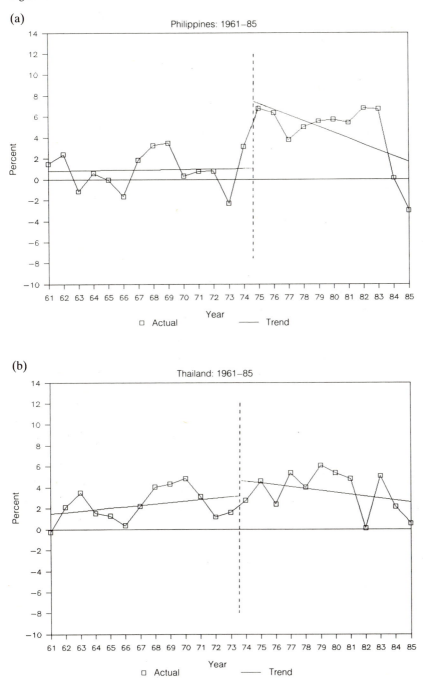

(a) Philippines: 1961–85

(b) Thailand: 1961–85

Figure. 5.7   Foreign exchange reserves/four months' imports

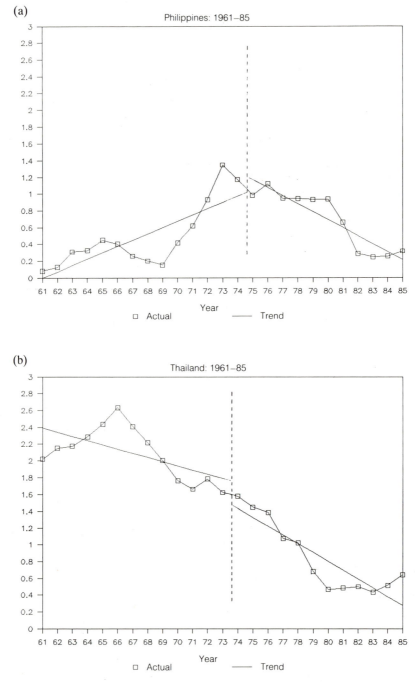

(a)

Philippines: 1961–85

(b)

Thailand: 1961–85

194

Figure 5.8 Total taxes/GDP

(a)

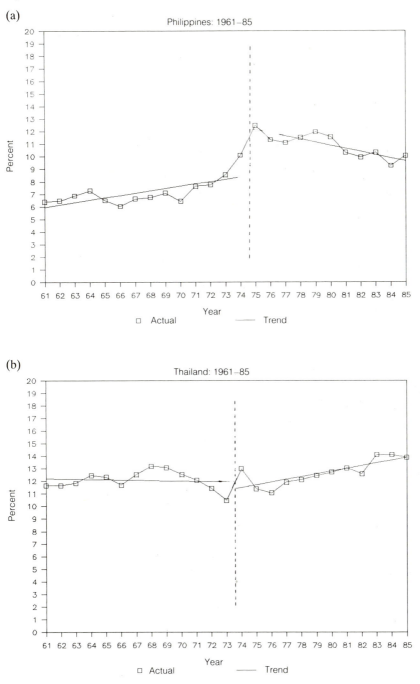

Philippines: 1961–85

(b)

Thailand: 1961–85

Figure 5.9   International trade taxes/total taxes

(a)

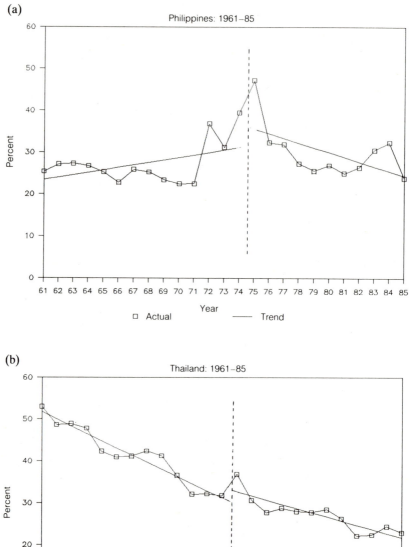

(b)

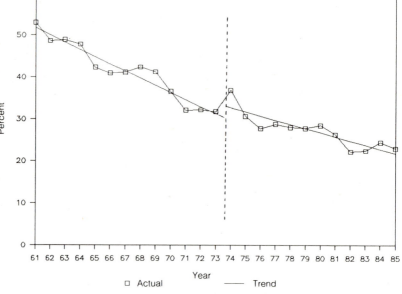

196

Figure 5.10   Government deficits/GDP

(a)

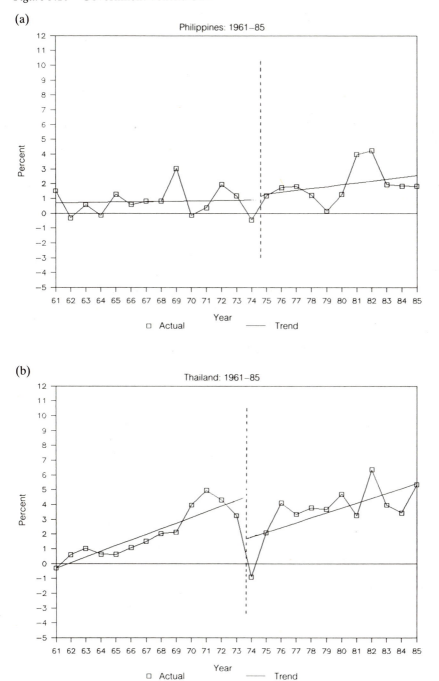

Philippines: 1961–85

□ Actual   —— Trend

(b)

Thailand: 1961–85

□ Actual   —— Trend

Figure 5.11   Annual rate of change of money supply

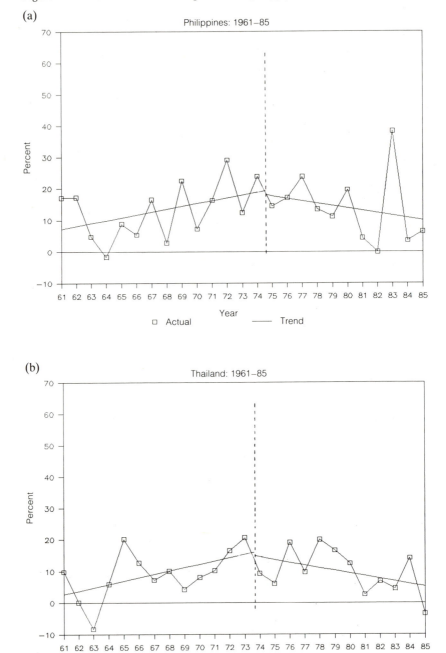

(a)

Philippines: 1961–85

(b)

Thailand: 1961–85

198

Figure 5.12   Annual rate of inflation

(a)

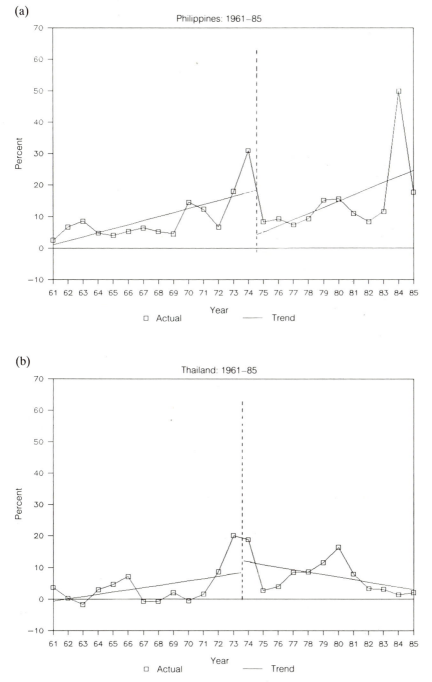

(b)

199

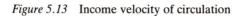

Figure 5.13　　Income velocity of circulation

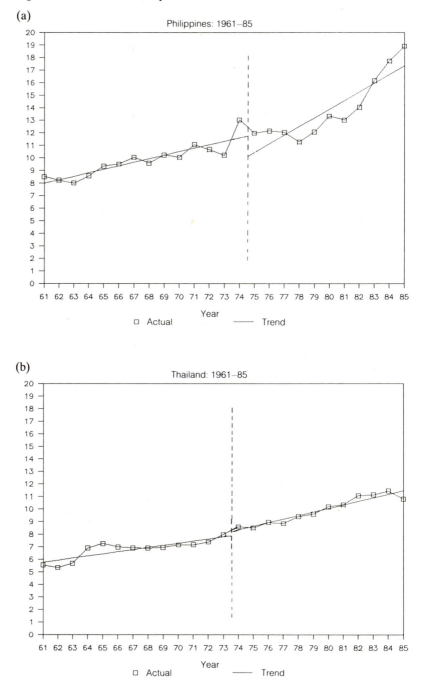

(a)

Philippines: 1961–85

Year

□　Actual　　　——　Trend

(b)

Thailand: 1961–85

Year

□　Actual　　　——　Trend

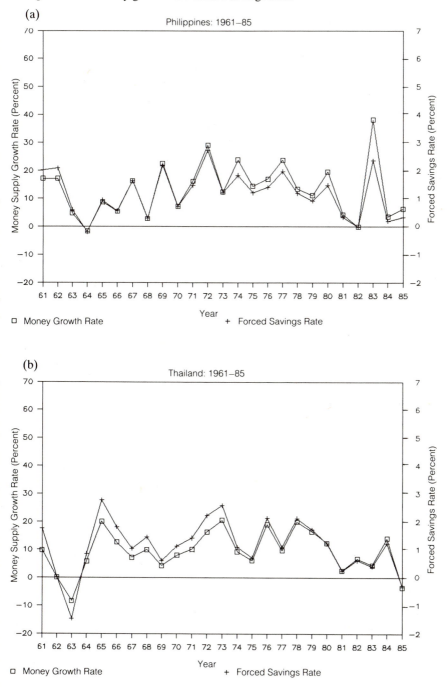

Figure 5.14 Money growth and forced savings rates

(a)

Philippines: 1961–85

(b)

Thailand: 1961–85

Figure 5.15 Real rate of interest

(a)

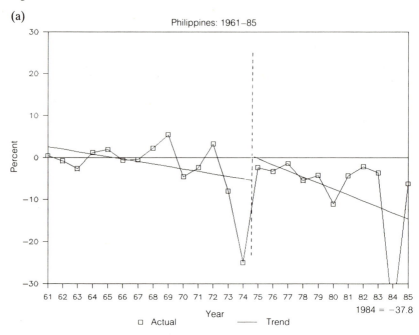

Philippines: 1961–85

□ Actual   —— Trend

1984 = −37.8

(b)

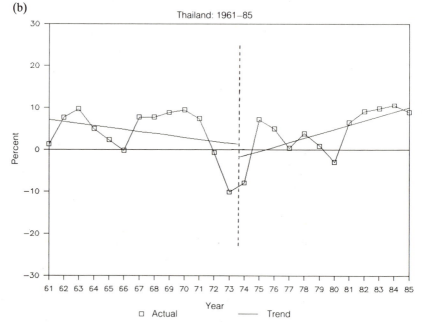

Thailand: 1961–85

□ Actual   —— Trend

Figure 5.16   Gross domestic savings/GDP

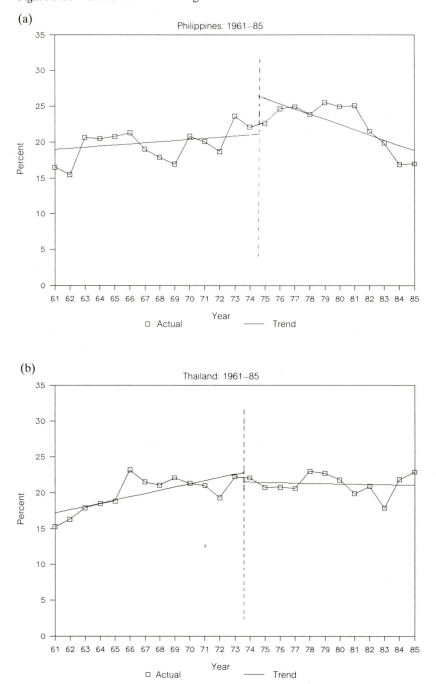

Figure 5.17   Change in savings deposits/gross savings

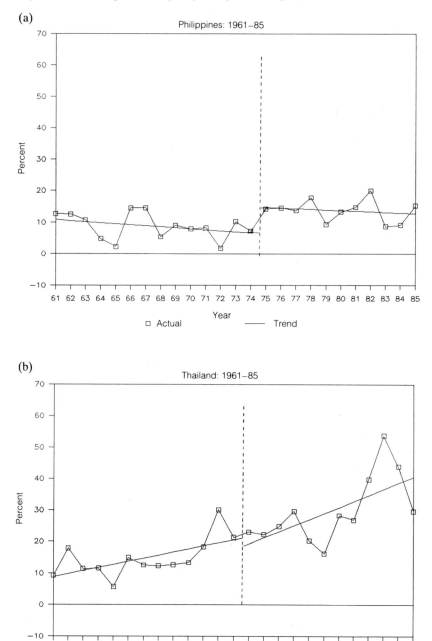

Figure 5.18   Index of real exchange rate (1980 = 100)

(a)

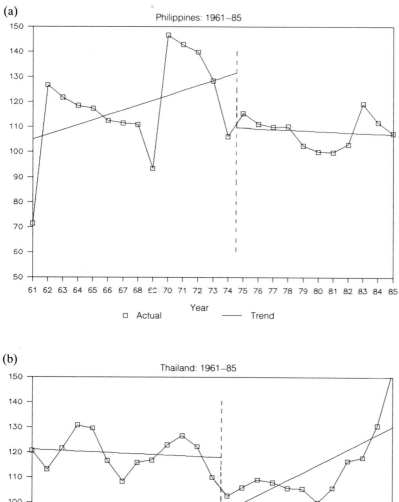

Philippines: 1961–85

Year

□   Actual   —— Trend

(b)

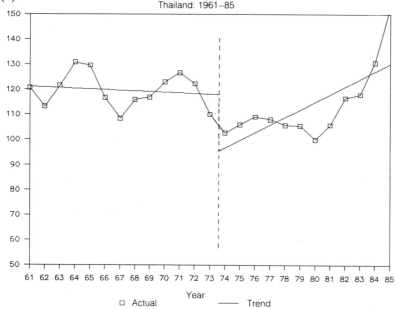

Thailand: 1961–85

Year

□   Actual   —— Trend

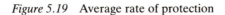

Figure 5.19   Average rate of protection

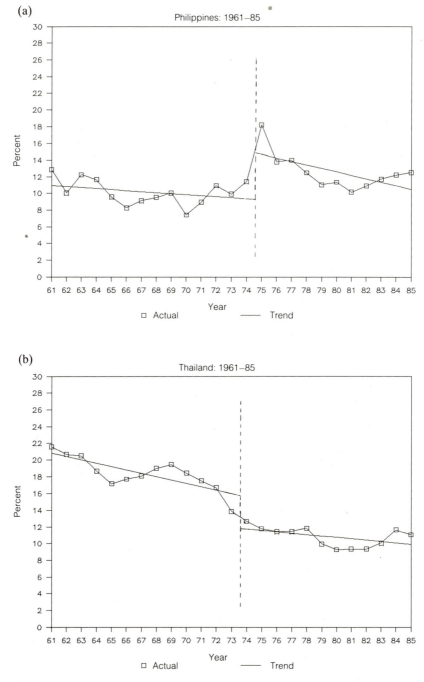

Figure 5.20 Net inflow of long-term foreign capital/GDP

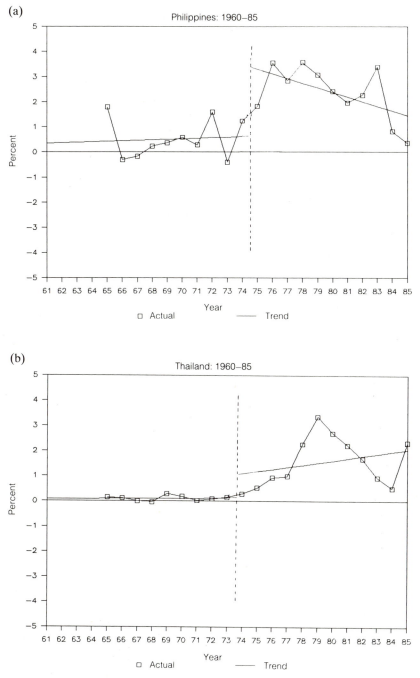

(a)

Philippines: 1960–85

(b)

Thailand: 1960–85

207

Figure 5.21   Index of labor disputes

(a)

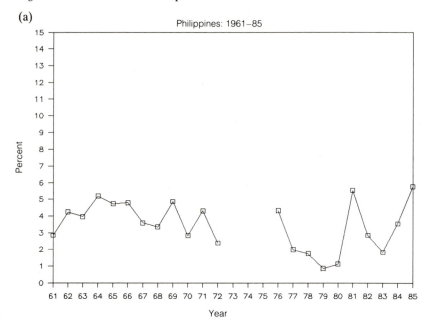

(b)

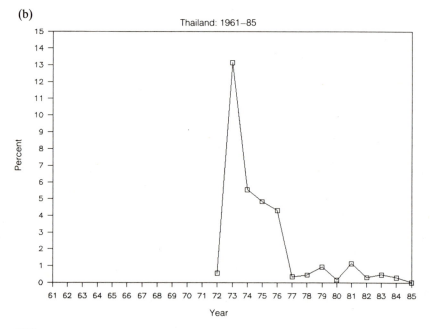

Appendix

Definition of variables

(definitions not spelled out for self-evident variables)

External terms of trade = Unit value of exports divided by unit value of imports

Exports = Exports of goods and services

Imports = Imports of goods and services

Trade balance = Imports minus exports

International trade taxes = Export duties plus import duties

Government deficits = Central government deficits excluding public enterprise accounts

Money supply = M1

Annual rate of inflation = Rate of change in GDP deflator

Income velocity of circulation = $(P_t \cdot Q_{t-1})/M_{t-1}$, where

P = price level

Q = nominal GDP

M = money supply (M1)

t = time

Forced savings rate = $(dM/dt)/PQ$, where

dM/dt = change in money supply

PQ = nominal GDP

Real rate of interest = Nominal central bank discount rate minus the annual rate of inflation

Savings deposits = Time, savings, and foreign currency deposits

Real exchange rates = Real exchange rates are derived from nominal exchange rates and relative wholesale price ratios of the five major trading partners using trade shares as weights.

Average rate of protection = Import taxes divided by total imports of goods and services

Index of labor disputes = Total number of workers involved in industrial disputes as percentage of total industrial employment

Data sources: The Philippines

Variable and Source

Unit values of exports and imports: IMF, *International Financial Statistics,* Yearbook, 1988

Real GDP: IMF, *International Financial Statistics,* Yearbook, 1988

Exports of goods and services: IMF, *International Financial Statistics,* Yearbook, 1988

Imports of goods and services: IMF,

International Financial Statistics, Yearbook, 1988

Foreign exchange reserves: IMF, *International Financial Statistics,* Yearbook, 1988

Total taxes, import taxes, and export duties: IMF, *Government Finance Statistics,* 1982, 1985, 1988 (for post-1972 data); *Philippine Statistical Yearbook,* various issues (for pre-1972 data)

Government deficits: IMF, *International Financial Statistics,* Yearbook, 1988

Money supply: IMF, *International Financial Statistics,* Yearbook, 1988

GDP deflator: IMF, *International Financial Statistics,* Yearbook, 1988

Nominal rate of interest: IMF, *International Financial Statistics,* Yearbook, 1988

Gross domestic savings: Computed from data in IMF, *International Financial Statistics,* Yearbook, 1988

Time, savings, and foreign currency deposits: IMF, *International Financial Statistics,* Yearbook, 1988

Real exchange rate: Computed from data in IMF, *International Financial Statistics,* Yearbook 1988; and IMF, *Direction of Trade Statistics,* various issues

Net inflow of long-term foreign capital: World Bank, *World Debt Tables,* various issues

Number of workers involved in industrial disputes and total industrial employment: ILO, *International Labour Statistics,* various issues

Data sources: Thailand

Variable and Source

Unit values of exports and imports: IMF, *International Financial Statistics,* Yearbook, 1988

Real GDP: IMF, *International Financial Statistics,* Yearbook, 1988

Exports of goods and services: IMF, *International Financial Statistics,* Yearbook, 1988

Imports of goods and services: IMF, *International Financial Statistics,* Yearbook, 1988

Foreign exchange reserves: IMF, *International Financial Statistics,* Yearbook, 1988

Total taxes, import taxes, and export duties: IMF, *Government Finance Statistics,* 1982, 1985, 1988 (for post-1972 data); *Statistical Yearbook of Thailand,* various issues (for pre-1972 data)

Government deficits: IMF, *International Financial Statistics,* Yearbook, 1988

Money supply: IMF, *International Financial Statistics,* Yearbook, 1988

GDP deflator: IMF, *International Financial Statistics,* Yearbook, 1988

Nominal rate of interest: IMF, *International Financial Statistics,* Yearbook, 1988

Gross domestic savings: Computed from data in IMF, *International Financial Statistics,* Yearbook, 1988

Time, savings, and foreign currency deposits: IMF, *International Financial Statistics,* Yearbook, 1988

Real exchange rate: Computed from data in IMF, *International Financial Statistics,* Yearbook 1988; and IMF,

Direction of Trade Statistics, various issues

Net inflow of long-term foreign capital: World Bank, *World Debt Tables,* various issues

Number of workers involved in industrial disputes and total industrial employment: ILO, *International Labour Statistics,* various issues

Significance of trend lines: Philippines

NS = Not significant
+++ = Significantly positive at the 98 percent level of confidence
++ = Significantly positive at the 95 percent level of confidence
+ = Significantly positive at the 90 percent level of confidence
--- = Significantly negative at the 98 percent level of confidence
-- = Significantly negative at the 95 percent level of confidence
- = Significantly negative at the 90 percent level of confidence

Variable	1961–74	1975–85
External terms of trade (deviations from trend)	++	--
Annual rate of growth of real GDP	NS	--
Exports/GDP	NS	+++
Trade balance/GDP	NS	---
Foreign exchange reserves/four months' imports	+++	---
Total taxes/GDP	+++	--
International trade taxes/total taxes	+++	--
Government deficits/GDP	NS	++
Annual rate of change of money supply	NS	--
Annual rate of inflation	+++	NS
Income velocity of circulation	+++	+++
Real rate of interest	-	NS
Gross domestic savings/GDP	+	---
Change in savings deposits/gross savings	---	---
Real exchange rate	NS	NS
Average rate of protection	NS	--
Net inflow of long-term foreign capital	NS	-

Significance of trend lines: Thailand

NS = Not significant
+++ = Significantly positive at the 98 percent level of confidence
++ = Significantly positive at the 95 percent level of confidence
+ = Significantly positive at the 90 percent level of confidence
--- = Significantly negative at the 98 percent level of confidence
-- = Significantly negative at the 95 percent level of confidence
- = Significantly negative at the 90 percent level of confidence

Variable-1961–73		1974–85
External terms of trade (deviations from trend)	+ +	− −
Annual Rate of growth of real GDP	NS	NS
Exports/GDP	NS	+ + +
Trade balance/GDP	NS	NS
Foreign exchange reserves/four months' imports	− −	− − −
Total taxes/GDP	NS	+ + +
International trade taxes/total taxes	− − −	− − −
Government deficits/GDP	+ + +	+
Annual rate of change of money supply	+ +	NS
Annual rate of inflation	NS	NS
Income velocity of circulation	+ + +	+ + +
Real rate of interest	NS	+ +
Gross domestic savings/GDP	+ + +	NS
Change in savings deposits gross savings	+	+
Real exchange rate	NS	+ + +
Average rate of protection	− − −	−
Net inflow of long-term foreign capital	NS	NS

6

Summary and Conclusions

6.1 Introduction

The methodology we have brought to bear in this volume is most aptly labeled comparative analytical economic history. This chapter presents a brief defense of that approach in relation to other recent analytical efforts and then proceeds to a brief summary of our findings and conclusions.

Our effort has been focused on the investigation of differential patterns of growth in different parts of the developing world as they move out of their infant industry protection subphase and are impacted by largely similar exogenous shocks. As our laboratory, we have traced the performance of our six countries through essentially one complete cycle of relatively favorable and unfavorable external shocks and not tried systematically to update their experiences to this point in time, i.e., the 1986–90 period of post–debt crisis adjustment efforts is not explicitly dealt with. However, to the extent we can perceive the makings of a real, secular break with the past, e.g., in the case of Mexico during recent years, this may be most conveniently thought of as a shift to the East Asian pattern of development.

As is well known, in the early postwar period investigations into the development process may be characterized as having started with the notion that there exists a "typical" developing country whose expected performance over time can be captured by cross-sectional research across all such systems at varying levels of per capita income, with deviations from this pattern left to as yet undefined additional analysis. Increasingly, such work, largely by Chenery and his associates, shifted from an all-inclusive effort to understand the pattern of transition growth for all countries to a differentiation by countries' typological characteristics, on the one hand, and the increased use of the LDC historical laboratory as a complement to the cross-sectional analysis, on the other. Kuznets' seminal work in describing modern economic growth relied more heavily on the eyeballing of statistics in contrast to Chenery's more sophisticated regression analysis and was from the beginning much more characterized by the utilization of historical materials in the "magnificent dynamics" tradition of the classical school. Other, more recent, strands of relevant research include the optimizing individual country CGE model approach as well as even more recent efforts in the so-called "new growth theory" arena to seek an explanation of country performance divergence in terms of externalities of various types.

The methodology deployed in this volume is clearly to be located closest to the Kuznetsian tradition. It does have a substantial deductive component in the sense that it begins with some theoretical structure derived from macroeconomic development theory, whether of neoclassical or classical origins; but it is clearly also inductive in the sense that it bases itself on an analysis of the comparative economic history of developing countries, focusing on different subcategories or types of developing countries in the search for regularities.

Such a methodology is certainly casual when compared to deterministic models, on the one hand, or timeless cross-sectional econometric analysis, on the other. Nevertheless, we believe it to be potentially much richer in terms of gaining a better understanding of underlying behavior. It is more likely to take us down the road to the sort of modeling that economists much prefer, i.e., toward the point where patterns established in the past can be used for predictive purposes once the same or similar initial conditions are given. This latter point provides the basis for the "three-by-two" comparative approach that we have used in this volume, i.e., the effort not only to isolate the main dimensions of the three subcategories or typologies offered up but also to compare the two members of each of these subgroups for which the initial conditions are not too much at variance.

Comparative analytical economic history represents a form of purposive or inductive story telling. This is indeed what renders the approach admittedly rather casual. But if the story proves to be both interesting and persuasive and manages to encompass key aspects of behavior, it may also amount to the beginnings of wisdom in moving us toward a more rigorous explanation of the observed differentiation of behavior, perhaps as well as some of the other methods that have been cited. Of course our approach can be criticized for its failure to allow for alternative interpretations of the same story, for skirting some issues, and omitting some counterexamples. But while a more refined use of the economist's impressive analytical apparatus may serve to obscure this fact, such blemishes are by no means peculiar to the comparative analytical economic history approach, i.e., we indeed are a long way from a value-free science deploying any of the approaches that have been mentioned. Nor do we believe in the necessity of making either/or choices. It would indeed be our hope that more rigorous theoretical as well as econometric methods can eventually be married to our proposed line of reasoning.

Our attempt in this volume has thus been to tell reasonably plausible stories about six developing countries, divided into three subpairs each representing larger families, if not the entire spectrum of Third World types. In chapter 2 we endeavored to construct an analytical scaffolding to help us organize these stories within a coherent, political-economy-tinged causal framework. We are convinced that much can be learned by comparing the responses across these three families, as well as differences among members of each, to similar exogenous shocks. Whether or not we have been persuasive will ultimately depend on the eating of the pudding presented.

6.2 Some general findings

The analysis of development policy change carried out in chapters 3–5 has highlighted interfamily differences in the pattern of policy evolution within three distinct types of LDCs. While differences *within* each of these families are also instructive – and occasionally provide an especially strong test for the usefulness of our methodology – the more significant differences in behavior are clearly those that are demonstrated to exist *between,* rather than *within,* families. In this concluding chapter, we intend to summarize these findings, render the family-specific features more explicit, and attempt to draw lessons from observed differential behavior, with an eye to providing some guidelines for future policy reform. Average values for the main policy variables we have been focusing on for our six countries in both the "good" and "bad" periods are presented in table 6.1 for overview convenience.

The reader should notice that the most significant interfamily difference in the long-run pattern of policy behavior revealed by our comparative empirical work resides in the marked contrast between the more or less linear trend of depoliticization of policy making observed in the East Asian countries and the more oscillatory pattern of policy evolution in the Latin American cases over the period of observation. In the East Asian countries substantial depoliticization occurred on all fronts, although not simultaneously, and the movement gained momentum through time in small cumulative steps rather than by the large leaps and bounds that have all too frequently characterized policy evolution in Latin America historically and often implied policy fluctuation and reversal. The Southeast Asian case once again seems to be intermediate in this context.

A good illustration of the gradual but steady depoliticization of various markets in some sequential order is provided by the case of Taiwan between 1950 and 1985 (see figure 6.1). In the international trade sector, for example, customs duty rebates on exports (1956) were later complemented by the establishment of export-processing zones (1966). The

Table 6.1 Policy variables, average values

Variable	Mexico		Colombia		Philippines		Thailand		South Korea		Taiwan	
	1	2	1	2	1	2	1	2	1	2	1	2
Rate of growth of real GDP (%)	7.0	4.5	5.7	3.6	5.4	3.2	7.5	6.3	9.6	8.2	9.1	8.0
Exports/GDP (%)	9.2	12.6	14.2	13.4	17.1	19.1	18.2	22.9	11.1	32.5	19.4	50.4
Trade balance/GDP (%)	0.8	-1.6	-0.3	0.6	0.9	4.5	2.3	3.5	9.8	3.9	2.8	-4.1
Foreign exchange reserves/four months' imports	0.6	0.6	0.8	1.9	0.5	0.7	2.1	0.8	0.8	0.4	1.0	0.9
Total taxes/GDP (%)	7.8	13.6	9.9	9.9	7.2	10.9	12.1	12.7	9.7	14.9	11.2	15.4
International trade taxes/total taxes (%)	21.9	15.2	23.3	20.0	27.3	29.9	41.5	27.3	19.0	16.6	27.6	24.4
Government deficits/GDP (%)	2.1	6.0	0.8	2.7	0.8	1.9	2.0	3.6	0.9	1.8	-0.5	-1.3
Annual rate of growth of money supply (%)	13.2	36.9	22.6	23.2	13.0	13.8	9.0	9.8	28.2	23.6	18.8	24.4
Annual rate of inflation (%)	4.8	37.6	16.6	22.7	9.3	14.9	3.6	7.4	16.6	15.9	4.2	8.8
Income velocity of money	8.7	13.0	7.3	9.1	9.8	13.9	6.8	9.9	12.0	10.5	7.5	4.9
Real rate of interest (%)	5.0	-6.6	-2.7	4.7	-2.1	-4.7	4.4	4.3	2.1	-5.1	6.9	0.4
Savings/GDP (%)	18.5	25.2	19.4	18.6	19.6	22.5	19.9	21.3	11.4	25.4	19.4	31.2
Change in savings deposits/total savings (%)	12.9	25.8	8.6	24.7	8.7	13.7	14.7	29.9	40.4	19.2	25.4	37.7
Forced savings rate (%)	1.5	2.8	3.1	2.8	1.3	1.0	1.2	1.0	2.4	2.3	2.3	4.9
Real exchange rates (1980 = 100)	115.0	120.3	126.9	107.6	117.7	108.2	119.7	113.4	114.0	115.2	116.8	113.9
Average rate of protection (%)	12.4	7.3	10.6	10.6	10.1	12.6	18.4	10.8	8.3	6.9	14.0	8.2

1: period of favorable shocks
2: period of unfavorable shocks

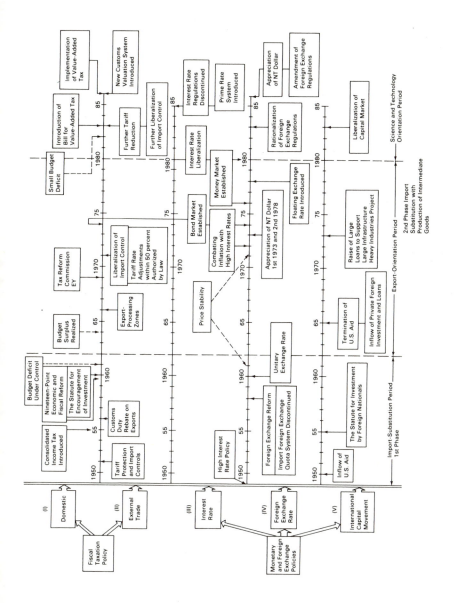

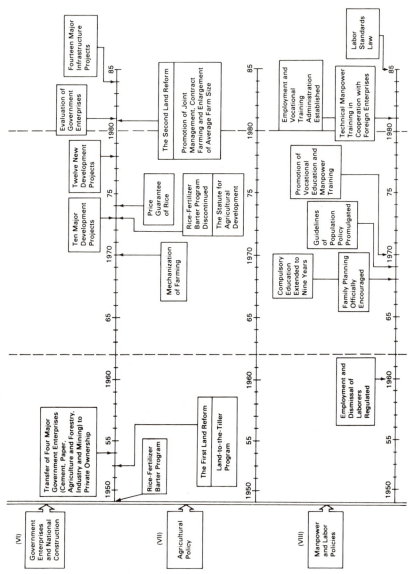

(VI)

Government Enterprises and National Construction

Transfer of Four Major Government Enterprises (Cement, Paper, Agriculture and Forestry, Industry and Mining) to Private Ownership

Evaluation of Government Enterprises

Fourteen Major Infrastructure Projects

Ten Major Development Projects

Twelve New Development Projects

(VII)

Agricultural Policy

Rice-Fertilizer Barter Program

The First Land Reform

Land-to-the-Tiller Program

Mechanization of Farming

Price Guarantee of Rice

Rice-Fertilizer Barter Program Discontinued

The Statute for Agricultural Development

The Second Land Reform

Promotion of Joint Management, Contract Farming and Enlargement of Average Farm Size

(VIII)

Manpower and Labor Policies

Employment and Dismissal of Laborers Regulated

Compulsory Education Extended to Nine Years

Family Planning Officially Encouraged

Guidelines of Population Policy Promulgated

Promotion of Vocational Education and Manpower Training

Employment and Vocational Training Administration Established

Technical Manpower Training in Cooperation with Foreign Enterprises

Labor Standards Law

1950 55 1960 65 1970 75 1980 85

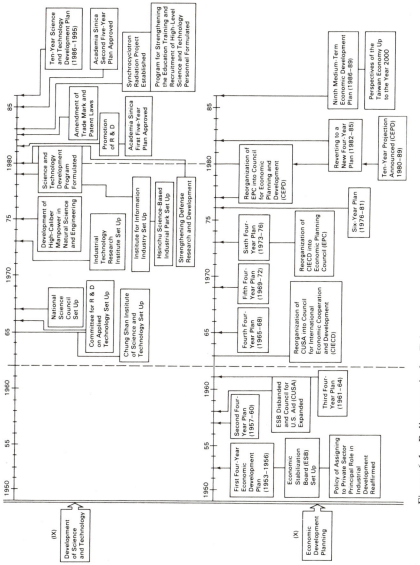

Figure 6.1 Policy matrix for Taiwan economy

related liberalization of import controls took the shape of some early shift from QRs to tariffs but did not gain momentum until 1971. Not until the mid-eighties did the system clearly appeal to a new ideology, that of the principle of international competition not only in foreign but also in domestic markets – a far cry from the xenophobic and autarkic appeal of the earlier import-substitution era. Another example is provided by the evolution of tax reform measures (consolidated income tax introduced in 1955, followed by comprehensive tax reforms in 1970 and the introduction of a VAT in 1983), all adopted in order to broaden the tax base in response to threats of a budget deficit and shift the burden from agriculture to nonagriculture-based activities. (More on this below.) Suffice it to note here that an examination of the policy changes not only legislated but implemented over time in such a (successful) case also provides us with hints as to desirable, if not necessarily optimal, patterns for the sequencing of reforms.

The contrasting stop-and-go trend in external monetary management in the Latin American type of LDC is especially instructive. In the Philippines, for instance, we observed a clearly oscillating pattern of trade liberalization and exchange rate management: devaluation (1962) and decontrol (1960–65), followed by the reimposition of controls (1967), devaluation (1970), decontrol (1980–81), the renewed reimposition of controls (1983) and, finally, devaluation once again (1983–84). A similar pattern was observed in Mexico, particularly during the relatively more volatile downturn period of 1974–85. There we observed increased controls (1974), followed by a floating of the peso and depreciation (1976), increased controls in the form of higher QRs (1977), a reduction of QRs (1978–80), another increase in QRs (1981–82), a major devaluation (1982), and trade liberalization (1984). In Colombia, where oscillations were, in general, less pronounced, the trend toward trade liberalization, initiated in 1967, was maintained over a longer period but ultimately also reversed, during 1982–84.

The roots of these contrasting patterns of a more or less linear depoliticization trend in East Asia and oscillations around an unclear trend in Latin America can, we believe, be traced to the differential extent of growth activism and the consequent differential response to roughly similar exogenous shocks. In our East Asian cases we observed, in general, a greater tendency to allow growth to follow a more or less "natural" path, i.e., one dictated by the resource endowments and technological capabilities of systems as they respond to the inevitable exogenous shocks. This behavior pattern can be most clearly observed in the case of Taiwan, where policymakers responded to both major oil shocks by allowing growth to drop temporarily before recovery set in. Consequently, sustained high-level growth was soon resumed. Although behavior was less consistent in South Korea, deviations from trend there were also relatively moderate and, moreover, were corrected without long delays. In short, the fact that growth rates continued, on average, to be unusually high in both these economies is attributable to policymakers resisting the temptation to promote growth artificially, instead adjusting to temporarily adverse conditions and consequently placing themselves in a better position to exploit their human resources and harness their technological capabilities over time.

In contrast, the analysis of policy behavior in our Latin American countries, especially Mexico, revealed a tendency toward excessive activism during good times, with desperate attempts to maintain growth when times were relatively bad. Within the "intermediate" Southeast Asian family we observed a typically Latin American behavior pattern in the Philippines and an approximation to the East Asian pattern in Thailand. Thus, as the experiences of Mexico and the Philippines in our sample demonstrate most vividly, the strategy of growth activism ultimately proves self-defeating since it inevitably leads to sharp forced reversals in performance, including prolonged periods of low or even negative growth. In other words, the interventionist "Latin American" pattern is a more unstable one, with sharp fluctuations in performance, compared to the much greater stability of the "East Asian" case.

One important indicator of the underlying character of policy behavior is the manner in which growth is financed. As argued in chapter 2, a critical distinguishing characteristic of policy is not just the size of the overall tax effort but also the relative reliance on overt versus covert means of transferring resources from one group in society to another. The empirical results presented in this volume reveal substantial interfamily differences in these respects. To wit, we clearly found a pronounced greater tendency in our East Asian countries, and to some extent in Thailand, for governments to finance their expenditures through explicit taxation, in contrast to the Latin American cases. The tax/GDP ratios of Taiwan, South Korea, and Thailand were not only considerably higher initially than those of Mexico, Colombia, and the Philippines, but remained so throughout; only Mexico caught up during the late seventies and eighties. Moreover, in both East Asian countries, and in Thailand, the tax/GDP ratio showed a significantly positive slope even during bad times, whereas elsewhere, e.g., in Colombia and the Philippines, a significantly positive trend during good times gave way to no trend or a negative trend when times were bad.

It may also be noted that in the East Asian countries the tax/GDP ratio increased consistently despite a steady fall in the relative importance of international-trade-related taxes. This suggests that, over time, these countries were able to diversify their export tax effort by moving away from a regime in which primary producers and consumers carry the heaviest burden. In contrast, countries such as Colombia and the Philippines, while also reducing the role of international-trade-related taxes, failed to compensate for the decline in these taxes by diversifying their overall tax base, resulting in a slowing down of increases in the tax/GDP ratio, as in Colombia, or an actual reversal, as in the Philippines.

Tax efforts must, of course, be viewed in conjunction with government expenditure patterns. Mexico, for example, showed a steadily increasing tax/GDP ratio after the early seventies, but this is much less impressive when viewed against the backdrop of a rapid increase in government expenditures, giving rise to huge budgetary deficits. Such failure to finance escalating government expenditures through increased recourse to explicit taxation implied increasing reliance on implicit, i.e., inflationary, taxation. But even if budget deficits were not always smaller in the East Asian prototype – for example, Thailand had a larger deficit compared to the Philippines on average – the degree to which they were monetized differed systematically. East Asia was characterized by relatively lower rates of money creation as well as a differential response by the public to inflationary trends, reflected in differential levels and trends of velocity.

The more interventionist pattern of policy behavior in Latin America was seen to be associated with the greater tendency on the part of the government to use covert means to transfer resources, not only from the rest of society to itself, but also from one group to another. The major mechanisms for such resource transfers have been negative real interest rates and overvalued exchange rates. While the East Asian countries, plus Thailand, succeeded in maintaining positive real interest rates for most of the period under study, in Mexico and the Philippines, and to a lesser extent in Colombia, negative real rates were a common feature. This was not only due to higher rates of inflation, resulting from the enhanced monetization of government deficits in these countries, but also to the relative inflexibility of nominal interest rate management. The prolonged existence of negative real rates of interest, in turn, inevitably discouraged formal savings. This made it difficult for the government to finance its expenditures through internal borrowing, rendering it even more reliant, by necessity, on money creation and external borrowing.

Such excessive and prolonged reliance on the covert means of resource transfer is indicative of the fundamental inability of government to adopt polices that may be economically superior but politically more difficult. The same relative lack of political courage or inability to override interest group resistance may be found in the observed tendency, time and again, to postpone politically difficult decisions until it is very late in the day – when the remedy required is all the more extreme and difficult to swallow. This was particularly evident in the area of external monetary management where, in each country, the initial response to a deterioration in the trade balance invariably took the form of the reimposition or intensification of existing controls on imports rather than a devaluation of the usually substantially overvalued domestic currency. It was only when external imbalances had reached critical proportions and no other alternative was available that governments resorted to devaluation, which, because of the delays, now usually had to be carried out on a rather dramatic scale.

The tendency to push growth beyond its "natural" levels and finance such growth activism through covert rather than overt means thus lies at the root of the long-run oscillatory pattern of policy evolution observed in the Latin American type. Liberalization efforts, often initiated at the beginning of an upturn, could not be sustained as the improvement in the external environment encouraged governments to expand expenditures, financing them through money creation that inevitably led to inflation and balance-of-payments crises; this, in turn, given the reluctance of governments to adopt politically unpopular policy changes in time, was dealt with first by reimposing controls and ultimately by having to accept more severe changes in relative prices. On the other hand, as the experience of the East Asian type demonstrates, a more restrained, flexible set of policies and a greater willingness to rely on overt rather than covert means of transferring resources make it easier to maintain a depoliticizing trend over time.

In summary, our findings suggest that the determinants of the long-run pattern of policy evolution are intimately linked to economic systems' initial conditions. These conditions, given partly by nature and partly by the legacy of history, affect not only their initial level of income and welfare, but also their policy responsiveness and flexibility over time, i.e., the extent to which policy is likely to be accommodative or obstructive of some basic time-phased evolutionary change. The nature and pace of organizational/institutional changes that serve to alter fundamentally the quality of a government's intervention activity are, in other words, seen as related to several critical dimensions of a system's initial conditions, the two most important of which are the relative strength, or weakness, of what Kuznets called "nationalism," and the relative strength, or weakness, of the system's natural-resource endowment. The first dimension, which has been commented upon but not fully integrated into our analysis to date, affects the relative mildness and length of the seemingly inevitable primary import-substitution subphase of transition. The second makes itself felt in two ways. First, the larger the initial resource endowment, the more important are the rents emanating from the primary sector and therefore the more animated the struggle among various contending parties to appropriate these rents on their own behalf. Second, the more plentiful the natural resource endowment, the more exposed is the system to such exogenous shocks or fluctuations in the terms of trade. The amplitude and periodicity of these exogenous fluctuations moreover affect the rate of secular organizational/institutional change, i.e., the slope of the so-called long-term depoliticization trend.

6.3 Conclusions for policy: general

This volume has attempted to do two things: to propose an approach to the endogenization of development policy and to begin to test it against the postwar empirical experience of some actual country cases. It has become increasingly obvious to both LDC policymakers and donors/ creditors that the issue of a change in development policy, and the pros and cons of accepting or rejecting structural adjustment packages proposed by domestic and/or foreign critics, is not so much one of an inadequately shared understanding of the technical problems involved as it is a function of more subtle political-economy-tinged processes. After more than 40 years of a build-up in human capital in the Third World and of discourse between the donor/creditor and recipient/debtor communities, all parties have become increasingly aware that it is less a question of actors technically "knowing not what they do," in strictly rational scientific terms, and more of their responding knowledgably to less-well-recognized and, at least for some, partially obscured dimensions of the total environment. We would argue that if these dimensions and processes can be exposed to the sunlight of analysis and rendered more transparent the chances for understanding each other better and advancing the development process as a positive sum game will be substantially enhanced.

We obviously do not claim to have rendered policy making fully endogenous here. That is much too ambitious an undertaking, given the level of "noise" in the system, our inadequate understanding of the nature of the state, of learning processes, and a number of other complexities that have not as yet even been introduced. Moreover, rational expectations theory notwithstanding, we do not really believe that policy formation will ever be fully endogenized since a truly dynamic scenario will always have to leave room for differences in time horizon, individual personalities, and old-fashioned surprises. Rather, we would be quite content if we have succeeded in pointing the direction future policy-oriented research might take, recognizing, to paraphrase Goethe, that "the first step toward self-improvement is self-realization," i.e., enhanced transparency. It is "political economy" in this sense, tracing differential policy responses in different types of LDCs, rather than in tracing the implications of a class struggle among vested interest groups via the manipulation of a neutral or not-so-neutral government, that is being deployed here.

Our approach has endeavored to focus as much on the more difficult question of the "why" as well as the "what" of development policy change and performance. This represents a novel and more ambitious task, and consequently the efforts reported on in this volume should be viewed as a progress report on a hopefully continuing research effort, rather than the presentation of definitive findings. Nevertheless, we are obviously convinced that the approach we have taken is a fruitful one and likely to become more so as we continue to shape both the analytical framework and our empirical testing procedures. At this stage a few conclusions for policy would seem to warrant attention. Some flow directly from the work reported on; others are at least suggested by it.

We conclude that once the EO subphase of transition has been reached, an LDC government's attention should shift from watching prices *and* quantities (via a resort to rationing) to gradually watching quantities more and letting prices be more nearly determined by the market. In the case of monetary policy, for example, the application of the principle of "watching quantity" seems to constitute Friedman-like advice, namely that even the world's most experienced central bankers should watch the quantity of money (M) and forget about trying to control the rate of interest, letting it be determined in the loanable funds market. This suggests that the money growth rate should be limited to approximately the growth rate of GNP. In the case of foreign exchange management, the same principle implies moving to a relatively clean float system in which the quantity of reserves (R) is watched and the level of the FE rate is no longer viewed as "sensitive" for political and/or psychological reasons. It further implies that the quantity of FE reserves held should be limited to the relatively small, relatively constant amounts needed for transactions purposes, i.e., that an LDC should not afford the luxury of a large R.

The simultaneous application of such a focus governing both internal and external monetary management would not be accidental. In both cases money would be increasingly interpreted as what is necessary for transactions purposes, i.e., M as a domestic medium of exchange required for the internal division of labor, and R as a medium of exchange for international transactions purposes to accommodate the international division of labor. In both cases the focus implies an increasing emphasis on efficiency through decentralized choices by market participants.

Gradual depoliticization of course implies the increasing substitution of the market for government direct controls. As the interest rate is liberalized there is less need for credit rationing by political force, and as the FE rate is liberalized there is less need for FE rationing. While not all government interventions, e.g., import duties, are substantially reduced or eliminated, the most serious forms usually are over time. No government, DC or LDC, makes daily adjustments in its tariff structure, but it does make daily discretionary decisions with respect to the supply of money and the foreign exchange rate. Distortions by tariffs represent less of a case of oscillating inefficiency; this is one reason they are likely to be tackled somewhat later in the liberalization process.

Indeed, the sovereign state's exercise of monopoly power via the printing of money and the compulsory purchase of foreign exchange is far more damaging than the retention of import duties, at least for some time. In fact, depoliticization is largely coextensive with the acceptance of a new monetary philosophy, i.e., to regard M and R mediums of exchange suggests relative monetary inactivism, i.e., they are not to be viewed as purchasing power that can be artificially created and/or manipulated by the political will to achieve socially desirable purposes. This represents something of a rebellion against the postwar mainstream view in the industrially advanced countries that regards the creation of money as the augmentation of a socially desirable liquid asset that is being "held," mainly for psychological reasons, rather than spent aggressively to enhance the growth performance of the system.

In the EO phase the purpose of reform in monetary, fiscal, and foreign exchange policies is thus to identify the proper role and responsibility for government promotion efforts consistent with the requirements of dynamic efficiency in an increasingly complex economy. It decidedly does not mean a reduced role for government, but a different, perhaps more powerful, if also more even-handed, role. Organizational/institutional construction to facilitate the depoliticization trend, e.g., in the monetary and fiscal arena, is essential, as is appropriate government action in ensuring appropriately time-phased educational policies and the support of R & D and science and technology policies generally. Rendering exports competitive, via tax rebates, processing zones, and bonded warehouse schemes long before the domestic market is competitive and ensuring the emergence of nationalism in the Kuznets spirit during the post-IS phase requires interventionist acts by government – as does the conventional construction of overheads – equitably distributed – and even the occasional large-scale public sector directly productive activity, while financial markets are still narrow and imperfect. The key is the increased exercise of self-restraint in the use of macroeconomic policy and a switch of objectives from one of ensuring profits for the anointed few to building an accommodating institutional structure for the mobilization of the human resources of the many.

A flexible, pragmatic approach implies, moreover, establishing some time profile for various reform measures rather than the wholesale adoption of a "big bang" reform package oblivious of the fact that it indeed takes time for new institutions (ideas and organizations) to replace the old. In a reasonably democratic society subject to normal political pressures and administrative constraints a government certainly cannot be expected to do or undo everything at once. Some transition period must be allowed on the path to gradual liberalization since concessions to political reality must always be made if reforms are to be sustained.[1]

Purchasing power management by means of an expansionary monetary policy represents a quick solution to the felt needs of growth promotion, in contrast to the deployment of tax and expenditure policies operating through the various line ministries (e.g., expenditures on education, financial infrastructure, transportation, science, and technology) that have perceptible, if slower, growth-generating effects. A cardinal argument against government deficits and monetary expansion is that a country needs to gradually curb the natural urge for "quick fix" solutions and instead shift its policies to stimulate growth via overt ("on-the-table") taxation and productivity-enhancing line ministry expenditures.

However, putting all the emphasis on "cutting the deficit," though meritorious from the anti-inflationary point of view, may actually be bad (at least, untimely) advice from the political standpoint because it requires a politically mature social consensus concerning how the new tax burden is to be equitably shared. The Latin American type of developing country, for example, may have to live with some inflation for some time to come; settling some problems through inflation is almost a "given" that cannot readily be relaxed because the political art of consensus formation has yet to be developed as depoliticization proceeds. What is reasonably needed is a gradual move toward an equilibrium rate of exchange and an equilibrium rate of interest in the presence of some inflation.

While, for the above political economy reasons, the LDC central banker probably has to continue to be something of a money printer, he can try earlier to become a clean floater, i.e., if he cannot initially keep his eyes on the quantity of money he can at least keep them off the foreign exchange rate. In this way the opportunity for trade within the international division of labor is isolated from mild levels of domestic inflation. Moreover, if there is indexing or, still better, if there exists a flourishing financial market outside the commercial banking system, the maintenance of an equilibrium rate of interest is also safeguarded. Although fiscal reform aimed at full "taxation with consent" is postponed, there is no major resource misallocation, either internally (because an approximation to equilibrium interest rates prevails), or externally (because an approximation to equilibrium foreign exchange rates prevails).

---

[1] This is, of course, a matter of considerable debate in the context of the current East European reform movements. These countries differ markedly in their initial conditions; moreover, those that could legitimately be labeled developing countries have to tackle the additional constraint imposed by their socialist past, including the absence of any private sector and of even the rudiments of the institutions required for the effective depoliticization of macroeconomic policy. Only time will tell whether the adherents of selective gradualism or of the "big bang" theory are correct in such a context.

Consequently the private sector may do well based on an external orientation in line with efficiency orientation dictated by the international division of labor. For the private sector this represents the perfect case of "classical inflation" according to the equation of exchange where all absolute prices keep on doubling but, given the indexing of interest rates, cause no distortion of relative prices internally or internationally. Inflation can do less damage (e.g., distort relative prices less and/or add less to the administrative costs of indexing) if it proceeds more or less evenly through time.

To translate the motto "limit the quantity of money" and "treat M and R as media of exchange" into policy action requires LDC organizational reforms whereby the relatively independent status of the monetary authority is increasingly recognized. A central bank jurisdictionally independent of and somewhat protected from the pressure for money printing by the executive branch of government would be one indicator of such a willingness to accept increasingly the discipline of the market. The emergence of such a functionally specialized "organ" may well be the inevitable evolutionary consequence of an LDC gradually coming to emulate certain organizational features of systems that have already graduated into modern growth.

This trend is analogous to the generally observed increased reliance on decentralized decision making over central planning as a consequence of the rapidly growing complexity of the mature economy. Along this road there are interactions between the slope of the long-term depoliticization trend and the severity or amplitude of oscillations around that trend occasioned by shocks emanating from the external environment. The more frequent and severe such oscillations, leading to temporary retreats back into the import-substitution-like policy syndrome, the more delayed the progress of long-term organizational and institutional reforms and, consequently, the prospects for timely graduation into modern growth. But as recent events, not only in Latin America but also in Eastern Europe – not explicitly part of our analytical landscape – indicate, the long-term trend seems clear and virtually inevitable. The critical questions that remain are related mainly both to speed and sequencing, both of which can, of course, spell the difference between a relative "success" and "failure" for several generations of LDC citizens.

These questions can be placed in somewhat sharper focus by a more detailed analysis of the "typical" fiscal sequence of reform. In the normal budget-deficit-prone LDC case, total government expenditures G will normally exceed total revenues T, producing a budget deficit $D = G - T$ (indicated on the horizontal axis of figure 6.2) that is covered, as we have seen, by inflation-generating money creation, $dM/dt = D$. In our dualistic economy, the current total tax revenue is the sum of T_a (taxes on agriculture) and T_q (taxes on nonagriculture), as represented by some point X on the tax line $T = T_a + T_q$. To avoid increasing the money supply, dM/dt, the main purpose of fiscal reform is to arrive at a new tax point Z on some higher tax line ($G' = T'_q + T'_a$). A tax reform can thus be represented by the vector ($\overline{c}$) in figure 6.2.

In the natural-resources-rich LDC, T_a consists mainly of international-trade-related indirect taxes (i.e., indirect import and export duties), while T_q encompasses internal taxes, both direct (income and property) and indirect (sales) taxes. From the viewpoint of tax administration, it is, of course, much easier to levy indirect, especially trade-related taxes, due to the "point-specific" convenience of their collection at borders and major harbors. In contrast, direct taxes are more difficult to administer because of the necessity to maintain personal contact between tax collectors and individual taxpayers, plus the need to maintain an auditable tax record, which is a near impossibility where modern bookkeeping is not yet a common practice, especially among spatially dispersed farmers in the rural areas. Land taxes are rare; where they exist, they are usually administered by local governments and eroded by inflation. In fact, farmers, along with the bulk of urban income recipients, are usually exempt from income taxes. For a primary-product-exporting economy with the usual colonial heritage, the ratio T_a/T_q (i.e., the slope of $0X$) is therefore initially likely to be large, since trade-related taxes must be relied upon, mainly for administrative reasons, to yield the lion's share of total government revenue.

In the primary IS phase, a case can be made that the policy significance of import duties as a "protective device" (i.e., for infant industry protection) was an innocent by-product of the fact that the central government needed larger revenues and only rationalized the imposition of duties as a protective device *ex post* via the infant industry argument, riding on the coattails of the need to create a synthetic nationalism via interventions. It is certainly also fair to state that the postwar history of IS growth has been largely coincident with the necessity of tariffs as a revenue measure, plus a psychology calling for the government to generate the requisite level of cohesion or nationalism by performing important growth-related functions, including protection. This helped usher in a chapter of interventionism from the very beginnings of the postwar transition growth effort.

We can, therefore, assume that tax reform in the EO phase begins with a tax structure (X) showing a heavy reliance on trade-related taxes on agriculture (T_a) as a point of departure for the analysis of fiscal reforms in the typical LDC. Any potential tax reform vector ($\overline{c}$) can then be decomposed into the additive sum of a structurally neutral component ($\overline{a}$) and a revenue-neutral component ($\overline{b}$), (i.e., $\overline{c} = \overline{a} + \overline{b}$ in figure 6.2). By keeping the tax structure (T_a/T_q) constant, the purpose of $\overline{a}$ is to

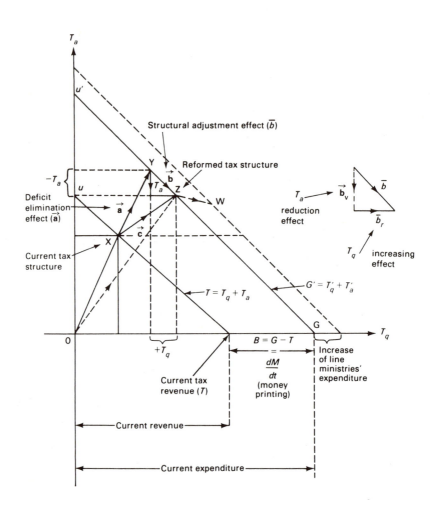

Figure 6.2 Fiscal reforms

eliminate the budget deficit (dB/dt). While this represents the much heralded customary "advice" to a deficit-prone LDC, it is also unrealistic unless it is accomplished by revenue-neutral reforms implying the increase of some taxes (e.g., T_q) to compensate for the reduction of other taxes (e.g., T_a). Since LDC governments can seldom tolerate an absolute reduction in revenue, all realistic tax reforms must operate in terms of such a "substitution" via changes in the tax ratio (T_a/T_q).

While administrative difficulties, fraud, and evasion are often mentioned as bottlenecks standing in the way of tax reform, the real obstacle is undoubtedly the lack of a political agreement on the part of the urban industrial population to support such reform. The burden of these taxes falls on corporations and salaried consumers who have political influence. In contrast, trade-related taxes, whose burden falls more on spatially dispersed rural families (export taxes) and/or consumers (import duties), are often viewed as "warranted" in the sense that, since such taxation has been practiced so long and its burden is indirect, the victims hardly notice their existence. While a 50 percent import duty on Japanese cars might cause considerable dissatisfaction in the United States, taxi owners in Taipei pay higher import duties and do not complain because they have been paying them for well over 30 years. When export taxes (T_a) are collected at the ports, spatially dispersed farmers may hardly be aware that this long-established practice constitutes institutionalized discrimination.

Import duties are a unique tax in that there exists a strong vested interest group, i.e., the protected infant industrialists who are quite insistent that consumers should keep on paying a double penalty, including for their own inefficiency, as purchasing power is transferred to them via the government. While in the DCs such a protective tariff tends to be more of a temporary arrangement, i.e., to share the social costs of labor reallocation out of the "sunset" industries adversely affected by international competition, a protective tariff in LDCs tends to be a "growth promotion" institution for new industries and tends to resist an expiration date. It is, therefore, difficult to reduce import duties (T_a) in the typical LDC case, given that the concentrated, organized groups that are helped are keenly aware of the benefits, while the dispersed and unorganized victims are less aware of the costs. Thus, protective tariffs represent a relatively durable institution for covert income transfers and the manufacture of profits by political force both complementary to and consistent with the low-interest-rate policy associated with the printing of money.

The reduction of the burden on the agricultural sector, i.e., the reduction of overt export taxes and the elimination of the overvaluation of the domestic currency, which amounts to a covert tax on exporters, must be seen as representing a long-term historical trend. Virtually all DCs subsidize their agricultural sectors, while all LDCs exploit it at the beginning of the transition growth process when it is the only production sector that contains a "squeezable" surplus, or rent, especially in the natural-resource-abundant countries. In the successful LDCs, in the relative absence of a politically powerful "farm bloc," the reduction over time of the tax burden on their agricultural sectors must be traced in part to the traditional deep-rooted cultural belief that agriculture, as a way of life and as an insurance against dependence, is superior to urban industry and "merchants." It is these vested ideas – coupled with the fear of domestic unrest in the presence of foreign threats – that motivated the authoritarian governments of East Asia, for instance, to initiate the early postwar land reforms catering to the interests of the politically relatively powerless peasant class. It is also what now motivates the same democratizing governments to begin to subsidize agriculturalists via an artifically high rice price. The fact that landlords rather than a dispersed peasant class dominate in the more typical Latin American case – and that we have seen precious few instances of real land reform there – undoubtedly has a cultural as well as a political economy explanation. But the fact is that when agriculture, for this as well as other reasons, continues to be unable to make its historical contribution to the society's overall growth the transition process is severely hampered.

A priority-oriented approach to reform in our inflation-prone, dualistic economy suggests itself as a three-stage process. The first stage involves monetary reform, via a relatively "clean float," to move the system toward an equilibrium exchange rate, on the one hand, plus monetary decontrol with or without indexing to move it toward an equilibrium interest rate, on the other.[2] At this stage, the printing of money is usually permitted at a smooth and steady pace as a concession to government's inability to raise taxes, given the aforementioned political resistance of the urban industrial class.

In the second stage a revenue-neutral tax reform $(\bar{b})$ is carried out over a number of years during which the resistance by vested interest groups (urban taxpayers and urban infant industries) is gradually overcome. As a consequence, the government will eventually renounce its policy of printing money as rationalized by "growth promotion." With respect to import duties, resistance to their reduction will gradually be softened once urban consumers realize that they have been paying for years for the inefficiency of domestic industries. Such consumer awareness will gradually gather momentum as import liberalization proceeds and there is more opportunity to travel abroad and compare domestic and world prices.

---

[2] This amounts to a gradual government decontrol of private financial transactions so that what is often referred to as a "black" or curb market charging "usurious" interest rates is legalized. The ultimate objective is to establish a more competitive financial system.

Indirect nonagricultural taxes and, especially, direct income taxes, once installed, usually have a "progressive" feature that makes them GNP-elastic, i.e., they can be counted on to produce the structurally neutral effect ($\bar{a}$ in figure 6.2) that closes the budget deficit gap over time, provided government household expenditures do not increase as rapidly. Reform in the first stage should therefore be helpful in producing a sufficiently high GNP growth rate to make it possible for the government eventually to close the budget deficit.

Finally, in the third stage, given its increased revenues, the government can now think in terms of increases in nonhousehold line ministry expenditures (e.g., education, health, science and technology, agricultural research, roads, etc., moving from point Z to point W in figure 6.2) in order to promote growth through long gestation period investments. Such projects, based on the economic principle of externality, are intended to provide a better environment for the operation of private entrepreneurs, specifically in the large-scale, more capital- and technology-intensive industries. The success at each stage is, of course, a prerequisite for keeping the budget deficit under control in the second and third stages.

Seen in this three-stage perspective, our first-stage advice is to try to disentangle purchasing power management from growth (i.e., to move toward "natural" exchange and interest rates) so that the government becomes less of a direct growth activist. This advice does not, however, imply throwing out the "growth baby." When the first and third stages are viewed together, in fact, it clearly suggests the replacement of a quest for "growth with haste" by the insistence on "growth via efficiency-oriented steadiness," well illustrated by our Thai country case.

In addition to discriminating against consumers, tariffs annoy economists by violating Pareto optimality in rendering the domestic relative price structure out of alignment with international prices, according to the effective protection literature. What is even more important is that the accompanying covert income transfers from consumers to some producers inhibit the so-called infant industries from ever becoming healthy adolescents by learning to compete in the domestic market (when protected positively) or in the international markets (when protected negatively). Even if they wanted to, Philippine textile producers, for instance, cannot compete with Hong Kong in world markets if they have to pay import duties on imported cloth or other imported inputs. Nevertheless, the attack on structural protection of this type should probably not constitute a high priority reform item since it may represent a temporarily necessary concession to both the vested interest groups who want to keep protecting the "infant" and the vested idea that it is one's patriotic duty to support the country's domestic industries. The very durability of protection even in the successful East Asian cases indicates that it is not a major cause of policy instability. As long as consumers continue to subsidize their infant industries, either out of ignorance or patriotism, even in the export-oriented phase of transition, this does not do too much damage. Tariff reductions will become politically feasible – though by no means easy – only when the consumer responds to the increased transparency of his losses by refusing to continue to support the industrialist position.

During the EO phase, since consumers in world markets are, of course, naturally selfish in their attitude toward the exporting LDCs, the sovereign power of the latter, as great as it may be internally, cannot be used to exploit foreign buyers. Therefore, if protective tariffs must be maintained for some time, tariff rebates, export-processing zones, and bonded warehouses as transition devices can and do contribute to an earlier integration of the export sector with world markets in order to reap the harvest of competitive efficiency without tackling the "moral issue" of domestic consumer discrimination head on. Taiwan and South Korea followed such a policy of fostering early growth in external markets while continuing consumer exploitation in their internal markets for some time, and did well. Thailand represents a less extreme case. Under such arrangements relatively high protective tariff walls can and have been maintained until a relatively later date (approximately 1982 in Taiwan) when consumer awareness (as well as foreign pressure) finally became too powerful.

A movement toward scheduled tariff reductions represents a healthy evolution philosophy toward one of temporary protection (for sunset industries) as practiced in the DCs. However, such "scheduled" tariff reductions can only come later in the external orientation phase, i.e., only after such industries have demonstrated their competitive efficiency in world markets. Contrary to the ordinary Linder thesis, the world market can thus be seen as a laboratory for experimenting with competitive fitness. Once the fear of competition with foreigners in foreign markets is reduced, the domestic economy can fully open its doors to accept similar competitive pressures at home. The timing of an open door policy must, after all, be judged in the light of the historical background of a market-oriented epoch of colonialism during which foreigners were feared economically as well as politically. It takes some time for some LDCs to overcome this dual type of xenophobia.

The ideal stages for a realistic tariff policy may thus be seen as follows: first, during primary import substitution, mainly for revenue reasons but disguised by an infant industry motivation, the LDC is likely to establish a fairly high protective wall for everything except capital goods. Second, once EO becomes feasible, this may well entail protection at somewhat lower and more uniform levels – with as much shift as possible from QRs to equivalent tariffs, accompanied by the introduction of tariff rebates and export-processing zones. If the FE rate is now more or less cleanly floated, the elimination of the artificial over-valuation implies that the incomes of primary product exporters will no longer be transferred to become windfall profits of the urban industrial class. Domestic consumers may continue for some time to fulfill their "historical mission" by subsidizing domestic producers in the presence of a substantial tariff wall. But, finally, a third stage is likely to entail gradual harmonization and scheduled (preannounced) across-the-board reductions in all tariffs, with the exception of a few cases of secondary import and export-substitution industries promoted for political and/or scale economy reasons. This stage would naturally blend into the occasional short-term protection and subsidization of "sunset" industries in the DCs.

Postwar development has been witness to a process of politically enforced "overurbanization" via the use of various government policy instruments, i.e., the overvalued FE rate, tax preferences for urban industrialists, money-printing-supported bank finance to meet the investment demands of mainly urban borrowers, compulsory government food procurement programs to support rationed food supplies for urban consumers at artificially low prices, etc. The sharp contrast between the crowded urban way of life and the relatively stagnant rural hinterland of these LDCs is more pronounced in the relatively more natural-resource-abundant LDCs. Here also organized/unorganized sector wage gaps are larger, and there is a greater tendency for rural populations to migrate from stagnant agricultural areas to crowd the cities and create large so-called urban informal sectors. All this occurs mainly because the natural-resource-based economic rents have been siphoned out by political forces to build up urban industry excessively instead of supporting agriculture along with complementary rural industries in a balanced growth context.

Given our political economy interpretation, the underlying causation for the so frequently encountered LDC rural stagnation, as well as the means for modernizing the spatially dispersed rural sector, should no longer be regarded as a mystery. Politically, economically, culturally, and technologically sensitive urban areas that ultimately represent the base of modern science and technology, including the capacity to produce inorganic fertilizer, agricultural machinery, and new seeds, are usually overbuilt early on. A more gradual urbanization strategy would provide a much better opportunity for linking these forces of modernization to the rural backyard. While an acceleration of such "linkages" via the line ministries' expenditures on road building, rural electrification, adaptive research, etc., is likely to be reserved for the third phase of any fiscal reform movement, a good start can be made earlier on by ensuring that the deviations from a market-oriented approach in the earlier stage are minimized, i.e., that the virtually inevitable early import-substitution phase be kept as "mild" and brief as possible. Balanced rural-urban growth via a decentralized pattern of industrial location would then permit local agricultural producers to dispose of their agricultural surpluses in small towns in exchange for modern inputs as well as the modern attitudes and practices that accompany the spread of science and technology – without the political, social, and economic costs of premature large-scale urbanization. The development of the farmer as a full human resource, along with the medium- and small-scale rural industrialist, will bring substantial productivity gains as a by-product, while avoiding the excessive and costly early urbanization process that is so typical of the contemporary natural-resource-rich LDCs.

In fact, the urban-oriented strategy of the typical contemporary LDC constitutes a perversion of the historical experience demonstrated by such successful, now mature, countries as England and Japan, i.e., the fact that an agricultural revolution is normally the precursor of an industrial revolution. This was demonstrated by Taiwan in the early sixties as it shifted from traditional rice and sugar to mushroom and asparagus production as part of an agricultural-processing-focused export drive that preceded the better-known export surge of labor-intensive manufactured goods based on imported raw materials. Farmers thus learned to produce wave after wave of new products to supply both nearby and distant markets, given a profit-seeking environment equally strong and a natural resource endowment equally weak as that typical of the industrial entrepreneurs of Hong Kong and Singapore. This was also demonstrated in the post-1978 liberalization movement in China where the rural sector was successfully modernized by, first, achieving agricultural productivity gains via a shift to a more market-oriented "responsibility system" and subsequently enhanced linkage to secondary crops and rural industrial producers in domestic markets. It has since ground to a halt because complementary balanced liberalization affecting urban state industries has not been forthcoming. The failure of the typical Latin American LDCs to modernize their own agricultural sectors can be said to be due less to a shortage than to an overabundance of the rent – yielding natural resources that lie at the heart of the "urban first" politicoeconomic strategy we have been analyzing. The Thai case represents a version of the East Asian prototype and the Philippine case a version of the Latin American prototype in this regard as well.

A market-oriented approach to rural modernization is impossible as long as the rent-seeking political forces deny farmers the purchasing power that rightly belongs to them – via the continued overvaluation of the domestic currency, the heavy burden of export duties, the use of the inflation tax, etc. As compared with the reduction of import duties that exploit consumers in the urban sector, the reduction of export duties thus represents a more urgent task within a priority-oriented reform program.

In the context of our three-stage evolutionary approach to reform, the floating of the exchange rate in the first stage returns to farmers their own purchasing power that has been covertly taken away from them and helps initiate a market-oriented approach to rural modernization. A reduction of the export duties in the second stage, by giving farmers back more of their purchasing power, continues this process. Finally, in the third stage, the previous neglect of public sector investments in human and institutional overhead capital can be corrected.

There are strong indications, including the focus of the World Bank's 1991 *World Development Report,* that the international community and the developing countries themselves are about to emerge from the trauma of the so-called debt crisis of the eighties and return to the basic development problem of the sixties and seventies with all its attendant opportunities and choices. There are also indications that the severity of the crisis of the past decade may have served to shake loose some of the ingrained habits of policymakers as they respond to external shocks. It is, however, less clear whether, if and when the pressure is off – relatively speaking, of course – either by way of debt write-offs or sell-offs, the fundamental lessons governing the political economy of secular policy choice will have been learned. It is hoped that this volume, focused on one full cycle of experience (1960s–80s) in the open economy setting, will have made a contribution to this process. Even increasing transparency and enhanced learning by all the actors should pave the way for a sustained depoliticization trend with reduced oscillations around it, as more and more Third World countries attempt to navigate the final lap of their transition to modern economic growth.

Bibliography

Akrasanee, N. "Trade and Employment in Asia and the Pacific." Manila: Council for Asian Manpower Studies, 1977.

Baldwin, R. *Foreign Trade Regimes and Economic Development: The Philippines*. New York: Columbia University Press, 1975.

Chenery, H. B. "Patterns of Industrial Growth." *American Economic Review* 50, no. 4 (September 1960).

Chenery, H. B., and M. Syrquin. *Patterns of Development, 1950–70*. Oxford: Oxford University Press for the World Bank, 1975.

Chenery, H. B., and L. Taylor. "Development Patterns Among Countries and Over Time." *Review of Economics and Statistics* L. no. 4 (1968).

Corbo, V. and S. Nam. "Controlling Inflation: Korea's Recent Experience." Discussion paper no. 207. Development Research Department, The World Bank (October 1986).

Corbo, V. and S. Nam. "The Recent Macroeconomic Evolution of the Republic of Korea: An Overview." Discussion paper no. 208. Development Research Department, The World Bank (February 1987).

Corden, W. M. "The Exchange Rate System and the Taxation of Trade." In *Thailand: Social and Economic Studies in Development*, ed. T. H. Silcock. Canberra: Australian National University Press, 1967.

Corporación para el Fomento de Investigaciones. *Controversia Sobre el Plan de Desarrollo*. Bogotá: 1972.

de Rosa, D. A. "Trade and Protection in the Asian Developing Region." *Asian Development Review* 4, no. 1 (1986).

Fei, J. H. C., and D. Pauuw. *The Transition in Open Dualistic Economies*. New Haven: Yale University Press, 1973.

Fei, J. H. C., G. Ranis, and S. Kuo. *Growth with Equity: The Taiwan Case*. Oxford: Oxford University Press, 1979.

Garcia, J. G. "Commercial Policy in Colombian Development Plans between 1967 and 1982: Theory and Practice." Mimeo. June 1985.

Garcia, J. G. "Macroeconomic Policies, Crisis and Growth in the Long Run: Colombian Country Study." Mimeo, vol. 2. The World Bank, May 1988.

Garcia, J. G. "The Timing and Sequencing of a Trade Liberalization Policy: The Case of Colombia." Mimeo. The World Bank, October 1988.

Ghani, E. "Timing and Sequencing of Stabilization and Liberalization: A Study of Mexico in the 1980s." Mimeo. Operations Evaluation Department, The World Bank, 1990.

Haggard, S. *Pathways from the Periphery: The Politics of Growth in the Newly Industrializing Countries.* Ithaca, N.Y.: Cornell University Press, 1990.

Ingram, J. C. *Economic Change in Thailand, 1850–1970.* Palo Alto: Stanford University Press, 1971.

Intal, Jr., P. S., and J. H. Power. *Trade, Exchange Rate, and Agricultural Pricing Policies in the Philippines.* World Bank Comparative Studies in the Political Economy of Agricultural Pricing Policy. Washington, D.C.: The World Bank, 1990.

Kamas, L. "External Disturbance and the Independence of Monetary Policy Under the Crawling Peg in Colombia." *Journal of International Economics* 19, No. 3/4 (November 1985).

Kamas, L. "Dutch Disease Economics and the Colombian Export Boom." *World Development* 14, no. 9 (September 1986).

Kuznets, S. *Modern Economic Growth: Rate, Structure and Spread.* New Haven: Yale University Press, 1966.

Li, K. T. *The Evolution of Policy Behind Taiwan's Development Success.* New Haven: Yale University Press, 1988.

Oshima, H. T. "The Transition to an Industrial Economy in Monsoon Asia." Economic staff paper no. 20. Manila: Asian Development Bank, 1983.

Power, J. "Responses to Balance of Payments Crises in the 1970s: Korea and the Philippines." Staff paper series no. 83-05. Manila: Philippines Institute for Development Studies, 1983.

Ranis, G. "Towards a Model of Development for the Natural Resources Poor Economy." In *Kim Jai-ik Memorial Volume,* ed. L. Krause. Berkeley and Los Angeles: University of California Press, 1991.

Remolona, E. M., M. Mangahas, and F. Pante, Jr. "Foreign Debt, Balance of Payments and the Economic Crisis of the Philippines in 1983–84." *World Development* 14, no. 8 (August 1986).

Reynolds, C. W. "Why Mexico's 'Stabilizing Development' Was Actually Destabilizing (With Some Implications for the Future)." *World Development* 6, no. 7/8 (July/August, 1978).

Rhee, Y. W., B. Ross-Larson, and G. Pursell. *Korea's Competitive Edge: Managing the Entry into World Markets.* Baltimore: The Johns Hopkins University Press, 1984.

Scitovsky, T. "Economic Development in Taiwan and South Korea: 1965–81." *Stanford Food Policy Research Institute Studies* XIX, no. 3 (1985).

Silcock, T. H., ed. *Thailand: Social and Economic Studies in Development.* Canberra: Australian National University Press, 1967.

Solis, L. M. *Economic Policy Reforms in Mexico: A Case Study for Developing Countries.* New York: Pergamon Press, 1981.

Torigoe, N. "The Economic Development of Thailand." *EXIM Bank Review* (1986).

Trescott, P. B. *Thailand's Monetary Experience: The Economics of Stability.* New York: Praeger, 1971.

van Wijnbergen, S. "Growth, External Debt and the Real Exchange Rate," in

D. S. Brothers and A. E. Wick, eds., *Mexico's Search for a New Development Strategy.* Boulder, Colo.: Westview Press, 1990.

Wade, R. *Governing the Market: Economic Theory and the Role of Government in East Asian Industrialization.* Princeton, N.J.: Princeton University Press, 1990.

Westphal, L. E., and K. S. Kim. "Industrial Policy Development in Korea." World Bank Staff Working Paper, no. 263. Washington, D.C.: The World Bank, 1977.

The World Bank. *Philippines: A Framework for Economic Recovery.* Washington, D.C.: 1987.

Zabludovsky, J. "Trade Liberalization and Macroeconomic Adjustment," in D. S. Brothers and A. E. Wick, eds., *Mexico's Search for a New Development Strategy.* Boulder, Colo.: Westview Press, 1990.

Zedillo, E. "Mexico's Recent Balance-of-Payments Experience and Prospects for Growth." *World Development* 14, no. 8 (August 1986).

Statistical Sources

Bank of Korea. *Economic Statistics Yearbook.* Various issues.

The Central Bank of China. *Financial Statistics.* Various issues.

Food and Agricultural Organisation of the United Nations. *Production Yearbook* 1952.

Fei, J., G. Ranis, and S. Kuo. *Growth With Equity: The Taiwan Case.* Oxford: Oxford University Press, 1979.

Fields, G. S. "A Compendium of Data on Inequality and Poverty for the Developing World. Mimeo. Cornell University, March 1989.

International Labour Office. *International Labour Statistics.* Various issues.

International Monetary Fund. *Direction of Trade Statistics.* Various issues.

International Monetary Fund. *Government Finance Statistics.* 1982, 1985, 1988.

International Monetary Fund. *International Financial Statistics.* Yearbook, 1977, 1979, 1988.

Inspector General of Customs, Taiwan, Statistical Department. *The Trade of China.* Various issues.

Jain, S. *Size Distribution of Income.* Washington, D.C.: The World Bank, 1975.

Nacional Financiera, S.A. *La Economía Mexicana En Cifras.* Mexico City: 1981.

Philippines National Statistical Board. *Philippine Statistical Yearbook.* Various issues.

Republic of China, Directorate General of Budget, Accounting and Statistics. *National Income of the Republic of China.* Various issues.

Republic of China, Directorate General of Budget, Accounting and Statistics. *Yearbook of Labour Statistics.* Various issues.

Thailand National Statistical Office. *Statistical Yearbook of Thailand.* Various
    issues.
United Nations. *National Income Statistics.* Various issues.
United Nations. *Yearbook of International Trade Statistics.* Various issues.
United Nations. *Yearbook of Statistics.* Various issues.
UNESCO. *Statistical Yearbook.* Various issues.
The World Bank. *World Debt Tables.* Various issues.
The World Bank. *World Development Report.* Various issues.
The World Bank. *World Tables.* Various issues.

Index